Volume III

Adventure
in Meditation

Books by Carol E. Parrish-Harra:

Adventure in Meditation: Spirituality for the
   21st Century, Volume II
Adventure in Meditation: Spirituality for the
   21st Century, Volume I
The New Dictionary of Spiritual Thought
The Book of Rituals—Personal and Planetary Transformation
The Aquarian Rosary—Reviving the Art of Mantra Yoga
A New Age Handbook on Death and Dying
Messengers of Hope

Volume III

Adventure in Meditation
Spirituality for the 21st Century

by
Carol E. Parrish-Harra, Ph.D.

SPARROW HAWK PRESS
TAHLEQUAH, OKLAHOMA

For information contact Sparrow Hawk Press, Sparrow Hawk Village, 11 Summit Ridge Drive, Tahlequah, OK 74464-9215; Telephone 918 456-3421; FAX 918 458-5501, E-mail lccc@sanctasophia.org

---

Library of Congress Cataloging-in-Publication Data
Parrish-Harra, Carol E.
Adventure in Meditation Vol. III: Spirituality for the 21st Century
    A course in meditation presenting psycho-spiritual technologies to aid practitioners in living more consciously, leading to higher awareness and soul infusion. Tutoring available. Includes ageless wisdom teachings and tools for overcoming barriers to individual growth.

Editing by Mary Beth Marvin
Book design and illustrations by Marianne Sansing
Book cover design by Nell Thalasinos

ISBN No. 0-945027-15-X: $17.95
1. Meditation—tutoring available, 2. Spirituality, 3. Ageless wisdom teachings, 4. Psycho-spiritual technologies, 5. Agni Yoga teachings, 6. Bibliography.

Library of Congress Catalog Card Number
95-71835

Manufactured in the United States of America

*Dedicated
to those who carry
the light of
ChristoSophia
to the world —
You are the light of the world!*

Volume III Contents

Editor's Note. An asterisk indicates terms which may be new to some readers, terms which will be found in *The New Dictionary of Spiritual Thought* by Carol E. Parrish-Harra (Sparrow Hawk Press, 1994), a companion volume of 1100 words, concepts, and symbols helpful to the present work. The asterisk is used only with the first appearance of the most unfamiliar words to minimize distraction. *The New Dictionary of Spiritual Thought* contains terms and phrases related to spiritual sciences, esoteric Christianity, astrology, metaphysics, ageless wisdom teachings, and more. Available from Sparrow Hawk Press, Sparrow Hawk Village, 11 Summit Ridge Dr., Tahlequah, OK 74464, 918-456-3421 or 800-386-7161. $14.95 plus shipping/handling—$2.75 first copy; $1.00 each additional.

Most biblical references are taken from the King James Version or the Peshitta Bible, the classic version of the Holy Bible as translated from the Aramaic (Syriac) text—the language of Jesus—by renowned scholar George M. Lamsa.

Volume III List of Figures

Introduction

The mystical way is the unique creation of a life of art, music, and movement. The art may be a visible, tangible artifact, or it may be service or other expressions of love freely given but most often unseen. The music may be sung silently in the heart, or we may chant as we drive in our automobile, as we work in the garden, or take a walk. The movement may be the grace of healing hands, words of comfort spoken over the telephone or in prayer. All play a part. The magic of the mystical life occurs when this inner creation contacts and blends into the outer.

Mystics perfect their skills as they become comfortable with the silence, the soul's nursery. Our task in the quiet is to determine flaws in our character, then make the effort to cure disharmony. In *meditation and *prayer the mystic observes, carefully gathering lesser self into the true Self. As you and I advance in this process, doing the work as it comes to our attention, we dissolve obstacles. We face more squarely the consequences of our actions and look for meaning in our distresses, discomforts, and diseases. We make amends and enhance our sensitivity so that we "miss the mark" less frequently.

On the way to illumination we may encounter visions, voices, ecstasies, and raptures that could lure us into folly. We hold these phenomena in the light of love and wisdom, and we sincerely question. Turning to others more wise, we listen with the outer ear, then turn inward, weighing each for guidance in decision-making.

In volume 1 a foundation was established for instructive meditation and spiritual practices. The pyramid approach to high consciousness helped achieve an understanding of the tools and purposes of each level. In volume 2 distinct barriers which impede spiritual growth and expansion of consciousness were explored and self-examination processes were suggested for the necessary introspection to break through to desired *"aha's."

Volume 3 is intended as a companion to volumes 1 and 2. Should the reader encounter difficulty with concepts presented here, it may be necessary to refer to volumes 1 or 2 or *The New Dictionary of Spiritual Thought* for clarification. In fact, it is recommended that these resources be close at hand for support. The reader should before long recognize that volumes 1 and 2 introduced concepts and technology at the more basic levels. If concepts were not well understood, the reader may want to review. Volume 3 builds upon that foundation while spiraling concepts and technology to more elevated levels, stretching the mental body of the reader in the process.

Now we advance to the very heart of meditation, to what is occurring out of sight as our inner creations blend into outer reality. Awakened now and aligned to the higher, our personality must concede to soul growth as it interfaces with soul and its service. In this era of rapid advancement, we celebrate the many ways that await outer expression of our inner beauty.

Acknowledgements

A number of dedicated people have consistently held this meditation course on track over the years. Each fulfilled his or her part in order for Sancta Sophia Seminary to present volume 3. Now the course is complete.

The Reverends Stan and Helen Ainsworth joined me in the first efforts. Their contributions and persistence enabled the seminary to offer this comprehensive effort.

A series of accomplished meditation tutors have given generously of themselves over the years. Anonymous service reaps great rewards in the larger scheme of things, we are told. Numerous behind-the-scene guardians have encouraged, inspired, and loved those entrusted to their care. Letters testify to lives touched by meditation. The tutors are rewarded by glimpses of the divine as true disciples grow under their guidance.

Many coworkers have contributed as these three volumes matured. My delightful editor, Mary Beth Marvin, has diligently assisted at every juncture, with editorial expertise, skillful critiquing, and personal encouragement. (She never let me leave home without an enjoyable task so I would not be bored in airports and aloft.)

Marianne Sansing, our typesetter, does wonders with her combination of computer and illustration and design skills. She has worked closely with me to achieve volumes that are eye-appealing. I am grateful to my dearly loved secretary Lucille Perry who helps me stay on track while I balance my beloved projects and a hectic schedule. I am indeed grateful to Nell Thalasinos for designing the cover series around the peacock motif. I love the similarities and the differences in the covers. Thanks, Nell. I am sure our late dear friend, Norma Hallstrom, is rejoicing with us in a task well done.

Others who assisted this wonder-working team are Joyce Whitfield with her well-organized mind and helpful suggestions; my husband Charles Harra who has always shared the challenges of the Work with me; Finbarr Ross, C.E.O. of Light of Christ Community Church, who navigates so well the details of publication and our organization.

A special thank you to Maureen Waters, editor and publisher of *Mentor* newsletter, for presenting volumes 1 and 2 with the Athena Award for Mentoring Excellence, 1996 and 1997, respectively. We are grateful for her acknowledgement of the importance of mentoring and revitalizing this practice in the powerful and numerous ways she does. Keep up the good work; the word is spreading.

To those who will enjoy these ideas, insights, and practices in the years ahead, I will stand with you. Indeed, we are each *a point of light within a greater Light,* and thus the Plan on Earth will be restored.

The Pyramid of
Meditation Development

Introducing the Pyramid of Meditation Development

Our journey begins at the base as we contemplate the choice and commit ourselves to the ascent. Each level includes a skill to build, a work to do, and a result—all leading to the desired evolution of consciousness. Each level presents its challenge as we build inner tools with which to know anew.

Level 1. Here we master relaxation and centering to escape the distractions and domination of the body. (Lessons 1 and 2, volume 1.)

Level 2. Passive meditation stimulates the inner senses and teaches receptivity to High Self's impressions. Here exists guidance for the personality level of life and the building of the cup in which impressions are caught. Purification work is begun through passive techniques designed to exercise inner senses and to provide training for the spiritual practitioner. Purification heals and helps all of humanity as well as the disciple. (Lessons 3-7, volume 1.)

Level 3. Will is the necessary constituent of this level. The cup built by passive meditation is in place. Now active meditation begins inner focus; the focused mind pierces the veil and accumulates information vibrating to the keynote or seed thought. As we break through into the Cloud of Knowable Things, the cup collects the precipitation and organizes it into understandable and usable ideas. (Lessons 8, 9, volume 1, and lessons 1-4, volume 2.)

Level 4. Purification of ego is the primary work as one approaches soul infusion. The miasma created by old thoughtforms and personality's strong desire currents forms clouds that distort the wisdom gleaned from the light of the Soul. Here we confront the shadows. We consciously intensify clearing in order to embrace wisdom. (Lessons 5-9, volume 2 and lessons 1-3, volume 3.)

Level 5. Soul alignment is our great goal. As meditation practices are established in the personal life, the human soul ascends toward its true purpose. *Remember, ye are Gods.* Soul-alignment meditations guide the initiate—personality and Soul—into right relationship . . . into enlightenment. (Lessons 4-9, volume 3.) Hurrah, we reach the summit!

Meditation is truly a doorway to the world of spiritual realities. Your progress depends upon you. Embrace the quest!

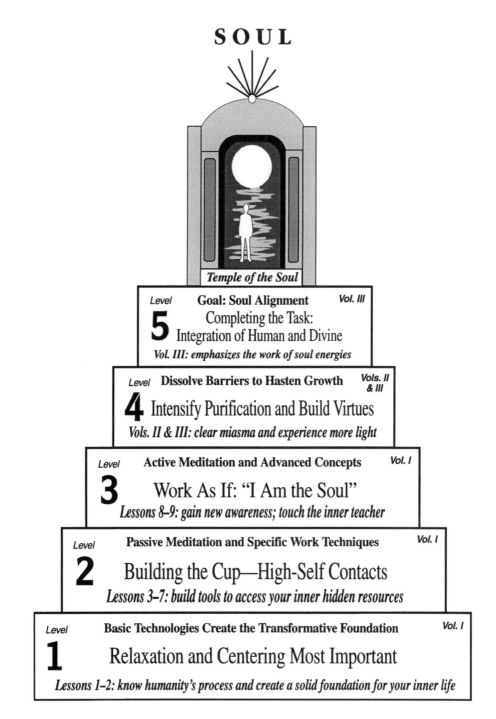

S O U L

Temple of the Soul

Level **5**	**Goal: Soul Alignment** Completing the Task: Integration of Human and Divine *Vol. III: emphasizes the work of soul energies*	*Vol. III*

Level **4**	**Dissolve Barriers to Hasten Growth** Intensify Purification and Build Virtues *Vols. II & III: clear miasma and experience more light*	*Vols. II & III*

Level **3**	**Active Meditation and Advanced Concepts** Work As If: "I Am the Soul" *Lessons 8–9: gain new awareness; touch the inner teacher*	*Vol. I*

Level **2**	**Passive Meditation and Specific Work Techniques** Building the Cup—High-Self Contacts *Lessons 3–7: build tools to access your inner hidden resources*	*Vol. I*

Level **1**	**Basic Technologies Create the Transformative Foundation** Relaxation and Centering Most Important *Lessons 1–2: know humanity's process and create a solid foundation for your inner life*	*Vol. I*

Figure i. The Pyramid of Meditation Development.

The Nature of Spiritual Maturity

The spirituality that goes deeper than pieties and cover-ups,
one that . . . insists once again
that "not all those who say 'Lord, Lord'"
are prayerful people, is again asserting itself.
—Matthew Fox
On Becoming a Musical Mystical Bear, 1972

A persistent impulse lives within the human heart — a demand to express. *Spiritual guidelines provide a framework for that expression. Each *religion, culture, or caste defines a collective perspective of what it expects of its people and provides ways for acceptance, rejection, and growth. Those who achieve the ideal are venerated as elders — wise, enlightened, holy.

In the *Maya and other indigenous traditions, for example, fifty-two years is recognized as a significant cycle. Those younger than fifty-two years of age are considered youth and those older are elders. Different expectations are placed upon each group. All cultures define ways to face challenges and protect status quo, and we usually have little idea of how present guidelines have evolved.

Thus, personal maturity becomes the goal. Maturity has many interactive components, however, which intricately link to all the *barriers we have discussed but also involve much more. Most of us would agree that immaturity is a serious barrier to personal and spiritual growth; now we begin to recognize that, conversely, personal psychological maturity leads to spiritual maturity. Yet, if we asked a hundred people to tell us what they mean by maturity, we would get an astonishing array of opinions.

For instance, one man complained that a neighbor repaired cars in front of their retirement complex. He thought the neighbor had enough money to buy a new car or get it fixed at a garage. When it was suggested that some people enjoy working on their cars as a hobby, the man sneered, "Yes, if they hadn't grown up yet." Apparently he equated maturity with not doing your own car repair. He thought his attitude proclaimed a higher level of maturity. His activities, however, were almost exclusively limited to watching TV, drinking, and complaining.

> . . . those who come to psychotherapy with genuine intent to grow are those relative few who are called out of immaturity, who are no longer willing to tolerate their own childishness, although they may not yet see the way out.
>
> —M. Scott Peck
> *Further Along the Road Less Traveled*

What Is Maturity?

Is anyone totally mature? Perhaps, depending upon how the word is defined. Or, is this even an appropriate question? Let us look at difficulties in answering. Esoterically we think of the *soul maturing as it evolves through certain steps labeled *"initiations." We often hear "old soul" used as a reference to maturity.

Paradoxes and Complications

We usually equate maturity with growing older and view a person acting immaturely as childish. While all of us grow older, some of us seem to fall short of the expected maturity. Psychologists contend certain people become fixed at particular age levels; contemporary encounter groups make a game of judging the age level of each response participants make. Most of us have encountered surprisingly mature behavior in little children, while ordinarily stable adults fall apart. While certain behaviors may typify a given age level, this does not help much in comprehending maturity in its broadest sense.

A great deal of what we consider "immature" relates to emotions. Some see management of emotions as the sole criteria and judge highly emotional people to be less mature than those who seldom display emotion. But many aspects of maturity involve attitudes and perspectives quite apart from emotions.

One illustration involves what we might call "reality checks" while driving a car. If we drive with preconceived notions about what other motorists should do or what we expect them to do, we are not in a state of mind to react quickly to the unexpected. If we see a puzzling object in the road ahead and are uncertain how to proceed, we wisely slow down, rather than continuing at the same speed. Maturity relates to an open-minded alertness that becomes habitual; childishness relates to driving on recklessly — using the car as an extension of our *ego and its fantasies. If we add the emotion of anger or use the car to vent our frustrations and resentments, we exhibit even more immaturity. So we see that refusal to adapt to changing circumstances essentially constitutes an immature reaction, whether or not emotions are involved.

> The anger center in human beings works in exactly the same way as it does in other creatures. It is basically a territorial mechanism, firing off when any other creature impinges upon our territory.
>
> —Scott Peck
> *Further Along the Road Less Traveled*

As previously noted, we often equate conforming to societal or parental rules with maturity. As long as we "behave," we believe we are mature. This obedience may be necessary for comfort or the approval of others, yet we may be reacting from unconscious, conditioned responses, not true maturity. If we flout injunctions and customs of society, or of smaller groups within society, our maturity may be questioned. Rebellion, on the other hand, may be a sign of greater maturity, although deviation is not usually equated with maturity or desired behavior but often considered a sign of "childish" disobedience.

> It is wrong to demand that the individual subordinate himself to the collectivity or merge in it, because it is by its most advanced individuals that the collectivity progresses and they can really advance only if they are

free. But it is true that as the individual advances spiritually, he finds himself more and more united with the collectivity and the All.

—Sri Aurobindo, *The Future Evolution of Man*

It is difficult to evaluate the maturity level of some behaviors without knowing the motivations, needs, and total circumstances involved—without having walked in those renowned moccasins. How far may we go in judging others, or even ourselves, by looking at overt behaviors? Suppose we usually act in a manner most people judge as mature, but in a complex circumstance we behave in ways even we realize are childish. Does this mean we are no longer mature? Or, if this is only a temporary lapse, how many lapses are we allowed to still be considered "mature"?

If we synthesize the qualities of mature physical, emotional, mental, and spiritual development, our guiding concepts create an image of the fine person we can be. As we dissolve barriers and integrate these qualities level by level, we become that person. We move from "less" to "more," from potential, to demonstrate increased wisdom.

Maturity encompasses such a broad array of awareness, judgment, feeling, and behavior, we must organize its critical aspects into a framework for discussion, knowing we need to synthesize these in our day-to-day life.

Behavioral Maturity

We may talk about mature attitudes, but this is pointless until translated into behaviors. The idea of being mature is misleading because a state of being is implied in the question, "Am I mature?" This state of being does not reflect the reality of maturity as a collection of behaviors. When we try to examine behaviors, problems arise because behaviors may alter at any time, depending upon needs, possible choices, factors influencing another, and so on. In crisis, for example, what appears to be maturity and stability may in fact be a state of shock or even insensitivity to the situation and its effects. Generally, however, the quality and consistency of behaviors support reasonable judgments of maturity level.

When we focus upon maturity as behavior, we relinquish the idea of becoming totally mature. Rather than "Am I mature?" we ask, "What degree of maturity does *my* behavior reflect?" Similar behavior may represent quite different levels of maturity within various individuals. We must look beyond our behavior and into ourselves if we are to become more mature.

The first level of maturity is behavior which conforms to judgments of society or the culture. It is useful in the sense that agreed-upon social rules help us relate better to others and to act more effectively in most situations. Conflicts often spring from what "they" want us to do and what we wish to do. At times we think we may lose a valued part of ourselves if we conform, so we rebel. When we disturb society, despite the reason, we are apt to be seen as relatively immature. The greater the disturbance, the more immature we appear. While the revolutionist is always immature by this definition, rebellion in some cases may be a higher form of maturity than conformity or submission.

*Spirituality often reflects nonconformist views as the inspired self emerges. Tolerance of abuse or misuse of others may weigh upon our conscience, and in due time we rebel against an exploitation widely acceptable to others, as with slavery, for example. We may be aware of misuse of privilege for many years before it pains us so much, we revolt. Not to raise the issue would be easier; so, we see, rebellion may be the more mature choice. As we eliminate grosser forms of oppression and abuse of self and others, we encounter more subtle refined forms which require that we continue to refine our judgment: manipulation, power plays, exclusion, disguised threat and intimidation, body language, tone. We learn to read between the lines for more subtle clues of maturity. This often holds true of spiritual matters as humanity evolves toward its greater potential.

At times our responses may appear to be disruptive, hostile, even destructive. At this level we choose to follow our conscience instead of "the rules." Following "God's will" has been known historically to lead to strange behaviors, misery, even fanatical destruction. Nevertheless, when motives are clear, a response to needs — whether or not society condones the response — represents a higher level of maturity than blind conformity.

*Master Jesus found he was at odds with the religious authorities of his time. Not that long ago, most of society accepted slavery. Christians owned slaves without feeling guilty or immoral for doing so. Attention was focused more upon how Christians treated their slaves. Now, for most of us, the entire idea is unthinkable; a different level of perception has emerged.

> Maturity begins to grow when you can sense your concern for others outweighing your concern for yourself.
>
> —John MacNaughton

As social consciousness matures, we face more contemporary matters. Until recently, a woman's right to vote or own property was denied. Today we more readily embrace the rights of all as God-given, inalienable, not realizing just how newly sanctioned these concepts are. As concerns are raised, the conscience stirs and leadership develops to resist what had been previously acceptable. Conscientious objectors are often influenced by religious tradition to resist aspects of military service. Others rebel against behavior unacceptable to their standards. Rebellion, then, must be evaluated to see if it reflects lower or higher awareness.

As spiritual maturity expands, we rethink concerns that once occasioned no discomfort. When consciousness changes, so does lifestyle. Consider questions such as sexual behavior, vegetarian diets, abortion, the death penalty, euthanasia, refusal to pay taxes. Add to these the issues you contemplate to see how you reconcile your spiritual beliefs with society's accepted norms. In fact, contemplating such issues for oneself is a sign of spiritual maturity, and inner growth provides these challenges as we attempt to reflect in our outer life the changes happening inwardly.

Continued maturity is measured by a combination of four factors:
1. We become aware that a distinct difference exists between what we see as a personal need and what society would approve;
2. we become aware of the consequences of any behavior;
3. we make a conscious choice to do what we see is necessary;
4. we accept the consequences.

These factors are stated in terms of an apparent conflict with society, but this is not necessarily true. We may operate from a holistic view of what is needed and use our creativity to fulfill that need in a highly constructive, nonthreatening manner. We may choose not to rebel in any obvious way and forego a quick resolution of the problem to work for change in other long-term ways.

It may sound as though higher levels of maturity concern only behaviors involving interaction with society. But we find these levels in our internal, personal interactions in day-to-day living. An important consideration is the degree to which we are sensitive to our perceptions, as well as to perceptions of others. We realize maturity is not a simple concept, but the wellspring of behaviors established in consciousness rather than in automatic, perhaps unconscious reactions.

Ethical Living

Nine guiding concepts for ethical living are offered by the *Agni Yoga teachings as purposeful directives for those who desire to live in high consciousness. *Agni,* or fire, reminds us of the fervor of all who seek God. "Light" and "fire," used throughout the ages by saints and sages to speak of the divine presence, link us to all spiritual seekers.

In this time of integrating wisdom from humanity's past, each concept is important. Contemporary aspirants who seek a synthesis of experiences and disciplines from the past help our progress toward the long-promised "leap in consciousness." Themes, not rigid rules, provide an expanded vision of human potential. While each of us has a specific temperament and may be more attracted to certain concepts than to others, by honoring all, we integrate them and fulfill our commitment to live lives guided by ethical principles.

We have chosen the Agni Yoga themes and *virtues as our *seed thoughts for several reasons. Open to everyone, the Agni way is timely as we advance toward a more enlightened era. It facilitates the quest for greater knowledge, regardless of background or nature — scientific or devotional. Neither Eastern nor Western but encompassing both, it unifies our personal inner and outer realities. Modern spiritual disciples eagerly embrace this ecumenical and transformational esoteric practice. In this transitional period, with new spiritual technologies rapidly

Themes
Striving
Humanity
Self-sacrifice
Future
Freedom
Harmony
Community
Responsibility
Service

Fig. 1. Agni Themes.

Virtues		
Enthusiasm	Love	Harmlessness
Beauty	Purity	Fearlessness
Universality	Reverence	Humility
Leadership	Transformation	Joy

Fig. 2. Agni Virtues.

emerging, we appreciate this contemporary yoga, its insights and power.

Since it is important to use each seed thought several times, we suggest that a lesson is incomplete until you have meditated as instructed over a period of days. If meditations are extended over a very long period, the momentum is lost and relatively superficial experiences may result.

Not yet a clearly defined process, the Agni path continues to reveal itself as humanity builds communication capabilities with the soul, individually and collectively. As heart and mind merge, new levels of the *mental body form within the individual, as in the group. Meditation has a greater effect than most understand. Evolutionary work, meditations bless both ourselves and humanity — a service we render even as we seek enlightenment or salvation, for *salvation* means "enlightenment." To equate salvation with enlightenment is to affirm the truth and reconcile the Western and Eastern paths.

Agni Yoga introduces us to the term *co-measurement:* the ever-necessary adjustment of consciousness which helps us live wisely. Exposure to an assortment of ideas, philosophies, and cultures adds to the range of concepts from which we draw conclusions. These may or may not be consciously thought through, but they externalize in our responses to events of daily life.

Through integration of experience, events, and responses, we become increasingly able to know ourselves and to shape to some degree the direction our life takes. Using co-measurement to demonstrate maturity, we establish a lifestyle which synthesizes awareness of all aspects: 1) our needs versus society's approval, 2) making choices after weighing facts as best we can, and 3) willingness to accept consequences. Co-measurement utilizes all factors and acknowledges a need for sensitivity in shaping personal response.

We think of this as a tool to facilitate natural maturing. Some see the goal of maturity and embrace it, thereby reaching maturity more quickly and less painfully. Others

Co-measurement and Surfing

Imagine the skill needed by a surfer riding the ocean waves. S/he must consider pressure of wind; roughness of water; spacing, speed, height, and power of waves; length and weight of surfboard; and his or her own body weight. The integration of these determinative factors is co-measurement.

Fig.3. Co-measurement and Surfing.

cannot figure out how to help themselves or even what may be awry; they struggle through life, seemingly unable to realize their choices affect their experience. In this work we see inner contact as having an impact which helps us effect change.

Fluctuating Maturity

It is quite apparent, degrees or levels of maturity, "maturity quotients," fluctuate, just as our stability, emotional state, intelligence, health, judgment, and other characteristics do. This, of course, creates further difficulties in judging overall maturity. Our immediate needs, the kinds and degree of stress we endure, our physical and emotional state, critical events in our lives, our expectations and the possibility of their realization, tragedies and joys in the lives of family and friends — all, and more, affect the maturity level of our behavior. If we have built responsible and constructive habits, however, we tend to continue to demonstrate this through crises, and a positive response generally predominates throughout our lives.

Our level of maturity may be diverted from its usual pattern by three distinct changes in the flow of living. When life proceeds comfortably, most of us do fairly well, but we may quickly succumb to more childish behavior when we encounter a crisis.

A general guideline is: if in our normal behavior we are centered at a certain level of consciousness or *chakra, such as solar plexus or heart center, we may drop a complete level in the midst of major challenges, from solar plexus to spleen or from heart to solar plexus. Yet we sometimes respond to challenges in an inspired way, by "rising" to the occasion. Some people become angry and rebellious when their plans are not successful. Others may be calm and flexible, even when ordinarily they are petty, childish, and irresponsible. During a crisis, they may respond with maturity.

A further fluctuation may be seen between short-term crises and long-term stress. All of us may react immaturely when we reach our personal limits and stress becomes too intense, too complex, or too continuous, but these lapses are usually relatively brief. Thus, because of variation, even mature behavior fluctuates considerably, which only increases difficulties in evaluating this highly desired characteristic.

Balanced Maturity

Readily recognized as desirable, balanced maturity is observable in many ways. Yet any one component may get out of balance, causing us to act immaturely. For instance, we need to be responsive but not reactive. A mature individual must be sensitive, but over-sensitivity leads to over-reaction. Stable maturity reflects constant adjustment (co-measurement) and an ability to manage in a practical manner. But some people who appear stable are really phlegmatic, nonresponsive. We all know those who are hyper-sensitive and who resort to all sorts of petty demands. They are more readily seen as "immature." How we handle these people and their demands becomes a test of our own maturity. So we characterize maturity as heightened awareness, coupled with constructive — at least not destructive — responses for all concerned.

We want to persist in keeping open our judgments about these situations of criticism and revision; we hope to grow wiser through experience. Balance is particularly noticeable in those on the spiritual path, for we are constantly seeking to expand consciousness, finding positive ways to measure and respond. New awareness, which often accompanies meditation, can lead to behavior we later see as inappropriate. But willingness to persevere through this process of growth is an indication of maturity. Thus, we see maturity is not a sequence of stereotyped behavior modes, for as we expand our horizons, we inevitably face new challenges to our developing maturity. An analogy for maturity is *ripening fruit:* souls "ripen" as consciousness evolves. Life experiences help us learn as we go. A higher consciousness demonstrates maturing awareness.

Multiplicity of Components

Maturity has several interactive factors to be considered, both in ourselves and others. We will respond better to some components than others and maturity fluctuates. In spite of our efforts, pockets of immaturity will persist — single events or situations we do not handle well, though we are quite comfortable with others. If we are aware of this complexity, we are less apt to make snap judgments about others or to condemn ourselves too harshly when we feel we do not satisfy our own desired standards. It is important to become conscious of these situations as they occur and to rework them in the *nightly review.

Relative and Absolute Responses

Many feel that if we could only find "right" responses to all situations, we would have no problem with immaturity — like the child who thinks s/he will always know what to do and everything will be fine when s/he grows up. The truth is, our behavior is only relatively mature at any given moment. Our goal, then, should be to *function more maturely increasingly often*. As mentioned, reasonable conformity to society's rules is a sign of maturity, but exceptions must be made, and a different response may indicate maturity. When we do not know the best response, we create a perspective which allows new responses which may be more (or less) mature than our original solutions. We acknowledge that relativity of response makes it difficult to evaluate the maturity of specific behaviors.

Components of Maturity

All components of maturity are to be viewed in light of the features already described: each reflects a pattern of behavior rather than a state of being; each concerns fluctuating behaviors and balancing a range of responses; each is part of a total complexity, and under certain circumstances, deficiencies in one component may offset a more appropriate general response; each projects responses that may be judged as more or less mature. As in all behaviors, different levels surface at different times. Circumstances and past experiences influence how we will act and react in the future, as do our *glamours and *illusions. Specific triggers may change our reactions temporarily.

Constructive Use of Emotions

Probably no other component stands out as so clearly related to mature behavior as ways we deal with our emotions. Temper tantrums, pouting and withdrawal, rages and depressions, feeling hurt, exaggerated guilt reactions, and rapid emotional highs and lows are what many people call immaturity. Those more frequently seen as unemotional are often judged as more mature, implying that elimination of negative emotions would be ultimate maturity. However, this ignores evidence that even "love" may lead to distinctly immature behavior — witness those who remain infatuated with seriously destructive people.

Interest in the quest for spiritual maturity led *Abraham Maslow to list characteristics he felt identified the *self-actualized individual. This remarkable aid inspires us to take great strides toward attainment of spiritual maturity.

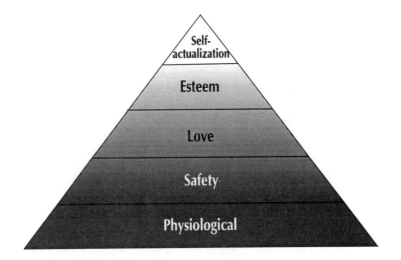

Fig. 4. Maslow's Hierarchy of Human Needs.

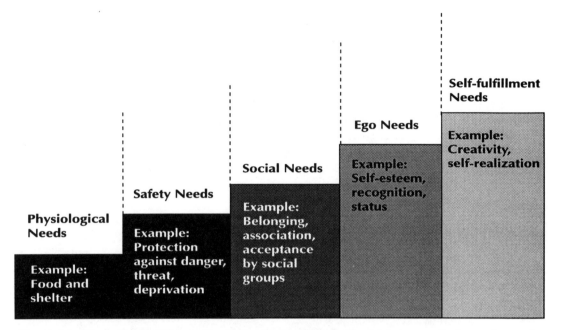

Fig. 5. Maslow's Table: Hierarchy of Needs Amplified. The higher we climb on the socio-economic scale, the more likely we are to discover more subtle needs, and as we become better educated, the more important our social attitude and inner needs become to our sense of fulfillment.

Sometimes maturity is measured by our continuing to function reasonably well in spite of feelings that threaten to overwhelm us. Forgiving instead of attacking is a more mature response. When pressures are too many and last too long, we may need to withdraw to "lick our wounds," or to seek help and solace. Certainly recognition and acceptance of these needs are signs of maturity. While we learn to handle rejection, failure, loss, and challenges, we must learn additionally to deal with achievements. Success may "go to our head" in such a way as to cause us to become arrogant and domineering, not considered mature attributes.

Responsibility

Much has been written suggesting that acceptance of responsibility is the true sign of emotional maturity. But this component goes far beyond mere acceptance. We each must discern responsibilities appropriate for us; be willing to absorb consequences of our decisions; continue to analyze how our judgments have produced

Maslow's List of Characteristics of Self-Actualizers

1. They avoid publicity, fame, glory, honors, popularity, celebrity, or at least do not seek it. It seems not to be terribly important one way or another.

2. They do not need to be loved by everyone.

3. They generally pick out their own causes, which are apt to be few in number, rather than responding to advertising or to campaigns or to other people's exhortations.

4. Their fighting is not an excuse for hostility, paranoia, grandiosity, authority, rebellion, etc., but is for the sake of getting things right. It is problem-centered.

5. They manage somehow simultaneously to love the world as it is and to try to improve it.

6. They respond to challenge in a job. A chance to improve the situation or the operation is a big reward. They enjoy improving things.

7. They do not need or seek for or even enjoy very much flattery, applause, popularity, status, prestige, money, honors, etc.

8. Expressions of gratitude, or at least of awareness of their good fortune, are common.

9. They tend to be attracted by mystery, by the unknown, unsolved problems and the challenging, rather than to be frightened by them.

10. They enjoy bringing about law and order in chaotic situations, in messy or confused situations, or in dirty and unclean situations.

11. They try to free themselves from illusions, to look at facts courageously, to remove the blindfold.

12. They feel it is a pity for talent to be wasted.

13. They tend to feel that every person should have an opportunity to develop to his highest potential, to have a fair chance, to have equal opportunity.

14. They like doing things well, "doing a good job," "to do well what needs doing." Many such phrases add up to "bringing about good workmanship."

15. They derive pleasure from knowing admirable people (courageous, honest, effective, "straight," "big," creative, saintly, etc.): "My work brings me in contact with many fine people."

16. They enjoy assuming responsibilities (which they can handle well) and certainly do not fear or evade responsibility. They respond to responsibility.

17. They uniformly consider their work to be worthwhile, important, even essential.

18. They enjoy greater efficiency, making an operation more compact or neater, simpler, faster, less expensive, turning out a better product, doing with less parts, a smaller number of operations, less clumsiness, less effort, more fool-proof, safer, more "elegant," less laborious.

Such worthy goals as self-realization, self-actualization, or *enlightenment seem overwhelming unless we learn to take small steps. How-to's become increasingly important in order to focus our will and make progress.[1] Accepting that the existence or seeming nonexistence of emotion and reaction does not determine degree of maturity, a critical factor becomes how we use our *emotional energies*. Any time we transmute emotional energy to more constructive responses, rather than our usual conditioned response, we build our capacity to act more maturely — which is true even if we occasionally relapse.

—John Curtis Gowan, *Development of the Psychedelic Individual*

Fig. 6. Maslow's List of Characteristics of Self-Actualizers.

negative or positive (useful) results; reduce our drive for reward, accepting responsibility and focusing upon doing what needs to be done just because — like Everest — it is there; know when to release responsibilities or alter our actions when change is indicated.

We achieve discrimination when we develop the wide range of integrative capabilities of the brain's right hemisphere and the analytical abilities of the left. As these interact, we retain the capability to evaluate (left hemisphere) and to receive fresh insights (right hemisphere). Discernment, assessing from a higher level of mind, is considered a *gift of the *Holy Spirit. As discrimination develops, we discern an appropriate response, not reacting from judgment or our mere rational, analytical, decision-making ability. We are able to gather information from all our sources and then use spiritual judgment to find our own right-action.

As we grow wiser, we see our acceptance of responsibility as necessary for growth, satisfaction in life, and to fulfill our role as an adult. If we become compulsive about the amount or kinds of responsibilities we assume, we are functioning immaturely from ego needs and unconscious conditioning. So, responsibility is an important component, as is maintaining a reasonable balance.

Respect

True humility emerges from a respect for ourselves, for others, and for an agenda which contributes to the well-being of humanity. Any steps taken to perceive more clearly who we are lead to increased respect for all life. This reveals itself in attitudes and outward behaviors: patterns which free us from the false superiority of ego demands, and foster an acceptance and honoring of differences, and an enriching openness to life. We embrace, rather than reject, the greatest freedom of expression for ourselves and others. We acknowledge that disrespect for others often discloses a lack of self-respect.

Growth

Maturity, a dynamic factor, always accompanies personal development and growth. Without growth, we do not continue to mature. A static "state of being" does not represent a mature, realistic view of life. Maturity is willingness to relinquish established, more comfortable ways in order to grow and expand. More than acceptance of inevitable change, this means accepting the challenge to become our better self through continuous effort. A profound commitment! Acceptance may be merely surrendering gracefully. But embracing the challenge in order to become more is quite another matter.

Persistence and Continuity

A reasonable ability to persevere in the face of challenge is an important component of maturity. "Keeping on" is imperative to movement toward growth, particularly noticeable when we are plagued by negative stimuli and circumstances. Persistence helps us recognize that we are more than someone battered by life's vicissitudes. Continuity makes us more dependable and useful — not because we prove our worth in this way (our worth needs no proof) but because it allows the external part of ourselves to express our internal comprehension — as in, actions speak louder than words. By discriminating, we avoid the "just plain stubbornness" that binds us to yesterday's reality. In some situations giving up or giving in may show more maturity than clinging to the outmoded. Now we see clearly the value, as well as the need, for discrimination.

Commitment

One aspect of behaving maturely is our willingness to commit to goals — caring about the welfare of others, as well as our own, to support that which enriches the world around us and affirms Oneness of life. This particularly includes commitment to long-term involvement. Combined with responsibility and persistence, commitment enables us to participate in the richness inherent in the universe.

Trust may be the greatest challenge life offers. Dare we trust the universe to love us? In the Desiderata, it is written, *Undoubtedly the universe unfolds as it should,* and in so doing, each of us, as a child of the universe, is helped upon our way. And we read in Matthew 10.31 and 6.28, respectively, *Give no thought to sparrows, lilies of the fields.* Yet human experience rarely witnesses such trust. On the contrary, we often believe trusting is foolish or childish. Indeed, *being as a little child* (Matt. 18.3) invites spirituality and encourages childlikeness, not immaturity. Childlikeness represents trust, spontaneity, simplicity, and the ability to be in the moment, unfettered by glamour and illusion. Children exist in the here and now, responding to the experience of the less entangled present. As trust builds, so does our ability to respond to the situation of the moment without attaching so much history to it or withholding a part of ourselves "just in case."

Persistent reluctance to become involved with significant enterprises places serious limitations on our opportunities to act maturely and to grow. This self-limiting attitude stems from an assumption that commitment suggests restriction and loss of freedom, which, in itself, may create a seriously restrictive trap. In reality, commitment may take a form that expands and intensifies our outlook as we realize the potentials of the moment, setting ourselves on the path that leads to the spiritual maturity we desire.

Dynamic Monitoring

An essential element in developing maturity is the ability to look at ourselves to see the effects and implications of our behavior and to become sensitive to our own and others' needs, so that we function most productively. We may accept *guidance from others, but for the most reliable and consistent development of maturity, we must be able to examine the inner sources of our responses, then analyze the effects of our behavior. Monitoring cannot be continuous, but regular review and evaluation, together with alertness to need for change, serves us well. As we have noted, on the spiritual path we often use the questioning technique: *What is this trying to teach me?* We ask this even of our illnesses, our accidents, our relationships — not only of ordinary, unexceptional incidents. Furthermore, we observe others for models of behavior, as well as for behavior to avoid. All of us do this at times, but we improve and relate the process more clearly with pondering.

Indeed, use of psychotherapy or *psychospiritual techniques helps us with this loving monitoring, thus hastening spiritual maturity. We seek the wisdom of another, as well as our own, in order to see more clearly and integrate more consciously. Psychospiritual techniques and analysis with a wise individual serve today's *initiate in a manner not unlike the confessor or *mentor of the past. We recall that the basic Greek word *psych* means "breath, the principle of life, soul."

As we eliminate glamours and illusions, we see more clearly. We apply insights and, guided from within, we grow increasingly wise. Periodically, we choose "reality checks" from others we hold in high regard. With this assistance, we may reach even greater maturity than if we were to use only our outer intelligence and personal drive.

Additional Interaction

Other components are a part of this complexity called maturity. Developing a philosophy of life indicates greater maturity; willingness to drift along without any concern for purpose in life typifies childish behavior. Even those who live "in the now" look to the future for an idea of where they may be headed, and ask, "Is this where I wish to go?"

This awareness of direction relates closely to spiritual maturity. We ordinarily progress at a personality level by working toward immediate and long-term goals. The way we carry out this process indicates our maturity level. A sense of direction allows us to remain flexible but centered, applying persistence when appropriate. It helps us hold a higher purpose, a sense of "soul at work" within the framework of human life. The necessity for continual discrimination reappears constantly; without it, we blunder along ineffectually. Our expectations and the rewards we seek frequently reflect maturity or lack thereof. So it becomes quite clear that all of these components are interactive and mutually supportive.

Developing Maturity

Does all this complexity mean no one can develop or even measure maturity? No. Maturity involves a high level of conscious awareness, as opposed to conditioned, unaware responses. Thus, it is always amenable to our choices and creativity. We have only to look around to see many who demonstrate mature behavior quite consistently. What they do, we can learn to do. We remember as well, dissolving barriers to higher consciousness increases the likelihood of maturity. As we free ourselves from the restriction of glamours and illusions, we perceive more acutely with the eye of the soul.

Contemplating maturity while making an effort to apply our new knowledge impels us toward growth. But it is necessary to determine a personal concept of what mature behavior is in any specific situation. We evaluate the real possibility of acting in this way and anticipate constructive effects. We then test it and look at the results. We remember the guideline: *act enthusiastically to become enthusiastic* (or whatever quality is sought). Simultaneously, we explore our motivations for desiring a particular quality. Are we hoping to create a favorable image? Does this truly contribute to personal satisfaction? Does it strengthen self-love? When we respond in ways which seem to innately increase our ability to love ourselves, to lift our sense of self-esteem, we demonstrate greater maturity. If this line of questioning is too difficult to pursue alone, ask a trusted counselor or therapist to assist you.

Begin the practice of monitoring behaviors and evaluating their effects — upon yourself, as well as upon others. Do not become compulsive about this; rather, do a sampling fairly consistently. This may be done on occasion in conjunction with the nightly review, allowing you to obtain a reasonably sound view of your overall maturity and specific areas which may need attention.

> ### *Maturity involves a high level of consciousness, as opposed to conditioned, unaware responses.*

As we practice the nightly review consistently, a sense of maturity seems to evolve naturally. Observing ourselves, we come to see what actions trigger reactions and whether or not we respond consciously from our ever-expanding pool of wisdom, sometimes called *witness consciousness. When we can see the difference in light of our own high consciousness, new maturity has emerged.

As we choose our own direction, we are empowered. Spiritual life offers opportunity to know and to be—drawing our outer life and our inner adventure into closer relationship, enabling us to observe much in each experience as we access this broader approach.

As we better grasp our choices and deepen our commitments, we gradually move into a state of mind that invites maturity in all areas of life. By attending to the components discussed, we refine our discriminations and judgments—and more often the quality of our behavior improves.

Do not ask, "Am I mature?" Ask, "In what ways do I act in an immature manner? What things might I change? How can I change this? Are my standards realistic?" Such questions lead us to constructive answers. Recommended reading at the end of this volume provides further opportunities for progress.

Active Meditation Technique

We continue to use active meditation as our principal practice. Please see the appendix in volume 2 for a review of the long seed-thought meditation technique as introduced in volume 1. The following outline is presented for use until it becomes routine.

PROCEDURE FOR SEED-THOUGHT MEDITATION

1. Begin to relax with several natural breaths, singing softly or *chanting.

2. Read a brief piece of devotional material.

3. Close your eyes, and turn your attention within. Use your opening gesture. Become still, and continue to relax.

4. Now visualize the soulstar ten inches or so above your head. Focus upon this vibrating light, and cause it to expand its radiance, remaining clear and bright.

5. Draw the soulstar energy down to your solar plexus, creating harmony between the quiescent self and the restless ego. Now bring energy to the heart. Magnify your feelings of love-caring. Allow love to flow. Feel it flow through your emotional nature. Consciously bless the body. Feel love for it. Fill yourself with the positive energy of the soulstar. Radiate that love throughout your body; then emanate it into the space around you.

6. Now seek to lift your focus from personality mind to interact with *higher mind. We guide this shift by taking a breath and thinking, *I would be lifted from limited mind to Divine Mind.*

7. By focused intent and active will, we form a line of light to pierce the *veil that separates the higher from the lower.

Lift the line of light upward, extending through and about ten inches beyond the forehead.

8. Lift your *magnetized consciousness into the *Cloud of Knowable Things. With purity of mind, we form a magnetized consciousness by focusing on the seed thought while lifting and magnetizing it by the power of the heart. This magnetized line of light when lifted into the Cloud of Knowable Things, precipitates droplets. Just as moisture collects and drops begin to fall when climatic conditions are just right, we are creating precipitation.

9. We draw to ourselves that which is needed for ongoing spiritual progress. Ask to perceive, intuit, and know. Ask the great questions of the aspirant:

What is my part in the *mandala of human endeavors?

How may I serve the higher cause?

What is mine to do? What part of this is mine to do this day?

10. Now, we seek to bring the subtle impressions back to the conscious mind, blending the passion of our heart and mind together within the chalice of our own being.

11. Use the technique of acting *"as if," perceive yourself as a soul-infused personality, and focus upon your seed thought.

12. Capture the thoughts you have contacted, jot down the phrases, ideas, concepts, or insights that come — also any symbols, designs, or forms that enter your mind. Mentally ask questions of these impressions, knowing additional responses will come.

13. Now, speaking as a soul-infused personality, say the Great Invocation (see appendix), both as a service and as a way of expressing thankfulness for all you have received.

14. Conclude this work by speaking the sacred tone, *Om, aloud three times, and use your closing gesture. At this point you may choose to add healing prayers, special intentions, visualizations, or other prayer work.

To derive the most value from this volume you are encouraged to correspond with meditation tutors at Sancta Sophia Seminary. These knowledgeable people with extensive experience offer each person enrolled in the meditation course individual attention. They answer questions, provide guidance and helpful suggestions. The enrollment form provides tutors the background information needed to advise you appropriately. If you wish to enroll, complete the application as instructed on pages 240-241 in the appendix.

The Virtues of Soul Development

In this volume the twelve Agni *virtues are used as seed thoughts — two in each of lessons 1 through 6. Two words per lesson need not alter procedures. Continue to allot about ten sessions for the first seed thought, then move to the second word. New exercises are introduced in lessons 7 and 8. Lesson 7 presents a new meditation technique called soul alignment and lesson 9 a closing seed thought. As students finish each lesson, send your response to the meditation tutors, always indicating lesson number.

An interesting correlation may be made between the twelve personality virtues and the twelve *archetypes of the *zodiac. *Spiritual science suggests that the twelve virtues humanity is seeking to develop are spread throughout the zodiac, one to each *sun sign. Each of us strives to cultivate all twelve virtues to facilitate advancement on humanity's *path of initiation.

The astrological signs and their corresponding virtues are:

Aries — Enthusiasm
Taurus — Beauty
Gemini — Universality
Cancer — Leadership
Leo — Love
Virgo — Purity

Libra — Reverence
Scorpio — Transformation
Sagittarius — Harmlessness
Capricorn — Fearlessness
Aquarius — Humility
Pisces — Joy

If you have your natal chart, note your three major influences — sun, moon, and ascendant — and their assigned virtues. Can you see how your life experiences have been assisting you even before you had this information? It is a good idea to review all twelve virtues and acknowledge how well you express some qualities and which ones present more challenge. You may or may not choose to share your findings with your meditation tutor.

An interesting way to think of virtue is as energy. We desire to express that virtue with the capacity to let it flow through us with clarity and without distortion. When misinterpreted or expressed destructively, the energy becomes distorted, a vice. Thus, in building a desired virtue, we develop our ability to communicate that personal attribute ever more clearly. Naturally, we express less capably at first; as we improve our skills, our expression of these qualities improves.[2]

Along the way, we develop the ability to observe others expressing the virtue or quality upon which we are focused. The more we observe and focus, we begin to comprehend the quality or energy and to build it within our own nature. Qualities and energies are only understood because we have experienced them. This continuous observing, building, and reflecting affirms growth and encourages us as we strive to become all we might be. Seed-thought work cultivates our being, as well as our knowing.

Seed Thoughts

Your assignment includes two seed thoughts. Conduct several (ten recommended) meditations on the first seed-thought virtue, and then move to the second. When finished with both, mail your responses. If you wish to devote more sessions to a word, feel free to do so. If you have particular difficulty with a word, you may experience less satisfaction with the results, but do let the tutors know the nature of your problem so they may be of help.

Assignment

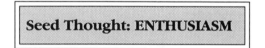

Seed Thought: ENTHUSIASM

Our first seed thought is *enthusiasm,* the virtue assigned to the Aries influence.

> The Greeks bequeathed to us one of the most beautiful words in our language — the word *enthusiasm — en theos,* a god within.
>
> —Louis Pasteur

Whatever you do, do it with vigor, enthusiasm, or fervor. Charge your life, your profession, your ideas with your unique and fiery spirit. One with fervor becomes a transmitter of fire, and fire ignites. Holy enthusiasm enables us to bring the fire of *spirit from higher planes through ourselves and into our work. Sustaining the fire through our personality vehicle transforms all our bodies — physical, emotional, mental, and spiritual. Thus, as we advance on our path of life, utilizing fiery spirit and will, fiery love and wisdom, we burn away all that impedes our progress. As noted by Perle Epstein, "In Jewish mysticism, enthusiasm is the great way for [one] to unite with the upper spheres and 'break through all skies in one act.'"

Seed Thought: BEAUTY

The second seed thought, *beauty,* is the virtue assigned to the Taurus influence.

> The ideals which have lighted my way, and time after time have given me new courage to face life cheerfully, have been Kindness, Beauty, and Truth. . . . The trite subjects of human efforts — possessions, outward success, luxury — have always seemed to me contemptible.
>
> —Albert Einstein

Beauty is absolutely necessary for one on the spiritual path, for it feeds the unfolding soul. Beauty is food for spirituality, just as we must have nourishment for the physical nature. Its presence prompts divinity to emerge and allows it to express more freely. Every creative person is trying to manifest beauty.

"When we express the innermost beauty of *Self, the *real* man or woman is born," the late Torkom Saraydarian has said. By encouraging beauty and expressing high ethics day to day, we give birth to the inner Self. Through the beauty of the emerging high consciousness, we bring Self to express on this plane.

As we build and express this virtue, our own ability to perceive beauty expands. At first, we perceive only material beauty; in time, natural beauty. Later we come to discern the subtle beauty permeating creation. Peace, harmony, and serenity are all aspects of beauty. In time, we see the beauty within the other, and only then do we become capable of seeing the beauty within ourselves. All of us have been told, *Beauty is as beauty does.* When we accept each being as a spark of divinity learning to express, we begin to recognize a profound beauty above and beyond the outer form.

Beyond the Ancient, Restless, Scanning Ego

Any discipline that makes us feel our own
inferiority is as wrong as one which makes us feel
our own superiority. Man is neither great
nor small. He is a channel through
which eternal principle is flowing.
—Manly P. Hall,
Self-Unfoldment by Disciplines of Realization[1]

T he word "ego" may be confusing because it conveys many different interpretations. To the *Freudian analyst, ego designates only one specific part of the fundamental structure of personality. Others use it to designate the total conscious self. Some *metaphysical writings designate the spiritual essence of a being — soul, inner self — as "Ego," written with a capital e. In other writings, ego is analogous to personality, false self, or *nonself.

In these lessons ego characterizes that part of mind which thinks it is separate from the Creator, which we may also identify as our nonself. We easily confuse it with personality — that energy focus composed of attitudes, self-concepts, conditioning, and characteristics, as well as other energies we use in the outer/physical/material world, because the ego part of our mind uses personality for its own purposes. As we become increasingly sensitive to the light of soul, personality becomes the vessel for soul expression, shifting its allegiance from ego to soul as soul-infusion occurs. When we identify with the real Self, personality still exists, but we appear to others to be quite different.

When ego is threatened or diminished, it (and we, to the extent we identify with it) becomes fearful and hostile. Ego may retaliate with anger, illness, or hurt. This response has a general coherence; it is expandable and dynamic, a force with which to contend!

We may have lost sight of the fact that we created ego as a consequence of believing we are separate. *We* endowed it with power! It seems to function as a separate and ruling entity within us, even pushes us around. It has an intense, insatiable desire for complete freedom, power, control, and eternal life. It exploits situations to win praise for itself in order to counteract its insecurities. It presents difficulties for everyone, but spiritually inclined students have a special need to deal with this ego and to recognize the situations it generates.

Subjugating ego power to conscious awareness is a major work involving spiritual techniques to check ego advancement and to diminish the power of the false identity. As we transfer our identity to soul, we build a witness consciousness to oversee ego. As we diminish ego, the true Self emerges. Known by many names, this real Self in Christianity is called the *Christ-Within, the *hope of glory* (Col. 1.27). On a mystical path we seek to be led by this Inner Presence.

What Challenges Does ego Present?

Most obvious problems arise from intense, fluctuating, and often contradictory demands of ego. While these may oppose society's injunctions and pressures, internal conflicts may be even more determinative. If raw desires of ego are given free reign, society quickly attempts to suppress them in an effort to prevent anarchy. As a result, we often develop feelings of guilt and worthlessness. So, each of us learns ways to control conditioning and excesses which cause such internal struggles. We become conscious of the duality with which we must deal — two "sides" of our nature which cannot be reconciled but with which we must contend. We seek ways to compromise, but compromises seldom satisfy for long. To anyone who has developed even a rudimentary awareness of an inner essence apart from ego, this duality presents a very real challenge.

Nonself, or ego, fights continually to obtain its twisted ends. Everything entering its experience is either incorporated or rejected, according to whether it increases ego's power and importance, insures continued life, or seems to fulfill some vagrant desire. Left to its own wishes, ego is entirely selfish — or self-centered, a term offering particularly clarifying insights. It is important to realize self-centeredness is a natural state of development, not bad-ness. An infant is self-centered — crying when it pleases, unconcerned with whatever its caretaker is doing, oblivious to whether Mom or Dad is tired. It wants what it wants, and now.

As we advance in years, we see self-centered behavior persists as long as we are centered in emotionalism. When we bridle emotions with the power of mind, we grow in skillful manipulation of body, emotions, and mind, working for personality's goals and becoming quite proficient in getting our way. Our desires form our focus, and our skills serve our desires. This is self-centeredness, or egotism.

That part of our nature which believes itself separate, ego, strains to dominate our entire nature for its needs and goals. Yet the quiescent

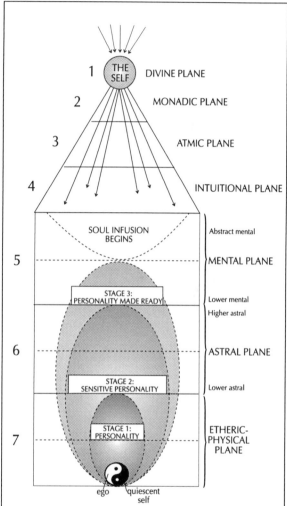

Fig. 7. Travels from ego to Divinity. Restless, scanning ego has been building its domain since its sojourn began. First claiming the physical nature, with time it becomes a dominant force over emotions and attitudes, creating beliefs and allegiances to satisfy its selfish purposes. As the light of the soul is invoked, challenge begins.

self waits, retaining an awareness of changelessness and complete-ness, of peace and joy. Basically, ego is insane, for it denies higher reality; so there is no real reasoning or compromising with it. An example of ego's inconsistencies is its treatment of the body — essential to our physical well-being and continuity — yet ego quite willingly reduces or destroys the body's effectiveness under a wide range of circumstances, perhaps to the point of holding *death as a reward, an escape from toil and misery.

We have created ego as a consequence of believing we are separate.

With the power we have given it, ego inhibits our complete-ness and wholeness at every turn. Our awareness of true creativity is fleeting and limited. Joy seems relative and temporary. Loving is only partial and spasmodic. Elation must be paid for by depression. We release anger, but we retain resentment. The ups and downs of our feelings and circumstances become the norm. To see the specifics that emerge from our ego orientation, we need only look around us and into our own mental and emotional roller coaster rides. As long as we listen to answers provided by ego, we trap ourselves in lives with no permanent satisfaction or joy.

In the language of the East, we remain upon the wheel of *karma with all its sorrow, frustration, and pain until we reach a highly developed level of spiritual awareness that provides passage from human life into the next level of experience, called *solar initiation. It takes a long time to see that nothing ego dictates brings lasting and real *illumination and peace.

As we have said, true joy — *samadhi* — is the ecstasy expe-rienced when personality and soul touch and begin to vibrate in harmony for a brief period. Now the true inner nature begins to have an impact. Along with happiness — the state of mind that fluctuates as personality experiences everyday life — we experi-ence joy, that sense of Oneness with the Great Life. It is joy that sustains even when outer life is miserable. With joy, we realize our inner connections and continue our quest, learning to face chal-lenges courageously.

What Can We Do about ego?

Though each individual must ask it for him- or herself, answers to this question have been sought since before recorded history. As a result, fascinating answers have been offered through the ages. All religions address the problem; philosophers discuss the nature of human ego at length. More recently, the fields of psychology and psychiatry are proposing answers with some claim of a scientific basis.

Psychology, often defined as the "science of the soul," is providing a modern means to bridge religion and science. Some psychologists satisfy their own egos (in this scientific, rational society) by denying religion and spirituality. Accepting a scientific identity, they are not ready for the soul work they will assume in time. Those aware of the important contributions the interface of ego with religion and spirituality can delight in their lives. In the future, psychology will advance even more boldly the convergence of science and spirituality.

Western and/or Christian Approaches

Most of us are familiar with Western, Christian attitudes toward ego. Lesser "self" (personality *and* ego) is seen as something which must be surrendered to God or to *the Christ. The initial step usually is known as "repentance." While assorted groups may wield somewhat different interpretations, a common thread fashions this lesser self as "innately evil" — malicious, sinful — and only divine intervention can redeem it and give it eternal life.

Through *prayer, worship, and surrender, we relinquish this lesser identity and personality to God's service. Personality will no longer wield its power to satisfy its own desires but is to turn from old ways of self-gratification. Pride must be replaced by humility, aggression by nonresistance, anger and hatred by love, taking by appropriate giving and receiving. One's faith community frequently determines the particular pattern, and applications of the basic process may seem quite contradictory.

*Esoteric Christianity similarly proposes the transformation of this nonself, postulating that our sense of self can mature and become part of the recast personality trained to serve soul in its journey to enlightenment. When properly understood, the *transformation process offered by Esoteric Christianity moves us toward the goal of Self-actualization; indeed ego is to serve purposes higher than its own. It is to become the Self, a vessel for soul, the *chalice for *Christ in you, the hope of glory.* The quest for keys to transformation is a natural outcome of loving the Creator and seeking to pursue higher will.

Eastern Philosophies and Religions

Christianity, as it has become largely crystallized, might now be called "churchianity." "Church" relates to *ecclesia,* translated "meaningful assembly." For many, *the salt has lost its savor* (Matt. 5.13), and hungry people have been led to look elsewhere for a way to fulfillment. For this reason, interest in Eastern religions, where we find elaborate and extensive treatment of ego, has grown in the West. The common theme — that we must destroy ego — is not because ego is evil but because it is illusory. We discover that, as long as we look upon ego as the true reality, we remain imprisoned by its pain and limitations.

Through meditation and conscious living, we prepare to experience an inordinate awareness of truth, and when we do, ego can no longer exist as it is. Its power lasts only as long as we believe we *are* ego. In that state we abide in an immense prison, bound by desires, notions, programming, feelings, ignorance, and consequences of actions that spring from that ignorance. The purpose of spiritual practices is to strip us of such illusion. *Lead us, O Lord, from darkness to light,* we pray.

Spiritual teachers generally agree that we cannot simply surrender ego. As a rule, Eastern approaches teach the necessity of experience, that unenlightened living takes place on the *involution side of life before we awaken to a larger picture. Wisdom teachings explain that soul puts down a personality through which we experience physical, *astral, and mental realms. This process of descent is the path of involution. We will get fully involved in these lower realms. In time, as ego becomes increasingly powerful and self-serving, some natural happening will bring about an awakening. We

The evolutionary arc is usually illustrated as:

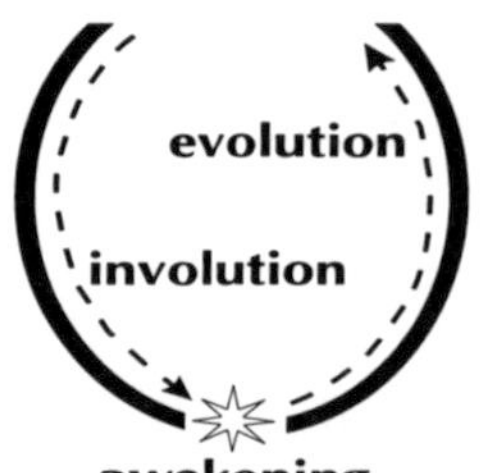

Fig. 8. Through Involution to Evolution.

cannot do this by ourselves; this occasion is triggered by *grace. Now personality integration and conscious soul maturity can begin. This path of conscious return, or *evolution, is the ascent of consciousness from matter to high awareness.

> If there exists a good and a wise God, then there also exists a progress of [hu]mankind toward perfection.
>
> —Plato

Our struggle with dark forces requires special knowledge. When we experience despair, a battle of the darkness within wages against the light within. We need support. Assistance may come from another, from sacred writings, prayer, observation, creativity. But we need guidelines to know where to turn at such challenging times.

> Aspirants usually bitterly resent the many cycles of darkness through which they go; they complain of the difficulty of working in the dark and of seeing no light anywhere; they forget that the ability to work in the dark or in the light is all one inherent capacity. The reason for this is that the soul knows nothing but *being,* and light and dark are—to the soul—one and the same thing. Above everything else, knowledge comes through conscious experiment, and **where there is no experimental activity no experience can be gained.** (bold emphasis added)
>
> —Alice A. Bailey, *Discipleship in the New Age II*

Let us return to the idea that ego is illusion. We need to consider what might be meant by illusion because we hear at least two arguments: 1) this dense and material world is the real world, and the unseen world is fantasy, or 2) this dense, material world is all illusion, and only the spirit world is real. In the beginning, we are pulled between what we know with the physical senses and what we perceive with a new part of our nature. Illusion means 1) not of the real senses, and 2) an erroneous perception of reality.

We are well aware that the five physical senses relate to the material world of sight, sound, touch, and so on. We may not be aware that *Wise Ones seek to guide us by pointing out the fallacies of limiting our beliefs and truths to the senses, for they know higher truths. One "false truth" is that the physical world is most important. By identifying this as illusion, we free ourselves to perceive a higher reality. The step from physical reality to nonphysical challenges us, but most spiritual teachers propose similar messages: "This is not the real"; "This is effect, not cause"; "Go higher." Sacred messages of all religions and traditions attempt to lead us beyond physical senses, knowing their powerful influences blind us and bind us.

In our modern quest for enlightenment it usually helps to separate spirituality from religion — considered by many to be the same. Spirituality is living in such a way as to discover, nurture, and express our own Inner Spirit. "Religion," from the Latin *religio,* means to realign to the source and includes practices or ways to reconnect. According to one's chosen tradition, these practices are then given serious allegiance.

I often compare religion to the handrail of a staircase. Life, the great teacher, provides lessons to help us advance step by step. As we learn, change, and progress toward high consciousness, we may hold on to the bannister or we may go bounding up the stairs without it. Religion is the pattern or way another used to achieve enlightenment, leaving directions for those who would follow. *Buddha provided his followers with the *"middle-road path." Master Jesus, the Christ, gave his truth to his disciples, who preserved that wisdom for those who would come later.

Remember, religion points to the past, and spirituality points to the future. We have no idea what may yet emerge from our own higher nature, our spirituality in bloom. As many discover the profound inner (veiled) messages of Esoteric Christianity, they find they are able to love and embrace the Christ more readily. They may have rejected the narrower *dogma Christianity traditionally has presented. A true understanding of TheoSophia and Esoteric Christianity excites those wishing to learn from within.

> If religion has failed, it is because it has confused the essential with the adventitious [coming from another source; not inherent]. True religion is spiritual religion, it is seeking after God, the opening of the deepest life of the soul to the indwelling Godhead, the eternal Omnipresence. Dogmas, cults, moral codes are aids and props; they may be offered . . . but not imposed . . . .
>
> —Sri Aurobindo, *The Future Evolution of Man*

TheoSophia is a philosophy built on inner knowing. It is the "theology," the study of God, "through *Sophia," wisdom. Esoteric Christianity preserves the mysteries of Christianity and emphasizes disciplines which enhance the Presence within. Meditation, a major practice, opens the gateway to an awareness of our mystical nature and provides the opportunity to reconnect Creator with Creation once again. As ways of inner knowing emerge, belief in mystical moments expands one's perspective of life. Harmony is established, and this Presence provides an inner knowing for which awakened ones long.

Each of us contributes to our specific group mind through development of the mystical aspects of our religion; every religion has a personal attunement to the Most High. Called by many names — inner knowing, sophia, gnosis — this personal attunement becomes the wisdom aspect active in our lives. To discover a personal alignment with the Christ, source of love-wisdom, is our goal. Remember too that as enough people of the Christian tradition awaken to its depths, Christianity will further unfold its potential.

As we enter the Aquarian era, the religion of the Holy Spirit — the *divine feminine — emerges. Nourished by the little-recognized and under-valued feminine, the mystical within now stirs, that we might truly become the sons and daughters of the Creator. This feminine aspect of God has been known historically as Shakti and Sophia, and it is often represented in an archetypal form as Mother Mary.

Since the term *sophia* has begun to be known to the public, we now need a deeper insight than just the Greek translation, "wisdom." Ever so accurate in itself, in a more fully developed sense Sophia can be considered "inner knowing" or the "wisdom of the heart." In Eastern and Russian Orthodox approaches, Sophia conveys the capacity to "realize a truth" regarding any area if one follows the inclination of the heart, ponders, and applies discernment. Sophia then guides us *from darkness to light, from the unreal to the real, from death to immortality.*

Sophia, our intuitive guide with her inner wisdom, becomes our companion as we walk the path of initiation — the feminine or mother aspect nurturing the infant Christ to maturity through first

Fig. 9. The Divine Feminine is the mother of the Christ within each of us, as this familiar icon personifies.

one stage of learning and then another. A good way to perceive this wisdom aspect, Sophia, is to identify the Christ part as active, growing, serving and Sophia as the watching-over, pondering, waiting part of our nature. Self-observation, inner knowing, the process of pondering and allowing are characteristics of Sophia. The goal readily perceived is for us to "thinketh in the heart," or to become "love-wisdom." This active-passive combination synthesizes into ChristoSophia, the love-wisdom, Christ consciousness of the initiate.

*As we transfer our identity to soul,
we build a witness
consciousness to oversee ego.*

Commonalities

Christianity, as well as other religions, sees ego as something to be transformed, subdued, or eliminated in order to attain higher states of consciousness. Methods to accomplish this vary. Even drastic procedures, the basis for most asceticism, have been developed. Flagellating the body, home of ego, is believed by some to be a practice aimed at ego's destruction. Reducing oneself to a homeless beggar may be seen by others as a way of diminishing our mortal power. The more rigid disciplines of some *yogas were designed to refine the body and fuse ego with soul, with ego taking second place.

All of these methods share the weakness that the process itself can be usurped by ego to obtain its own ends, often in a quite distorted but powerful fashion. Ascetics may take pride in punishment or deprivation and/or compulsively resist any expansion into everyday living. When yoga disciplines become ends in themselves, growth is stunted. Once-humble *aspirants may assume an air of smug superiority; powerful aspirants may use their strength to persecute and demean. Efforts to punish and degrade ego might backfire and become egocentricity, for when ego is most fearful, desperation drives it to extremes which distort rather than transform it.

Approaches to ego Management

Transform ego

In recent years many psychological processes have been developed to deal with ego. With the increased acceptance of science and the humanistic, the fields of psychology, psychiatry, and sociology have begun to address this problem. Their definitions of ego depend upon their theoretical biases, but, in general, ego is seen as needing development and integration; ego management is considered necessary and desirable. The usual approach is to strengthen ego by healing our bruises and low self-esteem and to build healthy *self-esteem.

Within a spiritual framework this may be called "training the personality." The goal is transformation of personality into an integrated whole, a refined vessel that is sensitive to impressions. We seek to incorporate ego and its power into a harmonious unit desiring to serve the soul.

At the same time, we adopt disciplines and practices to guide ego so we can live in relative peace. These approaches see ego as an organization of intact and stable energies which enable us to deal adequately with the world. We find ways of relating to the world so that we more frequently trust ourselves and our social environment. Coping skills are cultivated. We are now able to respond more effectively, more pleasantly. Pain is reduced, our capacity to endure without disintegration increases, and rewards are more frequent. Psychological methods may be used in a common-sense, self-help manner, or they may involve professional guidance at great depth, as individually preferred.

Contemporary concerns have given rise to many "self-help" systems: positive thinking, assertiveness training, transactional analysis, encounter groups, est, and concept therapy, to name only a few. The very popular twelve-step programs bear a remarkable resemblance to the *probationary path of *ageless wisdom. Twelve-step, rediscovered and modern, has become an initiatory path for today's seekers. All of us can benefit from living such wise steps. If this is a new and interesting thought for you, advise your tutor. S/he will recommend additional information.

Psychological Management of ego

Limitations

- As long as we stay within the perception of ego as proposed by psychology, we exclude the existence and effects of our spiritual nature.
- The outward focus often stops with how we relate to the outer world and how we feel as a result; whereas, spiritual awareness and meditation encourage us to focus within and toward new discoveries of self, providing means for our inner and outer natures to harmonize.
- Power which emerges from an ego that becomes too strong (however we define strength) results in abuses which backfire disastrously and ruin the peace and joy we seek. We may settle for power instead of peace.
- Personality ego functions only in a world where everything is relative and subject to change within addressing the changeless reality, which is the Source.
- Thus, ego remains vulnerable to circumstances, to personal desires, and to abuses resulting from achieving freedom from inhibiting influences.
- Since goals of a strong ego do not involve a basic, unifying spiritual principle, our purpose for living has limited depth and breadth. Something is lacking for those who sense an existence beyond a powerful ego, and that something is the reason we launched the spiritual search originally.
- Psychological approaches may intensify the belief that we are dependent upon wellness, wholeness, and strength of ego for living. Without ego, we are nothing, we think. This is a reversal of the truth about the nature of our essence.

Advantages

- Psychological management of ego provides immediate ways to cope with conflict and pressures of daily living.
- It serves to free us to a reasonable degree from our mental and emotional prisons.
- It leads us toward greater stability and healthier self-esteem, from which we can then advance our personal development.
- For some, it can make the difference between functioning and not functioning, even between living and dying.

Fig. 10. Psychological Management of ego.

      In fact, all psychological work becomes spiritual in nature, if it diminishes barriers to self-awareness — a spiritual goal. We must be mindful, however, that all psychologists do not see themselves as part of a spiritual process, nor does this mean that psychological work automatically brings spiritual awareness. Serious spiritual students are advised to work only with a psychologist who respects their personal spiritual approach. Our spirituality is too precious to be placed in jeopardy, and trust between therapist and client is vital. Without ego, the true self still has access to all the powers of personality (even more) that can be used in dealing with the world. This is the most important difference between personality strength and spiritual awareness.

We recall a basic premise: *We cannot surrender what we do not have.* We move in our spiritual journey from instinctual, unconscious awareness to a powerful ego. Upon awakening, we transform this vigorous ball of energies into an integrated consciousness useful to soul. Think of maturing ego as the result of considerable human struggle. All the personal power we have developed may now be elevated.

Remember, human ego is most obnoxious at that point just before awakening or reawakening. We have gathered our skills and resources and, whether we know it or not, we are ready to bloom. We are eager, charged with self-centered power. Then, ta-da! — the bud bursts forth!

A Basic Spiritual Approach[2]

Through the ages, many means of dealing with ego have resulted in individuals gaining ultimate illumination. For those devoting themselves wholeheartedly to a single traditional path, rewards are often significant.

In both Western and Eastern religions the path to enlightenment is delineated, but meeting these instructions can present challenges which often lead to frustrations, especially without a support system. Countless instances of bigotry and intolerance flourish in all religions because of narrow perceptions. Or, we see attempts to water down the *universality of God to a vague humanism. Churches often foster guilt and fear; some people are terrified, some rebel, and some may flee to science or a more progressive spirituality. Responses vary from withdrawal to intense involvement with the things of this world. Abuses are not inherent in transformational teachings, but distortions arise from several sources: ignorance; difficulties in translating truth from language to language; failure to realize the deeper meanings within symbols, *myths, and words; and deliberate, though often unconscious, distortions by ego as self-protection.

> There is no doubt that the Scriptures are symbolic, and only a translation of those symbols can reveal the full beauty and comprehensiveness of their holy wisdom.
> . . . Consciousness continues to evolve even faster as

Paul and the disciples of Jesus comprehend the true
meaning of light and begin to teach. Only the apoca-
lyptic Revelation of John reveals the final truth that the
destiny of every human is to become a light being.
—Sarah Leigh Brown, *Genesis: Journey into Light* [3]

Some of us, if not all, are challenged to find our own way to
basic truths. We strive to recognize contributions of religion and
science to free us from entrapment. We may seek confirmation from
mystical approaches which encourage more freedom. We check
every reasonable source for methods, guidelines, and ideas which
seem most helpful.[4] We are challenged to become comfortable with
modifications and expansions of former "truths" as we grow,
keeping our mind open to new understanding. To allow these
subtle changes, ego must diminish. So let us examine some
approaches for accomplishing this.

Principles for Relinquishing ego

1. Recognize the source of ego as an identity separate from
soul which we have constructed.

By considering ego as our center and protecting it, we have
provided all its power through our allegiance to it as our identity.
Astonishing instability and changeability of ego confirm it to be a
product of that part of mind which considers itself separate from
God, thus vulnerable. This is illusion, because our essence and all
that is real are one-with-God. In truth there can be nothing else; so,
all that comprises ego and what it seeks is illusion. Since God did
not create it, it is not part of reality. On the other hand, our essence
is — and can never be anything but — a part of God. This truth
threatens ego, but the battle for survival is an ego struggle, a myth
we have built. By relinquishing ego, we give up nothing.

We are now ready to accept the task presented humanity by
the path of initiation — a walk from physical identity to soul
identity. Think of this as moving from aspirant to *Master through
conscious awareness, choice, self-observation, and self-discipline.
Remember, the entire spiritual journey is only the distance from
base of spine to top of head. Chakra by chakra, experience by
experience, we raise our innate spiritual consciousness toward
enlightenment.

2. Give up any attack upon ego. If we see ego as something to destroy, to fight, to control, we are bound to use a form of attack. If we see it as a battle between soul and ego, we get caught in a counterproductive cycle. We try to use ego's own methods, thus increasing anxiety and intensifying ego responses. Its reaction is always one of attack upon us, which we transfer to attack upon others. Neither can we ignore ego. We must be aware of how it operates in our lives — what it is doing daily; our responses, thoughts, and feelings reflect our identification with ego.

Attacks enhance ego identification in subtle as well as obvious ways. When we express hostility and anger in words or actions, we may feel justified or that our response is "natural." Not all attack is obvious. If we withhold forgiveness, we are attacking. At a deeper level, if we harbor a desire to hurt, thwart, or control, we are still attacking. Being "sweet" or a martyr may be regarded as forms of attack.

It is natural not to believe this rationale, another of ego's tricks. Our attack may become subtle, perhaps manipulative, and ego convinces us we are "nice" or "kind." Frequently we soften the attack as we refine the part we play, thinking indeed egotism is no longer at work.

Even those who feel that peace should be defended, even fought for, deceive themselves. Merely recognizing our many hidden ways of continuing to attack, so that we can then choose not to do so, consumes lifetimes. This process involves much more than what most people consider "harmlessness." But reducing our need to attack partially dissolves ego as an identity. We must realize attack in any form — aimed at others, ourselves, or ego — achieves ends established by ego, for within the *kingdom of souls, attack is impossible.

3. When we attack others in any manner, we attack ourselves. We are one in the Oneness. As we truly forgive others, we accept it for ourselves. We begin to see real Self, the perfection, the completeness that God created. This process progressively reveals the depth of absolute forgiveness. In time, we will move into a consciousness which truly knows there is nothing to forgive.

The eternal reality of our being can never be changed, hurt, or destroyed in any way, nor its oneness with the Creator reduced. If we consciously and persistently forgive while our deeper awareness is open and receptive, we become more aware of our true nature and that of others. Ego begins to fade — even without painful effort — into nothingness. In wisdom teachings of the Christ: We are *forgiven our errors as we forgive others.* Confucius put it this way: *One word may serve as a rule of practice for all one's life—reciprocity.*

4. Ego is the source of all fear. We can never know uninter-rupted peace until we are free from fear and its derivatives of hostility and guilt, along with all connected feelings of worthless-ness and depression, misery and pain. Ego uses fear and guilt to control our loyalty to it. It speaks loudest to us through our feelings, saying, if we make it stronger, we will not feel the pain or destructive emotions. When we are afraid, we grasp at whatever offers us freedom from fear. But ego's appeal is always deceptive, for ego is afraid. Its existence hinges upon our continued belief that this separateness is not only possible but true. With such a precarious basis for existence, no wonder ego *is* afraid. Ego's false identity with the body is the basis for fear of death.

Only acceptance and integration dissolve fear induced by ego. If we think of fear as solar plexus responses to **F**alse **E**vidence **A**ppearing **R**eal, we realize how establishing clarity will bring relief.

Recall, fear is the glue that holds together the many compo-nents of the *Dweller on the Threshold. Any progress we make in dissolving fear sets us free in ways we rarely anticipate. We can link ego and our knowledge of the *shadow or Dweller in many ways. In lesson 7, we will pursue the Dweller on the Threshold and the *Angel of the Presence at length.

5. Truth dissolves ego. The answer to attacks on the ego is in learning about ourselves, about God and creation. We turn especially to reality revealed to us by *High Self, the Christ-Within, or the transpersonal self. Our mystical moments grant profound gifts. As realizations speak truth to us, an inner knowing registers. Insights, flashes of illumination, remain with us, and we come to know even more is accessible. Each bit of knowingness — that very *truth that makes you free* (John 8.32) — prepares us for the next *revelation.

Anything which reveals truth to our consciousness serves to reduce ego's importance. In meditation we energize increasingly subtle levels. Rituals, disciplines, and outlets such as chanting and music elevate and expand our consciousness, invoking higher energies to merge with our own and thus move our selfhood toward higher reality. As we demonstrate that we are more than ego, our true nature is revealed step by step. When we recognize ego is functioning and choose otherwise, we shift toward truer reality, diminishing ego's influence. True, ego makes repeated and frantic demands for our allegiance, leading us into all sorts of emotional storms and negative feelings. So, we let the light illuminate the darkness, not by destructive action but by filling the nonself with more light.

6. We can and will develop awareness and discrimination. Another way to move toward relinquishing ego as our identity is to become increasingly aware of ego's machinations and maintain alertness to what one part of our mind does to the whole. We learn to recognize signs of ego domination. Over time, they become obvious. When we are not at peace — when we feel upset, angry, hurt, guilty, hostile, frustrated, helpless, depressed, or anxious — ego is ruling our reactions. Later, we learn to recognize less obvious signs — pride, smugness, judgment or rejection of others and self, desire for recognition and approval, and many other tokens of egotism.

> ### *The nature of the physical is to bounce between ecstasy and pain. Embrace wisdom to be free.*

Long ago, we began our efforts to build witness consciousness by observing ego at work and learning to identify its tricks. Such awareness may prevent us from drifting into excesses and delaying our growth toward truth. We not only guard against ego at work, but we are more frequently protective of the "kingdom of God," the state of consciousness wherein "I and the Father are One," and we see it more and more around and within us. Now we can become less preoccupied with vigilance against ego. We increasingly shift our awareness to standing *for* something, not *against;* this truth assists us even in our struggle with ego domination.

7. *All experiences of life intensify our identification with either ego or true Self.* When our entire human identity is with ego, duality is reflected everywhere in physical life. For instance, as we become involved with metaphysical studies, we become intensely aware of duality expressed variously as personality versus soul, ego versus High Self, good versus evil, and so on. By stressing the duality of our nature, we produce internal strife. As we weary of the conflict, we learn to see beyond it. We remember, *I am the Soul,* our daily affirmation.

> *I am not the body, I am not the emotions, I am not the mind. I am the user of the body, the user of the emotions, and the user of the mind. I am the Soul.*

Reality ultimately involves only God — there is nothing else. We come to know some darkness abides in the best of us and some goodness in the worst. So, we comprehend the universal principle of duality/polarity, even as we transcend it.

The Hermetic Principle of Polarity

Everything is dual; everything has poles; everything has its pair of opposites; like and unlike are the same; opposites are identical in nature, but different in degree; extremes meet; all truths are but half-truths; all paradoxes may be reconciled.

—The Kybalion [5]

The popular saying, "There is but one power in the universe," reminds us of the principle of Oneness, even though we know this power expresses as duality in the material world. We confuse soul and ego. We generate a willingness to experience what life dispenses, knowing these are opportunities to grow.

At a particular time and place, we may find we are in a kind of void, a space where we are unsure what we believe. We have abandoned old ways without a firm grasp on the new. We attempt to use past lessons to help us through hard periods. When nothing but trouble (with no apparent reward of conscious learning) comes our way, we reach out to wiser ones to assist us through our crises, and we continue to grow. *The nature of the physical is to bounce between ecstasy and pain. Embrace wisdom to be free.* [6]

8. Ego orientation and identification are not *sins, but errors to be corrected. Many earnest, sincere individuals, as well as some religious groups, equate ego with sin. However, the view that ego stands for sin implies that our identification is fundamentally negative, and this intensifies feelings of worthlessness and despair. Our "fall" from heaven and the consequent identification with ego are not evidence that we are of little worth. Ego is neither negative nor sinful; it is a point of identity making false assumptions. That part of our mind which conceives itself as separate is mistaken. But its errors can be corrected. We can be "saved." We learn to think of life as an opportunity: the "original blessing."

*Salvation is merely the right-mindedness we need to achieve before we can know One-mindedness. *Right-mindedness* is another way to say our minds are cleared of glamours, illusions, and confusions. We clarify by dissolving the barriers of fear, unforgivingness, attachment, low self-esteem, and anger. We free our lives of nontruth, and our lives become sacred as our consciousness more accurately comprehends and responds to the love-wisdom of ChristoSophia. We may say we now live more enlightened lives, as we journey from darkness to light.

Removal of barriers makes it easier to give our whole nature to Lord Christ — teacher of angels and of humanity.[7] Actually, the goal is not distant, for it exists here and now within each of us. We could reach it instantly, but for our long identification with ego and its powerful resistances and barriers to Self-realization. So we now *will* ourselves to go through a *purification process called the path of initiation, known by many as *"purgatory."

9. We give up nothing when we relinquish ego. This is one of the most difficult principles to accept. At times, we advance so slowly we feel the task to be almost beyond us. We seem to believe we need ego to function in this world: to relate to others and to circumstances, to control our environment enough to assure our safety and success, to make us feel like we are somebody, to obtain whatever happiness may be found in this trouble-filled world. Actually, personality — the expression of ourselves which deals with and relates to the world — is not the same aspect of our being as ego. True, it is often shaped by ego and used for ego's ends, but our higher consciousness also influences it. Personality merely reflects influences which bear upon it, like a clear crystal vase into which any color may be poured.

We see the truth of this easily when we think a moment about personality's contradictory nature — the "Dr. Jekyll and Mr. Hyde" stereotype, recognized as true, to a degree, of all humankind. While personality is a rich array of characteristics, ego is a specific focus, like sunglasses that tint our environment. Imbalances, programming, glamours, illusions, experiences, and outside influence all play upon personality. Since integration is our long-term goal, observation helps us identify and appreciate personality's resources, while practices prepare it for higher purposes. As it is freed from distortions, personality is able to reflect more clearly the light, love, and power directed from higher realities upon it.

While in traditional Christianity "heaven," "purgatory," and *"hell" describe various states of consciousness, there is no reason to believe these states only exist on the nonphysical side of life. All may be experienced now. In his wonderful book, *Opening to Inner Light,*[8] Ralph Metzner teaches *heaven* as that state of being centered in the divine; *purgatory* is when we are in the fires of purification, and *hell* is when we get stuck. Purgatory is therefore the struggle with glamours and illusions. We put them, and thus ourselves, in the cleansing fire.

Spirit, which we intrinsically are, needs a mechanism to function in the material world; soul, a distinctive unit of God consciousness, is the intermediary that assists the process. Spirit begets soul which begets personality. Soul projects personality through which it gathers experience in the dense physical realm. Personality serves soul in the same manner as the brain serves mind.

A critical question: What major influences act upon my personality? If bent upon serving ego's desires, we have a focus with varying levels of stability and drive. Ego focus intensifies ego identification and actions but has little meaning beyond the moment. However complex or altruistic ego may appear, its veneer is very thin. In most people it is rapidly stripped under stress, and we fight viciously for survival.

As we relinquish more and more of our identification with ego, we find we lose nothing in the process. Our personality continues to function in the world under higher guidance but in our own unique way. True, it may modify considerably and contain periods of uncertainty as changes occur, but we may be assured this aspect can be transformed through the influence of high consciousness. The basic structure with its individualized responses remains; we do not become saintly clones. Our ups and downs are ego's efforts to assert itself, and we learn to manage these. We discover that not only is ego unnecessary in dealing with the world, but we function with increased peace of mind, joy, and power despite ego.

Applications of the Basic Spiritual Approach

Ultimately it becomes clear: We must relinquish or dissolve the separative ego if we are to move forward on our path to illumination. The whole process of meditation is designed to help aspirants go beyond the need for ego identification. You are already changing if you are meditating, internalizing these lessons, and practicing suggestions. Guidelines become increasingly valuable as we realize the tricks of our own ego and desire to push beyond ego responses in order to continue our move toward Self.

> *Personality serves soul*
> *in the same manner*
> *as the brain serves mind.*

Instructions, with the assistance of tutors, prevent stumbling blocks often found in religious systems. When people "see the light" or become keenly aware of a desire to intensify their spiritual search, they naturally seek assistance. If they depend upon outside authority for confirmation of success, such reliance may become a trap and abort an intimate, personal mystical relationship with the Infinite that may have initiated the quest. Some simply turn over responsibility for their spiritual growth to another or to a system of discipline that promises certain results. Many older spiritual paths included the support of a guru to direct spiritual seekers, just as Christianity honors Jesus. These approaches have served well — to a point; it is easier to be an obedient child than a mature adult. However, when we are ready to become Self-actualized, we move from obedience to another to becoming wise in our own right without diminishing respect and love.

By suggesting ways to deal with ego and by outlining the principles of a basic spiritual approach, we hope the process you have begun will be further intensified. We have discussed only part of the important issue of ego relinquishment. As specific questions or comments arise, continue to include them in your correspondence to the meditation tutors.

Assignment

Seed Thought: UNIVERSALITY

Our first seed thought for this lesson is *universality, or nonseparativeness,* the virtue assigned to the Gemini influence.

> Our mystical experiences are unitive experiences. They may occur on a dark night with the sparkling stars in the sky; at the ocean; in the mountains or fields; with friends or family; with ideas; in lovemaking; in play; with music and dance and art of all kinds; in work; in suffering and in letting go. What all mystical experiences have in common is this experience of non-separation. . . . The unity that mystics celebrate is not a loss of self or a dissolution of differences, but a unity of creativity, a coming together of different existences.
>
> —Meister Eckhart

Universality (nonseparativeness) is the guiding consciousness of all life, where no separation between life forces exists. These life forces flow into each other, overlapping and embracing. In all situations the wise one stands for *omnipotence: one spirit and one existence. The consciousness of *at-one-ment is necessary to be free of the false identities of the lower nature.

Universality would have us dissolve prejudices and programming that segregate us into collectives. As separative ideas dissolve, we realize all humanity is becoming one family. We strive to comprehend the great truth that all the *cosmos is one *lotus slowly opening. We assume a position of relating to Life and all events from the perspective of universality.

This new era is a time for reconciliation of dualities by our discovery of a new, more inclusive level of mind. The forthcoming Aquarian influence acclaims the power of each to unite in oneness.

From time to time, moments of *cosmic consciousness break through to illumine human life. These experiences enrich the collective awareness of humanity and keep it attuned to the higher. For additional understanding, read *Cosmic Consciousness* by Richard M. Bucke.[9] This anthology of diverse informative and historically accurate experiences of the Light addresses the Oneness.

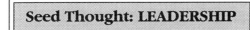

Seed Thought: LEADERSHIP

Our second seed thought, *leadership,* is the virtue assigned to the Cancer influence.

> Can you love people and lead them without imposing your will? Can you deal with the most vital matters by letting events take their course? Can you step back from your own mind and thus understand all things?
>
> Giving birth and nourishing, having without possessing, acting with no expectations, leading and trying not to control: this is the supreme virtue.
>
> —*Tao Te Ching*

Spiritual traditions offer a variety of ideas, some challenging our cherished beliefs. One of spirituality's important concepts, hierarchy, is difficult for individuals who think of democracy as the chosen and only way. In spiritual studies we learn that hierarchy exists among the holy ones and, we are reminded, seekers choose

---

Leadership

Leadership is not something we do, but something we are.

It is not a challenge. Leadership is the reality of every situation we are in.

Leadership means being responsible for the person we are, for tasks we have to do, for activities in which we participate.

Leadership is not a mystery, nor a learned skill; it is belief in oneself, a sense of dignity and respect, of aliveness and importance—a realization that, if I am in a situation, I have a responsibility to participate to the fullest of my knowledge and energy.

Leadership means releasing negative opinions about self and others. It means affirming my beauty and sharing this confidence with others.

Leadership is helping others believe in themselves and their abilities.

Leadership is seeking peace and joy and understanding.

Leadership is not just being president of an organization, or chairman of a committee; it is believing, caring, sharing, and being.

Leadership means accepting myself and others and the daily tasks each confronts. It is being glad to say "Yes" to life.

—Rev. Marjorie Stuth, M.S.W., October 1990, Sancta Sophia Seminary

---

Fig. 11. Leadership.

to ask leadership, or guidance, from those who know. No voting or power-play is available to get ahead in spirituality.

Spiritual law offers the understanding that the responsibility for managing challenging situations falls upon the most aware. If we think we are the wisest one in any given circumstance, we are the one charged to struggle for clarity and perhaps solution. This may require change within ourselves. We recognize that by surrendering less divine traits, we become more divine. At times, aware ones must disengage to preserve integrity. *The task of management is to do the right thing; the task of leadership is to do what is right.*

Time and again in the refinement process we hear, "One cannot lead until one becomes a good follower." High consciousness must be demonstrated to gain admittance into the company of saints and sages. We surrender to the leadership of the Masters.

Understanding Inertia: Sattva, Rajas, Tamas

Man becomes what he believes himself to be.
If I keep on saying to myself that I can do a certain thing,
I shall surely acquire the capacity to do it,
even if I may not have it at the beginning.
—Mahatma Gandhi

We now introduce another obstacle to progress toward enlightenment: *inertia. It could be called a "no man's land," where a kind of deadness exists — a numbness needing to be examined, confronted, and solved. We must recognize inertia when it occurs in us from time to time. Saraydarian calls inertia a limiting state, a barrier to be dissolved — much like glamour and illusion.

More than just a troublesome emotional state of mind, inertia relates to the basic substance and process of the cosmos, one aspect of which has particular importance for this lesson.

The *Yoga Sutras of Patanjali describe the three electric qualities — gunas, they are called. These attributes pervade all levels of creation and facilitate creation by their interaction. They are positive, neutralizing, and negative influences. The positive guna pulls creation back to its point of beginning. The neutralizing guna functions as an activating quality. The negative guna results in a flow of creative energy toward materialization and density. The *Bhagavad Gita,* an Eastern epic of spirituality, presents a simple and wonderful explanation of gunas.

The positive guna (sattva) results in mental brightness, and the effect elevates. Filled with purpose and enthusiasm, we are strongly motivated to move toward our highest ideal in harmony with soul's inclination. When the neutralizing guna (rajas) dominates, we may be seen to be highly stimulated, but our actions are characterized by restlessness and activity for the sake of motion. Busy, but not inspired, we may be driven by frantic compulsions that push us first one way, then another. If we are under the influence of the negative guna (tamas), we are mentally and physically sluggish, poorly motivated, with feelings of inertia. These qualities result in important differences in how we feel and act.

These gunas, or influences, affect the currents within us and all aspects of our living (physically and nonphysically) — our movement, foods we choose to eat and whether we eat, our manner of worship, our speech, relationships with others, devotional or inspirational practices, how well our job or relationships are flowing. The better we understand these gunas, the more we comprehend what is going on within us and how to promote our own endeavors.

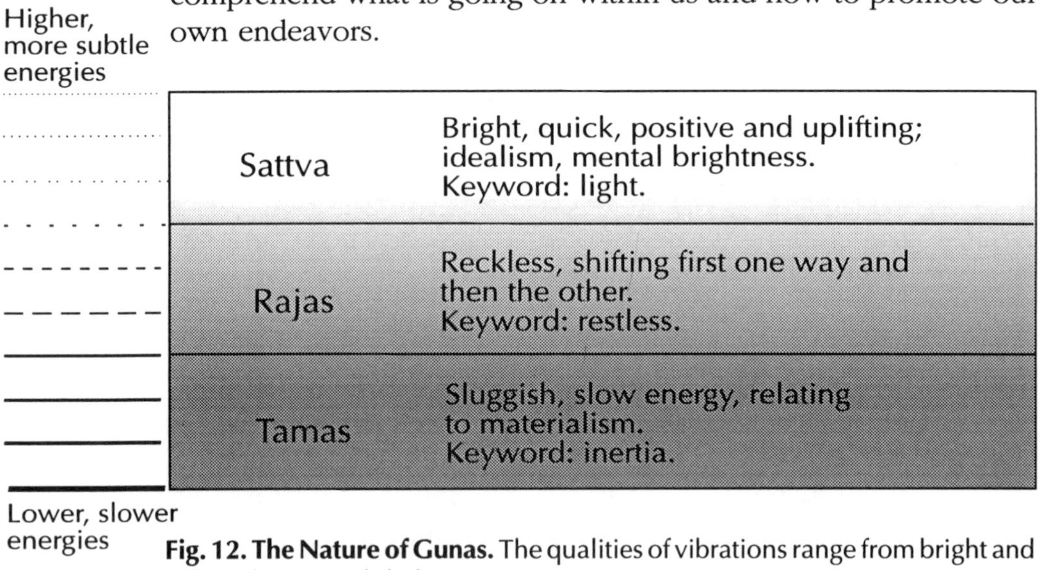

Higher, more subtle energies

Sattva	Bright, quick, positive and uplifting; idealism, mental brightness. Keyword: light.
Rajas	Reckless, shifting first one way and then the other. Keyword: restless.
Tamas	Sluggish, slow energy, relating to materialism. Keyword: inertia.

Lower, slower energies

Fig. 12. The Nature of Gunas. The qualities of vibrations range from bright and light to heavy and dark.

We can compare the anagrams live-veil-evil to sattva, rajas, and tamas. Each frequency impacts ego in its own way. Knowledge of these influences provides much insight. Spiritual growth addresses the qualities of the *gunas, as they are called in Eastern thought, in order to comprehend the effort needed to free us from limitation.

The dark night of the soul takes many forms. The most common are poverty, illness, despair, and depression — all of which may relate to inertia. Survival is the first goal during this period of great testing. We then must turn it into a period of gestation as we increase our faith and await comfort to come from within.

As our goal is to transcend such influences in nature, once conscious, we strive evermore consistently toward the positive influence (sattva) by learning how to reduce obvious and subtle effects of neutralizing (rajas) and negative (tamas) attributes. Each of the latter attributes contains complexities which make the process of consciously modifying them a tedious undertaking. Yet, we must resist currents that impede us if we are to progress spiritually.

> The gem cannot be polished without friction, nor men perfected without trials.
> —Chinese proverb

Outside influences which bring new ideas and energies or which carry impact may be needed to help us connect with higher or more stable currents. Examples may be any incoming energy, such as music, a movie, a counselor, AA meetings, or group therapy. Each has its influence, and we are either uplifted or pulled down by the energy with which we connect. Open-mindedness is readiness to allow fresh energy in and to feel capable of evaluating it. All of us must learn what lifts us and what paralyzes, what inspires and what depresses. As we come to know, we "feed" ourselves sattva — positive energy.

Variations of Inertia

At times, we all experience a heaviness that prevents constructive thinking and action. Our minds slow down, our mental processes dissolve into fuzziness, and we function as if under a thick substance or a black cloud. A range of feelings may accompany this state — all unpleasant. We do not care if the world goes on or not. We are in a "slump," we feel dull. Any duty — even preparing food to appease our hunger — becomes laborious and difficult. It is not unrelated to our actual busy-ness since it may be worse when little is demanded of us. We are bored. We seem tired. Nothing is worthwhile. We are miserable, but we are unable to generate the effort to change. Our reluctance to do *anything* is enormous. Spiritual students often experience periods when, after studying, meditating, attending to disciplines, we suddenly feel nothing is working. "It" is not real at all —"so what?" We may continue to slog along with "what is" because we do not know what or how to change. Nothing we do seems significant or empowering enough to make much difference in our lives.

As we experience this dullness over a period of time and if we struggle to do something about it, we may become aware of secondary negativities. We move into a kind of depression, a state of mind not necessarily associated with inertia, for these may be agitated depressions. We may recognize the appearance of defiance and guilt, of resentment and anger. We see escape is possible, but we are thwarted by our inertia. We relate these feelings to physical limitations: our energy must be low; we must be ill. We begin to doubt our personal worth and feel unloved and unlovable — but we do not care enough to make an effort to change. Old fears and anxieties creep into our thoughts as we lie awake at night, frustrated because we cannot direct our lives sufficiently.

In a contrary process, none of these emotions may plague us. Instead, an overwhelming feeling of uselessness, "blahness," and "I do not care about anything" may pervade our lives. Any attempt to move in a new direction just does not seem worth the effort. We may find this exasperating — or even this feeling may be absent. We are in stasis, motionless. The world continues to flow around us, but we seem to remain stationary.

One difficulty in dealing with inertia is the complexities that surround this state of mind. Physical ailments, for instance, exacerbate a sense of reduced energy and lassitude. While these prevail, we cannot do much. And this may be a good thing. The body needs rest to repair itself to take action again. If this period is prolonged beyond what we think is sufficient, we may become frustrated and despondent. While we really are not discussing physical problems under the term "inertia," physical conditions or low energy often contribute to the overall problem.

Inertia has many similarities to depression. While depression is filled with despair and pain, inertia usually has no strong, identifying emotional tone. Instead of being vague and threatening, any guilt associated with inertia clearly stems from not doing what we "should." At times we may confuse the condition with depression and react accordingly. Then we do feel "down."

Contemplated experiences and conscious effort register in the mental unit we are building, becoming the foundation upon which soul will build in the future—this life or in future incarnations.

At other times, we experience a distinct conflict. We feel a need to "get moving," but our gears seem locked in idle. This leads to all sorts of negativities. We expend our energies fighting other people, our circumstances, our lifestyle. We may express misdirected anger or frustration, so we may become active but in futile or counterproductive directions. This behavior brings about situations that occupy us for the moment, only to effectively distract us from the primary problem. The inability to sustain an endeavor or work toward an objective helps to define this empty state of being identified as inertia.

Sometimes events of living simply overwhelm us — problems crop up faster than we can resolve them. We may feel, "What's the use?" but we recognize this is temporary, at least at some level. We just want to escape for a while. This too is not inertia. But when such periods occur often or lethargy becomes a typical way of responding (or not responding) to the world, it becomes inertia. We may say or feel we just have no enthusiasm for life.

Self-doubt is often an underlying cause of inertia. Rather than make a wrong move, we hesitate until the opportune moment is lost. Even if we have no qualms about the move, self-doubt causes us to decide no action is the best action. Low energy and doubting our judgment or capabilities cause us to sink again into inertia, and this perpetuates our difficulty.

Had we been more energized, we could have mustered the effort we might have made, but too many reservations rest just below the surface of our mind. Self-doubt paralyzes us, simultaneously creating a negative attitude and revealing low self-esteem. As in depression, we misuse our skills and energy to block ourselves. Not wanting to err, we choose not to set much into motion — fear of risk, or perhaps fear of success! The resulting inertia may even be looked upon as "protection." Later, if we see the choice would have caused difficulty, we are presented a grand opportunity to justify our pattern of inertia. A decided answer is to work on low self-esteem and inertia simultaneously.

Shame, another hidden influence that locks us into inertia, has wisely been called "spiritual suicide" by recent author Vicki Underland-Rosow.[1] Only now are we beginning to recognize the psychological damage done by persistently plunging others into such negative pictures of themselves. The perpetrator often employs this tactic to feel superior, with little idea of the deep damage shame produces. The gunas are a new tool of understanding.

Inertia assumes such familiar forms, we may not easily pinpoint the precise nature of our difficulty. For instance, we all experience procrastination. We delay doing things for no apparent reason. We postpone until circumstances force us into action. When we do this frequently and habitually, we have surrendered to inertia. When we depend upon circumstances to move us out of inactivity, we are allowing outward situations to assume control of our lives. The resulting sense of powerlessness then adds to any frustrations we feel.

A healthy choice not to take action is far from inertia. Here we discriminate — weighing and determining a course of action which is, in fact, a choice to decline or to do nothing. Because it is the preferred course of action, it is not the result of doubt or lack of energy. We know we can choose to act if desired. Inertia is a numbness or apathy which precludes our making a choice.

Procrastination is inertia's twin; by delaying, we avoid decision and action. Some years ago, I decided to cure my procrastination by willing myself to action. When I became aware I was procrastinating, I vowed I would work posthaste to accomplish that task. For instance, if I found I was perpetually recycling a letter from the top of the stack downward, I answered it immediately. I affirmed, "I have time and energy for this now. Let me begin." By use of will, I could complete the chore. We gradually learn to identify activities we consistently avoid. Procrastination not only slows results but depletes energy — at least two or three times as much — by our delaying what could have been completed. Discipline, invoking will, is the antidote; recognizing the behavior must come first.

> There are risks and costs to a program of action. But they are far less than the long-range risks and costs of comfortable inaction.
>
> —John F. Kennedy

Chronic indecision is a form inertia may take. By not deciding, we avoid taking any active steps, thus losing by default. *No decision becomes a decision.* We live in a twilight zone that keeps us from acting. During this time, we may experience a minor degree of distress, frustration, or conflict, concealing the existence of the inertia influence (tamas). Perhaps we drift until pushed to a decision or impelled by another's actions.

At times, of course, we need to delay a decision until we have sufficient information or evidence; we may be wise to postpone taking action until a solution becomes clear. When we purposely defer decisions and responses for known reasons, it is not procrastination or indecision.

Boredom is another disguise behind which inertia hides. Weary of the humdrum, we settle into more of the same without enough "push" to get out. Often we acknowledge this by admitting we are in a rut. We seem tired — but when our interest happens to ignite, fatigue vanishes.

Some people find boredom so painful, they habitually seek that which may, in their experience, combat it. From the standpoint of the three cosmic influences, currents move from the heavy tamas influence to the restless rajas energy and deplete our personal energies, only to drop back into the stasis of inertia afterward. When we cannot get started until we get angry, this is what is happening. We often use anger to lift us from tamas to rajas, moving us into action at least for a while.

So we see, inertia can quickly become a significant problem, either rarely or chronically. We may find we fall into a pattern of drifting through life. We have periods when too many aspects of our lives are devoid of purpose; an emptiness seems to prevent positive movement. We avoid making an effort toward progress in any area. We allow circumstances to be the impetus for our responses. We simply let life carry us along, failing to invoke or apply will.

Sometimes we fluctuate between restlessness and apathy — traits which may be present only in certain aspects of everyday living, such as in our attempts to grow or to change. We may not be able to get started because we do not know the next step. When our typical mode of responding to life falls into any of these negative patterns, a barrier to spiritual progress forms. When we succumb to a period of disenchantment, we need a positive stimulus to move beyond it. We need reassurance and support to know there are steps to be taken to reduce this state of mind. Renewed dedication to meditation practices with another or a support group, or a period of regular study with a mentor may be just the help needed.

In the struggle to escape inertia, we may experience periodic bursts of will, erratic behavior, or sudden surges of activity we cannot control or maintain. This too is to be expected and may be brought under control, for just as we build any other skill, our spiritual dexterity increases with practice, such as right use of will, or better concentration, or sustained self-direction. Engaging another with us in the process helps us maintain direction until we can hold it for ourselves.

Ultimately, the spiritual quest demands we surrender our will to higher will. It is most common to think of obeying this axiom by aligning ourselves to acts that seem to be in keeping with actions of the higher world. At times, we remember we must surrender certain personal actions or inactivity to the higher guidance as best we can perceive it.

Once, when in a time of great passion, striving to be all I might be, I bemoaned my lack of perfection, I was then told, *One need not be perfect, but one must be willing.* Since then, I have sought with increasing consciousness to be willing to adjust and to realign.

I may not always know what is higher will, but I do know my willingness to come into alignment with that will.

We are challenged at times to remember our lack of alignment to higher will can consist of acts of both omission or commission. According to our personal temperament, we will find ourselves more inclined to action or inaction. An active temperament will lend itself more easily to a life of activity and be more pained by failings of commission. They ask, "How is it I did not try? I should have done something." They suffer quite seriously in regard to missed opportunity.

The passive or more hesitant one can live more easily with acts of omission. They suffer greatly over mistakes or acts executed foolishly. Their philosophy is "better to do nothing than to err." As we desire to know ourselves, we determine, "Am I an active or passive temperament?" Understanding our nature, we gain an important insight.

There are steps we can take to kindle our will. An effective way is to divide our plan into physical, emotional, mental, and spiritual levels of expression. We cannot just *will,* but we combine and practice techniques to influence basic self and thereby better activate a holistic nature.

The great desire of devotees is to activate enthusiasm — *en theos,* the God-Within. A combination of light, love, and will, this inner empowering agent flows ever more freely. Inertia, the opposing state, limits that joyful state for which we are striving.

How do we face inertia once it is recognized?

We are gentle to our body, perhaps nurturing ourselves with more rest, massages, or attention, and recognizing that some kind of exercise is necessary. Exercise does not exhaust, it generates energy. Martial arts are beneficial because, performed as designed, they balance the masculine and feminine forces, as well as stimulate the overall tone of the body. Allow time. It usually takes three or four weeks for a new practice to register its effects; many believe a moon cycle, twenty-eight days, is needed for the practice to "gel."

Acupuncture is another technique that assists energy flow from the *etheric into the physical form. Eastern traditions generally better understood gunas and developed methods to stimulate, relax, or balance the flow of energy (the gunas) that affects our every level. Such techniques are designed to help practitioners psychologically, as well as physically. Today, as we are becoming increasingly knowledgeable of subtle reality once more, we can reclaim these techniques to help ourselves.

As we better appreciate our bodily needs, we realize nutrition emerges as a top priority. Proper nutrition is fundamental to any holistic approach to sound health, resulting in energy for our total well-being which often has been ignored in the past in favor of more immediate needs. Any attempt to break cycles of inertia needs to address nutrition concurrently. Homeopathic and naturopathic approaches to healing provide a strong understanding of the energy nature and can assist us greatly in making desired changes.

> ## One need not be perfect, but one must be willing.

Music, affirmations, visualizations, keeping a peaceful center — all contribute to a more positive approach to life. However, we have to openly assert our desire to resist inertia. Less self-criticism and a more positive routine with plenty of rest and attention to the body help turn things around.

With our body more energized, we then focus on the words we use, making them positive and energy-producing as we stimulate the astral nature. Vivid, powerful, and nourishing words stimulate hope and new bursts of enthusiasm as we move toward a more eager, energetic rhythm. Music and chants add available energy, as do other healthy vibrations we encounter.

We must be prepared for change to occur; energetic bursts of restlessness erupt naturally and need to be channeled into constructive activities. When we are struggling with inertia, recognition of progress is important, as is the building of a more positive self-image. Self-doubts need to be recognized, examined, and dealt with openly, perhaps with the help of someone we respect. Self-love greatly assists the process of aligning our nature to the sattva influence. We may recall, we are more energetic and more eager when in love than under other circumstances; the same is true when we feel really good about ourselves. Inertia is resisted by a continued resolve to find the good or the better, and experimentation is necessary for progress.

> *Our spiritual dexterity increases*
> *with practice, such as right use of will,*
> *or better concentration,*
> *or sustained self-direction.*

In addition, inertia often causes us to let down protective boundaries — we become too lethargic to care. Indeed, in times of negativity, we need stronger boundaries and may have to ask another to help us reinforce our safeguards. Similarly, when pressure overwhelms us, we often give up our hopes, dreams, and wishes and yield to inertia — a common response to stress. We may lose our ability to cope with natural pressures of life, another reason a counselor or therapist can be helpful. Pressure itself is neither harmful nor negative within the bounds of our coping ability; but when defeated by the stress of a situation, we surrender hope, humor, and other emotions that generate the positive energy we all need to fuel our daily lives.

James Loehr, a sports psychologist and president of LGE Sport Science Center in Tampa, Florida, dismisses the notion that freedom from stress is a worthy goal. Comparing the world of business to sports, he helps executives build the capacity to respond well to pressure. "Stress," he says, "is clearly the stimulus for growth. And (rest and) recovery is when you grow. . . . If you focus on the process of what you're doing, get involved in the activity, and get into the rhythm of the activity, it will blank out the negative pressures and anxieties involved with the task."[2] Stress may be a major cause of inertia, when not confronted. Loehr's organization provides a formula from Sport Science workshops[3] for using stress productively.

> Life by the yard is very hard; life by the inch is a cinch.
> —Jane B. Burka and Lenora M. Yuen, *Procrastination*

We see how sad and unnecessary it is when pressures set us back. Accepting this, we rededicate ourselves to finding a way to shake lethargy and improve our responses to life's pressures and responsibilities.

Resolve alone does not solve "will" problems. A combination of daily practice, honest evaluation, and seeing positive results is necessary. As this occurs, we make a series of little adjustments to continue to make progress. It becomes a day-to-day achievement — practice makes perfect. Lack of stamina may be caused by imbalance on many different levels. Sometimes we need a physician, sometimes a counselor. Sometimes we must investigate chemical or nutritional imbalances.

STEPS FOR REDUCING INERTIA

Sattva, rajas, tamas — the three electric qualities, attributes, or influences — are present at all levels in the cosmos; their interactions are responsible for the material universe. However, we need not succumb to the idea that we must accept their influences; we dare not believe we are powerless to affect them. As we grow spiritually, our immediate goal is to reduce the power of inertia and restlessness in order to be more in tune with the uplifting influence of our own higher consciousness. We learn to be bright and clear *more* of the time. Here are specific steps to take.

1. Use introspection to recognize the influence of the inertia attribute as basic to a current inaction.

    a. While quiet and relaxed, look for thoughts and labels which conceal or distract from the basic inertia. The initial purpose is to face the presence of the tamas influence. Confront the "down," and see if its cause can be discerned.

    b. Do you tend to accept your procrastination, indecision, or boredom as "just the way I am"? Choose change.

    c. If you believe your state of mind and lack of energy have their source in physical problems, do you put off doing something about them? Are you in denial? Can you help yourself be ready to move forward in this process?

    d. Are you distressed by lack of movement but tend to assign it to a lack of personal worth? Use techniques from earlier lessons to change this attitude.

    e. Do you blame your feelings on other circumstances? Are you ready to heal those feelings? Examine blame and shame.

    f. Do you assume you can do nothing when you feel like this because of your inadequacies — imagined flaws, self-created limitations, lack of self-love or self-esteem?

Answers to these and similar questions help us eliminate peripheral feelings and assumptions. We realize we are accepting the heavy tamas energies and begin to reverse the process.

2. Make decisions on a conscious level. When we put off deciding or simply do not make a decision, this is really a decision and should be faced. Discussion with another could be helpful now. Take your notes with you and proceed.

3. Establish an improved decision-making process. Most action demands a decision long before it is executed. Decide your course, and invoke will.

> a. Separate decisions having far-reaching implications from daily-action decisions, and use this procedure for those having a broader impact upon your life. For instance, do not get involved in a detailed process to decide whether to do dishes now or later.

> b. Make your alternatives and pros and cons as specific as possible. Include facts, relevant information, and feelings. This step is more effective if you make lists.

> c. Look for ways to divide the total problem into parts, into smaller and simpler steps. Most major decisions involve several related, small decisions. Try to order them into a priority or time sequence. Bite-sized decisions provide experience and build confidence.

> d. When you have collected an array of alternatives, with their various ramifications, consciously move the problem into the subconscious, ask for a solution, and become involved with other activities. As for dream guidance, listen for and expect a response from the universe.

> e. Allow the decision (or sequence of decisions) to emerge. Do not try to make your conscious, rational mind take sole responsibility. Become open, receptive, as you watch for signs, impressions, and guidance. Use your conscious analysis for checking and evaluating.

> f. Make tentative decisions all along the way toward the final decision. If you had to make a decision now, what would it be? But do not be reluctant to change this for the final one. Grant yourself the right to change your mind as you integrate additional information.

g. Stay open to new data, e.g., facts or feelings of your own or others. Do not give your final decision to another; own responsibility.

h. Accept that we often need to make decisions with inadequate and limited objective data. This is a fact of life and there are no guarantees. We each do our best at a given time.

i. Postpone the final action decision until it is needed or most appropriate.

4. Develop "pump priming" devices to start moving out of inertia.

a. Start on a small scale rather than take on the whole job. Acknowledge you can do some part now — such as beginning to clean the attic or garage in a specific, limited way — then consciously quit. Set a timer and work at a task for x number of minutes. When the timer rings, stop. This provides a boundary to accomplish bite-size pieces without becoming overwhelmed by the magnitude of the task. You did the part to which you were committed for this point in time.

b. Similarly, plunge into any part of the problem any way you can. Even action without much thought is good if it gets us moving. At the same time, we realize this may throw us into a restless state, but we will deal with this once we understand the pattern.

c. Reward yourself for starting to move out of the heavy state: prepare special food, take time off to see a movie or play, buy something you have been wanting, read a book for fun, write a letter to a friend. After we complete a small, simple part, we find it easier to keep the task progressing toward completion.

d. Put yourself in a position where you *have* to get started — but do not take on too complicated a commitment initially. Start by making a list; this way we "cut the track" mentally before we physically begin.

e. Start with a project unrelated to what you really know you need to face. Inch into action. If you need to balance your checkbook, first look through a catalog, and move toward the real goal as you feel more energetic. Or putter a few minutes, freshening up the room before tackling a closet.

f. Steadily acquire interesting, state-of-the-art tools to assist you in doing jobs you tend to put off. A printing calculator is a time-saving device for work with numbers. New gadgets and appliances make kitchen work more fun. A walk-around tape player providing stereo music through lightweight earphones makes routine jobs more pleasant. Your own ingenuity will produce other innovative ideas.

5. Develop the habit of observing your feelings in relation to events so that you become alert to triggers which seem to generate a period of inertia. Notice whether this state is cyclical or if it appears with any kind of regularity. Falling out of "be here now" consciousness is a frequent cause of loss of momentum.

Think about your personal cycle. Are you a day or night person? Do you work well for one week, two, or three, before needing a break? How many hours of sleep do you need to feel good? Remember, inertia is always worse when we are trying to function out of our cycle. Are you energetic on vacation but not at home or at work? If so, examine.

6. Monitor yourself for restlessness or activities less productive than a focused effort. This may be a sign you have moved to rajas energy that ignites the desire to stall, yet appear busy. This energy may launch you, but do not stay with this scattered, unfocused type of activity for very long — it too becomes unpleasant. Seek to focus the energy positively as soon as possible.

7. Learn to live with inertia at times. Accept it, ride with it. Allow time for needed rest. It may have surfaced because you were out of balance in your activities — too much going out and not focused enough on your own personal needs. Immerse yourself in an easy routine; read light material for fun; increase physical activity in rewarding but not exhausting ways. Use inertia as an opportunity for calm introspection without concern for what you find. The answer lies not in merely increasing activity but in doing what truly creates release within the various aspects of self. Think of the present state of mind as temporary and restful.

Anything which introduces an orderly, conscious discipline into our lives — apart from those activities imposed upon us by circumstances of living, by our jobs, our homes, our lifestyle — reduces the frequency and intensity of periods of

Exercises for Building Will

Let us begin by acknowledging that will requires focus, moving our attention from a wide range, narrowing the picture to a single point of concentration. We adjust the inner lens. Will is accompanied by a feeling of effort and tightening. We build a

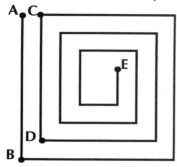

particular muscle to achieve this mental state. We realize the need to become single-minded for a period of time and yet retain our ability to shift to an overview perspective as needed. These two exercises (there are many) help us develop will.

Fig. 13. Mandala for Developing Will. Prepare this simple drawing for yourself on a large piece of light-colored posterboard.

First, draw the above mandala. Beginning at point A, keep your eyes fixed on the line and move toward point B. To maintain a tight focus on the line is the goal of this exercise to build will and concentration. Move eyes slowly but steadily. From point B, continue to hold focus and follow the diagram toward C, maintaining a steady but slow pace. Resist the tendency to begin moving more rapidly. Keeping the slow and steady pace governs the focus-building aspect (concentration) and is an important factor in achieving will.

Having arrived at point C, we proceed toward D. Now more focus is required because the parallel lines on either side seek to pull the eye off its course. Continue in the established pattern all the way to point E, paying particular attention to staying with the desired line and not speeding up your point of concentration. Note the tiredness you feel when you reach E. You have been exercising a mental muscle. Congratulations!

This exercise has been found helpful to many areas of daily life. A neighbor once used it and found his ability to skeet-shoot improved greatly.

The second exercise strengthens will and patience. Be comfortably seated with a large-size box of wooden matches in hand. Pour the matches out in front of you, and count as you begin to pick them up. One, two, three — concentrate as you pick up matches, allowing each count to register. At some point you will realize you have lost count. When you do this, return all the matches to the pile and begin your count over. Persist honestly and consciously for at least fifteen minutes. You need not do this for longer periods, but it is important to be consistent, repeating the exercise about three times a week for a few months. According to your ability to feel will at work and how clearly you can stay focused on the task determines whether you should persist for a longer period of time.

inertia. This is one reason why regular meditation, systematic study, improved nutrition, regular exercise, and similar disciplines bring us uplifting experiences. Preventive measures do not assure freedom from inertia but reduce the tendency toward sluggishness. They help us maintain a more consistent, positive attitude and higher motivation.

Physical activity, singing, and chanting are good tools for dealing with these challenges and wonderful energy builders. If you do not feel up to joining others, sing or move with an audio tape or the stereo to start and keep your energy flowing. The practice of self-love is important when struggling with inertia, so we indulge in things which give us a lift.

Review: Preparation for Completing the Task

Now we need to integrate what we have learned as we advance in our study of meditation. We discussed the brain mechanism (see vol. 1) humanity has acquired in the evolution of the species. Today, rational mind is our primary mechanism for functioning in the physical world. In meditation work we reconnect to inner realities and hidden talents. We know some are quite adept with *right-hemisphere capabilities and others are more *left-hemisphere oriented. Today, we observe society making new and strong attempts to understand both hemispheres, bridge them, and maximize both sets of resources. People who do so comfortably demonstrate extraordinary intelligence, often called "high creativity."

Mind-Soul Connection

*Esoteric teachings refer to our present stage of humanity as building new levels of mind or expanding consciousness. Individually we advance through our personal use of mind. Contemplated experiences and conscious effort register in the mental unit we are building, becoming the foundation upon which soul will build in the future — this life or in future incarnations. Our unconscious experiences continue with us in the *permanent mental atom to be reworked time and time again until they too become conscious. In such a way, lessons move from old patterns to integrated wisdom.

It should be clear by now that the strongest recommendation these lessons offer is persistence. The first challenge to which we must respond as we perceive ourselves as sincere seekers is to realize we can no longer "blame, shame, or play the game."

The successful completion of any project is dependent largely on the will of the researcher and the natural evolution of the spiritual effort. Mary Gray addressed the issues of will and evolution in *Spiritual Laws: Rules of the Evolutionary Arc.*[4]

> Man must know himself the arbiter of his own destiny. He exists in a world of law which permits him to govern the conditions by which he is surrounded — not perhaps of this life but of his future life upon the planet. With his own will of willfulness in one life, he sets into motion forces which will create not only the conditions of his future life, but the character and qualities he will have.
>
> A man frequently blames "conditions" for failure, but these conditions he himself created in an earlier existence. For good or for evil, what we are follows the pattern we shaped in other lives.
>
> This law at once condemns and liberates a man, according to its application. Yet, since all evolution is educational, one should not shrink from facing limitations one has helped create. By facing them, by overcoming them and by making use of the lesson involved, one may rise above the conditions and find freedom of environment in the next. Man must accept the truth of the laws of evolution and the development of the powers of the spirit through successive lives.

*Reincarnation

When a soul does not complete the human initiation journey in a physical lifetime, it reincarnates, bringing patterns from its permanent atoms to integrate with its unfinished work. Gathering information, it sets out once again with renewed vigor to experience the physical plane and to create adventures for learning, subtracting and adding qualities to its makeup.

The process of bringing forth lessons learned in previous incarnations is called *"recapitulation." Life to life, we follow a pattern whereby: we are born, we rebuild our persona and, once anchored in a new life experience, we bring into that mechanism previous awarenesses and karmic lessons with which to work. Soul continues to unfold through new opportunities. Reconnecting present to past, recapitulation helps soul continue on its path toward enlightenment. Usually we begin to reawaken to the pool of wisdom around the time of our first "Saturn return" (about twenty-nine years of age), astrologically speaking. For important insights, recall the shifts that occurred in your own life between ages twenty-nine and thirty-five.

The practice of meditation expands levels of mind for us to master. Usually seven levels are depicted from most dense to most subtle, representing unconscious to conscious. All experiences are recorded in the permanent atoms. We normally touch into various levels daily as a natural function of brain development: *reptilian to *mammalian and then *neocortex. Our unconscious programming underlies the level of conscious mind, out of reach, dormant until tapped. However, it is into this unconscious that the history of the species flows, along with the history of the individual incarnating ego. We can draw upon this history by accessing its pictures and symbols — archetypal mileposts which track, as well as guide, the human journey to high consciousness.

The individual history of the human being and its development residing in the permanent mental atom is a seed planted long ago and labeled *quiescent self. This quiet center contains powerful imprints, points of identity from good and bad past-life experiences, such as pain, valor, sacrifice, trauma, confusion, and service. Quiescent self with its imprints continues to move with developing ego through karmic (mostly subconscious) patterns until what is needed for growth is realized. Healings may occur through learning lessons, lessons brought to conscious awareness. Psychological or spiritual technology, such as past-life recall, may carry us to new knowledge and release us. Those experiencing life without a spiritual awakening move unconsciously through their karmic patterns. When awakening occurs, with it come opportunities to hasten evolution as well — to learn through means other than pain and pleasure, to advance more rapidly toward the incarnated soul's purpose.

At our present stage of evolution, the focus is on construction of the mental mechanism so we will be able to access more than our usual three lower mental levels. Our current wave of human consciousness is to advance and improve our mental capabilities. Some lead to the development of more refined levels of higher mind so humanity, individually and collectively, will be able to more clearly reflect divine mind. Currently and collectively, we are beginning to envision the "possible human."

Each level presents a new stage of growth and a level of mind the meditator has succeeded in building as a foundation for the future. As we meditate, we establish new levels of self and also participate in the evolution of the human group mind. Humanity is simultaneously evolving and refining its collective mind in order to reflect more perfectly human creative genius imprinted in every being.

> I do not believe . . . that an individual may gain spiritually and those who surround him suffer. I believe in advaita, I believe in the essential unity of man and for that matter, of all that lives. Therefore, I believe that if one man gains spiritually, the whole world gains with him and if one man falls the whole world falls to that extent.
>
> —Gandhi

We do not recall our divine potential easily, yet periodically we realize breakthroughs and see unique capabilities demonstrated as true possibilities through others: the loving nature of a Mother Teresa, the genius of an Albert Einstein, the multi-talented *Nicholas Roerich, the enlightened teachings of a Siddhartha Guatama the Buddha or Master Jesus, the Christ. Most men and women are content to be average, forgetting each of us is destined for greatness. We fail to remember our true essence — the waiting, encoded soul.

The unknown holds a natural fear for the unenlightened; denial is part of the process at this level, as are the other four steps of transition: anger, bargaining, depression, and acceptance. Anger occurs in those who have a great investment in ego, for ego dies a slow death. Behind ego lurk strong capabilities reinforced by lifetimes of pride and false identity, so ego greets awakening with suspicion, even reluctance. Poor self-esteem increases the struggle, while with healthy self-esteem, we can adjust and pledge allegiance to the higher.

Back now to the work at hand: understanding the influences of sattva, rajas, and tamas. Each of us automatically responds to these energies, whether we know of them or not. The goal is to be sensitive to sattva, the holy, the lightest. Inertia is a sluggish energy that easily becomes bogged down in matter and psychologically in materialism — tamas, the heaviest. We could think of this as confused allegiance. Akin to depression, under this influence progress on any level is hard to make because the fire and fuel are not blending.

 Imagine, in tamas — inertia — the candle waits, but no action happens between it and the fire; the potential is stymied in matter. The energy may try to ignite but does not catch.

Rajas, on the other hand, lies midway — restless like a faltering candle flame attempting to burn in a wind that shifts, starts, stops. Little or no sense of direction can be sustained in this pattern. When one is struggling with inertia, however, and rajas occurs, it is progress. We do not want to rest now, for shifting currents may be precipitating a more positive effort.

In sattva, high consciousness is alive, like a bright flame that consumes the candle — its reason for being. Passion is ignited, and this passion will, of itself, hasten experiences that purify the nature.

We have all heard the words, "Follow your bliss." Literally, this means we are to pursue what we love, what excites us. How do we discover what lifts us out of repose and arouses intensity? To be fulfilled, we must discover that which awakens passion and calls us to action.

Humanity advances either by the path of heart or the path of mind. Remember, the mind is but a doorway to the vast beyond. *Knowing* is much more than an intellectual process; it indicates an intimacy is desired. It is this deep need to know which opens the mind to exploration and discovery. When rigid or closed, the mind constructs a prison from which we seemingly cannot escape. If intolerant, the mind forms a barrier, like a dark forest of concepts — mysteriously entangled and too fearful to enter.

When the mind is open, the user controls the locks and defines the boundaries of acceptable exploration. The mind that quests longs for new awareness and calls the heart to its service. The desire to know and the rejoicing exultation at discovery make the heart sing. As these two great powers of personality merge to seek the

Lord of Life, the result is passion. Physical and beautiful when trained and elevated, passion is one of the yogas developed by the ancients. Blessed are they who find their passion, for it fuels those who dare to live boldly.

This is not just a religious quest; the human nature yearns to express fully. The child wants to become equal to the parent; the lover wants to be both self and partner. We hunger to merge into our Cosmic Self and to register that moment in our knowing nature. We agonize for the embrace; to touch "it" is the fulfillment of cosmic sexuality.

At profound moments, this merger occurs; and when it does, the wonder reverberates not only in the individual but into and through all humanity. The Holy and Wise record magical moments, stories build around them, mystery envelops them, and the impact rewards the entire group consciousness.

The dynamic flash of love, light, and power (true *agapé) leaves recipients reassured, empowered, and forever different. They have tasted sattva and are now driven to confront the forces which would hold the world, their companions, and their doubters in limitation. The imprint of their moment of bliss intrigues all.

Even as he proclaimed himself "the Light," the Christ tenderly alerted his disciples, *You are the light of the world*. The words prevail through time to today's disciples. At the same time, he presents guidelines: how to feed the flame and to grow in its light, even as it is carried within.

In these volumes you are being prepared to fan your flame, to invoke passion to fuel your life and to find your unique expression. To train means one is taught and encouraged to develop an endeavor to perfection; you are not being *trained* for the quest, you are being *prepared*. Your heart is to soften and to become compassionate, quickened by your devotional practices; your mind is to stretch, as you learn to penetrate the Cloud of Knowable Things. You are sensitized to invite ChristoSophia to come and dwell within.

To those who would call themselves disciples, I echo, *You are the light of the world*. I propose, "You are the hope of humanity." There are forces that would extinguish your light and the yet-to-be-born work of your soul. You need not fear these, for the angel of discrimination accompanies you. But you must respond energetically; keep yourself clear and honorable in motivation, observe your purpose, and confront your discovered flaws. A willingness to clear centuries of human selfishness, ego building, materialism, and competitiveness is required. Resolve is demanded of those who would carry the light; but, know, the light itself assists in burning away loosened miasma. As we do our work, the light keeps us compassionately mindful of the human condition, and we repay our debt to humanity for allowing us to learn through its collective.

When the mind is open, the user controls the locks and defines the boundaries of acceptable exploration.

Walking and living in light and love is not quite rational — not now, not ever. It is learning to live in a holy space. We do not quite fit; we are not quite "of the world," even as we are in it. We resonate to something less dense even as we are here: spirit.

Thus we confront inertia at every challenge. Stand strong and clear in the best understanding the spirit within can summon, and *resist not evil*. Know what is harmful, and proceed with that which is right. Allow negative voices that call to you to go unheeded. Avoid personality stuff that would slow you on the quest. Certainly these warnings are easier heard than done, but within each is an inner *Knower to assist, Sophia to guide. Walk hand in hand with ChristoSophia, the love and passion of the Christ, and utilize the inner knowing of Sophia — for you are the light, both for yourself and for others.

The wonder ingredient is curiosity. When we respond to awakening with interest and curiosity, we welcome the new. We become conscious of tools that help us stimulate energy and then engage our personality in the search with less struggle. While purification work is still to be done, rushes of sattva bring shifting interests and changes of allegiance, often confirming our path and a quickening of assurance.

First Tools of Disciples

- The ability to self-discipline begins when we discover our will.

- Realistic expectations of self and others provide endurance for life's challenges.

- Overcoming our desires for instant gratification allows us to plan and work toward a glorious future.

- Considering consequences and outcomes of our choices empowers us to make choices in keeping with goals and capabilities.

Fig. 14. First Tools of Disciples.

Our personal will may choose alignment with the higher world; choice allows us to resist or refuse. As *lower mind opens to higher mind, additional insights provide guidance for making contact. Techniques vary, results differ, but mystics testify to the reality of higher dimensions. Experiences of the light flood humanity with wonder, direction, and information. Step by step, we ascend the *pyramid to high consciousness bathed in the light of soul.

Assignment

Seed Thought: LOVE

Our first seed thought is *love,* the virtue assigned to the Leo influence.

> Through gravitational pulls, magnetic Divine Love is
> coaxing all matter to melt into its bosom of space.
>
> —Paramahansa Yogananda

We are to learn to love with a new love. Love that you may sense the heart of the sun (not personality, not family). We strive to fall in love with something divine. When we find bliss in the midst of life, we perceive the word "love" in a new way. When we attain lovingness, it illumines our *aura and attracts *Hierarchy's attention. As it loves, humanity comes to know it is a part of the Oneness of the cosmos — not the most important part but a vital aspect of an advancing consciousness in the Divine All.

In learning to love, we must never underestimate the importance of self-love — not for survival, but to bridge from lesser levels of love to higher. The human nature advances in its ability to love and to care. The seed thought leads us through the four levels of love, but it is self-love that creates the bridge from personal love to impersonal. We often are reminded, one must love self before one can love another. Volume 2 explores the advancement of our love capacity well. When we are on a plane, we are told, "in the event of an emergency, the oxygen mask will drop. Put your own mask on before assisting anyone else." The same principle is at work here. We cannot provide what we do not have.

Seed Thought: PURITY

The second seed thought to consider is *purity,* the virtue assigned to the Virgo influence. Using the term "clarity" to define purity may help us rediscover the original meaning of this virtue. Purity is "without distortion."

> *Be an example to believers, in word, in behavior, in love, in faith, and in purity.*

1 Tim. 4.12

Purity. Purification of body, emotions, and mind eliminates obstacles between self and others and between personality and higher levels of our own nature. The work begins. To establish purity or clarity, we seek to eliminate distortions, even if revision comes slowly. Think about how a distorted window pane obscures or blurs the view. Glamours and illusions in personalities similarly distort our view of reality. Purification work cleans the filters — physical, emotional, and mental — so soul's awareness may be revealed through our open and expanded mind. We would know what soul knows.

Ask these questions: How might I best examine myself? What obstacles threaten my clarity? Perhaps honesty is an example. Can I, a student of truth, consistently express honesty? To others *and to myself?* To what degree? Can I come to understand purity/clarity is achieved a bit at a time as I adjust my perspective? Dare I commit myself to the sharpest clarity I can express today? I will monitor myself consciously as I refine my nature and live more in keeping with my truth.

See the Procedure for Seed-Thought Meditation outlined in the appendix, page 238.

Congratulations — Reach for Illumination!

A narrow gate marks the boundaries of the bridge to be crossed as we advance toward the solar angel. The picture of the *guardian angel watching over the little boy and girl as they cross a bridge over the *abyss illustrates our quest. This interface of spiritual guide and humanity epitomizes our journey. Just as the nativity scene reminds us of the Self-Within to be born, the guardian angel picture recalls to us our relationship to the higher world, with its guiding influence close at hand. The guardian is our solar angel, the little boy and girl our own masculine and feminine natures. We have to pass through the strait gate, step carefully, walk our path, and cross the abyss to enter the higher planes.

The path of initiation is the name given the process of releasing personality from its restrictive focus: ego, selfishness, and self-centeredness. Increased illumination of the mysteries of life advances us toward soul maturity. In our less evolved state ego uses each experience and opportunity for personal satisfaction. All situations are bent toward ego's own purpose — an eye through which narrow and self-serving perspectives operate.

Ego's domain consists of physical reality, the emotional nature, and accessible lower levels of mind. However, as these are increasingly integrated within the evolving personality, we embrace powerful moments of expanded awareness called by many names: joy, bliss, samadhi, peace, enlightenment. We step toward soul infusion under the guidance of our solar angel.

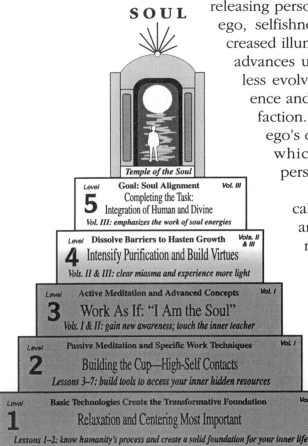

SOUL

Temple of the Soul

Level		
5	**Goal: Soul Alignment** Completing the Task: Integration of Human and Divine	*Vol. III*

Vol. III: emphasizes the work of soul energies

Level		Vols. II & III
4	**Dissolve Barriers to Hasten Growth** Intensify Purification and Build Virtues	

Vols. II & III: clear miasma and experience more light

Level		Vol. I
3	**Active Meditation and Advanced Concepts** Work As If: "I Am the Soul"	

Vols. I & II: gain new awareness; touch the inner teacher

Level		Vol. I
2	**Passive Meditation and Specific Work Techniques** Building the Cup—High-Self Contacts	

Lessons 3–7: build tools to access your inner hidden resources

Level		Vol. I
1	**Basic Technologies Create the Transformative Foundation** Relaxation and Centering Most Important	

Lessons 1–2: know humanity's process and create a solid foundation for your inner life

Figure 15. Level 5 Pyramid.

Solar Angel:
Companion on the Path

*The Yogi who is satisfied with the knowledge
and the wisdom, who has conquered the senses,
and to whom a clod of earth, a piece of stone
and gold are the same, is said to be harmonised.*
—*The Song of God*, VI/8 Bhagavad Gita

T he ultimate goal of humanity is to build an enlightened mind for the planetary being. The word "humanity" has its root in *manas,* the *Sanskrit word for "mind." If each of us is as one brain cell in the mind of the planet, we see the challenge: to bring each to a particular degree of high consciousness in order for planet Earth to experience its initiation.[1] *Humanity is the mental body for the planet* — thus the role of the human kingdom is defined. Each individual and group has a role in influencing planetary life. Meditation achieves a new importance in both individual and collective evolution.

The Domain of Personality

Gradually, personality's three bodies, as they are known — physical, emotional, and mental — prepare for a relationship with soul. Each body gradually matures in readiness for the

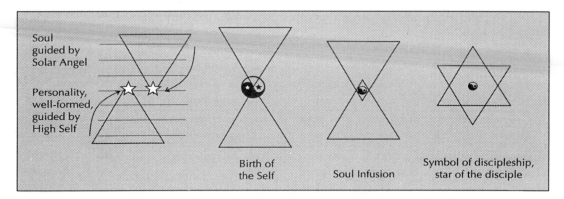

Soul guided by Solar Angel

Personality, well-formed, guided by High Self

Birth of the Self

Soul Infusion

Symbol of discipleship, star of the disciple

Fig. 16. Stages to Soul Infusion. Assisted by High Self, the integrated personality chooses maturing experiences as it seeks wisdom. Similarly, the densest point of the light of soul is cast Earthward, assisted by solar angel.

powerful influence of soul. This unit, containing the seed of divine nature (the quiescent self), evolves toward awakening and proceeds to build components through which soul can express within the human realm.

> One should not regard life upon the earth plane as unreal or less real than in the other worlds. Only the earthly existence provides the foundation for our further perfection and conscious existence in the Subtle Worlds. Only here, in the laboratory of life, can we acquire new stimuli and energies and immediately transmute them into higher accumulations for the further existence in the Subtle Worlds. Verily, conscious life on Earth guarantees the reality of life in other worlds. Precisely, there is a complete correspondence in the Cosmos. Therefore, the broader, the deeper our earthly consciousness, and the finer our sensations—the brighter and more beautiful for us is the reality of all the other worlds.
>
> —*Letters of Helena Roerich I*

Mind's three lower levels are fairly well established in modern humanity. The current focus is to refine and expand the conscious mind into more abstract levels. The head is the center of consciousness for the mental being. While the invisible threads deliver vital forces, the permanent atoms deliver unfinished business and energies to be transmuted. Telepathic thoughtforms flow through these threads in both directions. As the energy of the consciousness

Fig. 17. The Human Etheric Nature. Consciousness threads — life, consciousness, and creative — of the *subtle body connect personality with soul. Vital energy flows through these connections, carrying devotion, adoration, prayer, and meditation upward from personality, or downward as thoughtforms embodying impressions, inspirations, or visions of the future. The etheric body is slightly larger than and interpenetrates the physical body, interfacing the physical and nonphysical, and becomes the organized unit through which soul expresses on the physical plane. Various vehicles of expression constantly send messages back and forth to each other through this etheric form. Symbolized as a halo, the powerful mental levels blend and radiate light. Solar plexus is the seat of lower mind, power center of ego, and the point of reconciliation for the nature—both human and divine. Indeed, the whole is greater than the sum of its parts.

cord, called "light," flows into personality, it may be blocked by barriers: anger, jealousy, low self-esteem, guilt, fear, attachment, immaturity, inertia, egotism, unforgivingness, to name a few. Humanity will continue to discover new expressions of human potential as higher awareness unfolds.

Expanding the Ball of Knowledge

Through meditation, we refine the mind and access hidden inner wisdom. We approach High Self, that ball of knowledge gathered through many lives and experiences, by skillful passive-meditation techniques, guided imagery, and fantasy, and through learning the universal language attributed to basic levels of consciousness — archetypal *symbology and dreams. Activated extended senses and *psychic-development techniques apprise us of nonphysical realms; simultaneously we discover new maya to resist, as well as more personal and collective glamours and illusions.

The work of High Self (lower mental unit) is to utilize our experiences, consciously integrating them into a growing ball of knowledge. Thus, our resources continue to expand. That which we do not comprehend consciously accompanies us in patterns and experiences we will meet time and again — until they too are integrated into High Self. We learn to utilize High Self for help with personality issues and to stimulate soul contact. Inner work of this sort invites us to participate as leaders in humanity's collective life as windows of group awareness open.

Natural phenomena indicate levels of organization within abstract realms. We need to accept our *psychic capability as natural. Inner senses contain unique qualities and quantities of knowing, as do outer senses. Psychic development employs nonphysical sense organs that correspond to active chakras. Receptors activate and responses form. As we learn to translate this nonphysical language, we "get the message."

Spirituality is another matter. Here, we connect with the true inner nature. The Self-Within engages in dialogue and interfaces with subtler levels of life. "Dialogue" derives from *dia,* "to flow together," and *logue,* "logos," "the word." In spirituality, our spirit essence seeks to interact with the *Logos. As we identify with soul and harmonize with the energy of the Logos emanating to us, ego's control abates, its power diluted. By learning to observe ego and its tricks, the true Self may be liberated.

As we expand our perception of the multiple realities with which we interface, we repeatedly hear, *humanity is attempting to open the heart center.* But this does not tell us enough; we must know more about the solar plexus and the guiding light of mind. In ancient, more enlightened eras (e.g., India's high civilization), meditation pushed consciousness upward, from chakra to chakra. Humans advanced — from survival and instinctual, through sensation, to power/ego consciousness, paving the way for refinement. Great resistance resulted as ego power (solar plexus) grew.

Ancient wisdom teaches that the *Manu, Lord of Civilization, reversed the process of meditation techniques for the current human wave of consciousness, and it is to draw down the energy of the soulstar. Driving the currents upward so stimulates emotionalism in the human collective, the active, scanning ego mind seems ever ready for fight or flight. This challenge must always be overcome before the subtle energy of love can truly flow. So, to build a point of ego-calm into which soul may shine its influence begins our modern work: *centeredness. Like the Sun, soulstar shines upon the solar plexus with its two seeds of mind: the ancient, restless ego mind and the quiescent human seed of spirit.

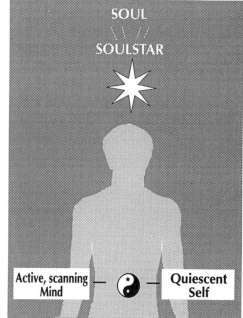

Fig. 18. Centeredness Is the Next Step. The light of the soulstar is brought down to illumine the quiescent self, fostering its growth. We consciously bring the light to the solar plexus, seeking to establish a harmonious vibration between the quiescent self and the restless ego. The solar plexus becomes the light center and thus illumines the rational mind.

Solar Plexus Components

The ancient, restless scanning ego veils the sleeping human seed (manas) called the quiescent self until such time as we begin to calm the ego.

The Master Djwhal Khul explains in volume 2 of *Discipleship in the New Age:*

> There are two points of vital light within the solar plexus centre [see figure 18], which makes this centre of dominant importance and a clearing house for centres below the diaphragm to those above it. One of these points of light is connected with lower psychic and astral life, and the

other is brought into livingness *by inflow from the head centre.* . . . [T]he centres above the diaphragm have only one vital point of energy, whilst the centres below the solar plexus also have only one, but that the solar plexus itself has two points of dynamic energy — one most ancient and awakened, being expressive of the life of the astral or lower-psychic body, and the other waiting to be brought into conscious activity by soul. When this has happened, the awakening to the higher issues of life makes the disciple sensitive to higher "psychic gift waves" (as Tibetan occultists call them) of the spiritual world.[2]
(italics added)

When energized, solar plexus awareness connects us to the nonphysical dimension, producing *clairsentience and *mediumship. Sensitive to presences, pain, and passion, it may be so attuned to the astral, we lose our ability to shut out invading impressions. Because this psychic center was highly developed in a previous era, many believe it need receive little attention now. However, since the natural process of recapitulation reawakens psychic abilities easily, the quiescent point must be understood. Centering exercises create a *stillness so the inner self may be discovered.

We expand the field of calmness at solar plexus and fill it with light. Holding the two points in mind, create a harmonizing resonance between them. We practice magnifying this field of brightness. As we stabilize our efforts, we gradually build a calm light center unfettered by ego demands and personality integration is facilitated. Later, *soul infusion will become the goal.

When we attune to the feeling, astral level, we perceive the phenomena of that plane. In learning to center and balance, we struggle to be free of the powerful instinctual grasp of body and emotions, sensitizing our nature to subtler feelings and thoughts. Becoming responsive to higher frequencies is a major goal for those practicing meditation.

Guiding our ever-changing consciousness requires effort. Meditation teaches us to shift levels, and discern contacts. The spiritual gift of discernment is precious, but not without cost; we learn through trial and error: overcoming rigidity and devotion to ego, becoming increasingly conscious, and detaching from limiting personality perspectives. As consciousness increases, we are better able to synchronize with the Plan being revealed at the edge of our expanding mind.

Think of conscious mind developing a relationship to the sensitive point we are calling High Self. The contributions of High Self feel right, not foreign or strange, for it is born of previous learning. Our awareness of High Self need not be an obvious experience of phenomena; it may be a deep sense of "rightness." As this reference develops, gradual shifts occur in personality. The more ancient, restless point of solar plexus still exists, but now in a healthier way — communicating its warnings but not so defensively as before. A kind of harmonizing of the duality within our nature begins, and we prepare for allegiance to High Self.

The energized High Self vibrates in response to conscious thoughts focused toward it. Remember: *energy follows thought, and thought is a thing; as we think, so we become.* So, as we invoke higher consciousness, we activate this High Self level. In turn, it vibrates throughout the mental plane, triggering a corresponding response from the downward projected energy of the soul (solar angel). Awakened and questing, the solar influence projects a new intensity into this subtler level of mind.

Just as soul, deemed feminine, guides the integrated human, High Self, considered a masculine point of consciousness, is the guiding influence of personality. Persistent interaction between the two points ignites a new creation: the Christ-Within. The divine potential of the human waits (generally considered sleeping) for this interaction. Now the new-born Christ-Within, the Self, steps upon the probationary path.

Sacred Art of Tibet and Russia

Tibetan Tanka of
Buddha of Wisdom

When we look into a mirror, we see the ordinary self of ego and illusion. Imagine how valuable it would be to have a special mirror in which the true Self would be reflected back to us. Meditating on these sacred...images (icons to the Westerner) reveals our true Self, speaking to a part of us that is beyond words, and awakening our own innate perfection.   —Anonymous

Russian Icon of Madonna
and Child

Fig. 19. Sacred Art of Tibet and Russia

Energies of High Self and soul (anchored by solar angel) must reach a crescendo to ignite this new consciousness which, on the Christian path, we call *Christ in us, the hope of glory.* Other approaches use the "Self," the "Atman," and other terms for this profound birth which leads us toward the gateway of liberation.

Referred to as **born again* in 1 Peter 1.23, this experience repeatedly marks the long journey from the people of Genesis to the "possible human." While this may be translated as referring to reincarnation — so taken for granted in the time of Jesus it needed no special addressing — consider how many times in each life we are born to new comprehensions. Each time scales fall from our eyes, we discover a new world, or we are made new, "born again" — much more plausible than believing we are "born" only once to our spiritual nature.

High Self guides integrated personality to subtler levels while solar angel projects soul energies toward the denser levels, flooding the mental body. At this interface, these two points of consciousness guard the way, creating the "strait gate." Simultaneously, the intuitive body begins its growth, making its contribution, flowing into the higher mental levels. When expansion of consciousness happens, and we have taken some scientific liberties in making this statement, we "know instinctively," for in the *collective unconscious rests the long history of human evolution.

Esotericists believe that upon this lowest level of mind (7) exists the foundation upon which the mental nature of the evolving species is built. It is generally accepted that humanity emerged from the animal kingdom about eighteen million years ago, when *individuation occurred. Innate experiences of knowing through psychic senses are submerged just below our usual level of consciousness. At times, a more conscious knowing

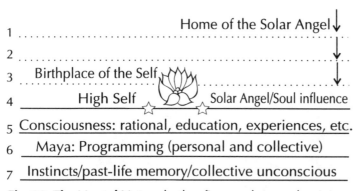

1 .... Home of the Solar Angel ↓

2 .... ↓

3 Birthplace of the Self ↓

4 ___ High Self ___ Solar Angel/Soul influence

5 Consciousness: rational, education, experiences, etc.

6 Maya: Programming (personal and collective)

7 Instincts/past-life memory/collective unconscious

Fig. 20. The Mental Nature both refines and expands, giving light to the levels below and receiving from levels above.

reappears in human beings, especially when unconscious survival instincts sense danger.

Level 6 consists of programming we have been subjected to: the *maya (collective hypnosis) of early life with its variety of happenings. Prior to establishing our separate ego identity, we are especially vulnerable to our family of origin, the society of which we are a part, and invading thoughts and feelings of others. Prenatal and early postnatal environments find us especially vulnerable. To heal, we re-examine our childhood and correct misleading and often deep imprints of these earlier periods.

As well as conscious programming ("this" is good, and "that" is bad, and "what will the neighbors think?"), young egos with few or no boundaries are subject to words, actions, and *thoughtforms without skill to differentiate. This whole level of self ultimately must be cleared of distortions, for here exist many barriers to enlightenment. Great amounts of maya, glamour, and illusion await dissolving by those choosing to heal, to embrace spirituality or the *will-to-good, whether or not they appreciate all of this. Many address these areas through work we know as healing-the-*inner-child.

Conscious mind (5) is really ego's tool for exercising its skills and integrating its capabilities in an individuated personality. Remember, mind is not brain. Brain is the physical mechanism, and mind is the consciousness operating the equipment as best it can. Mind is much more than is readily perceived by those oriented to mundane psychology.

This level of consciousness, 5, integrates the brain's left and right hemispheres. *Biofeedback registers human experience as brain-wave activity (beta, alpha, theta, delta). We have no way yet to record subtler inner levels of mind, such as *out-of-body experiences. Delta and theta vibrate to lower levels 7 and 6, making what awaits there hard to reach. However, as conscious mind learns how to capture and process impressions, more of our inner life emerges.

Recall, each level of mind begins as *mindstuff — free-floating mental energy — attracted by a magnetically charged, focused consciousness around which it coagulates into a working unit. Assisted by *contemplation, thoughtforms organize quite steadily. Energy centers — chakras, as they are called in the Eastern tradition — build in the *etheric body, responding to subtle frequencies.

Just as self-esteem helps us trust what we procure from within, we learn to observe when ego pretends defeat, assuming various disguises of spirituality. Personality's games persist; recall fear, anger, or curiosity are common reactions to the awakening experience.

The fourth level of mind, High Self, vibrates an awareness often blocked by ego. This *ball of knowledge from past experiences flashes higher guidance. A simple way to look at this may be that left hemisphere helps us function in the outer world; right hemisphere supports our inner reality, our wholeness or connection to group life. This fourth level receives the lowest vibrating point of solar angel. It is here that High Self and this lowest energy of solar angel arc toward one another to conceive and give birth to the Self, the Christ-Within, second birth, as we call it.

Expansion of consciousness, or second birth, brings advancement (initiation) as the third level of the mental plane accepts the developing new consciousness. Known by many names, we say the evolving soul builds the lotus, its petals of higher awareness unfolding as outer life is brought more and more into harmony with inner, permitting the energies from solar angel to influence the personality. This new self, nourished as well by the intuitive plane, continues to expand its sphere of influence. In time, the *lotus of high consciousness* will fill these subtler levels — until the fourth initiation, when it "breaks the chalice and sets solar angel free."

The levels of self, as indicated on the following two figures — before and after transmutation — reveal the story of humanity merging with divinity.

The step after transformation is called *transmutation* and happens quite purposefully. Purified of old resentments, heart must turn from emotionalism and sentimentality (high sensation) to become a steady channel for love. The currents of heart and mind must be stabilized to integrate feeling and knowing. Think of two great rivers flowing together. The dissimilar currents must cut appropriate new channels, blend, and establish new patterns within personality.

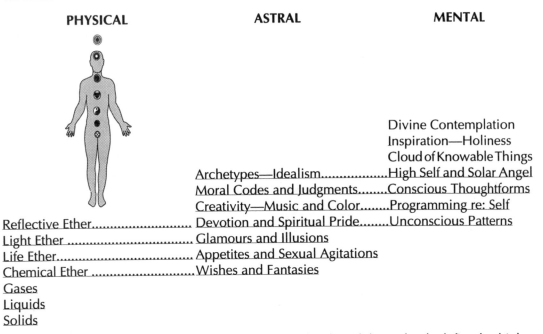

PHYSICAL **ASTRAL** **MENTAL**

Divine Contemplation
Inspiration—Holiness
Cloud of Knowable Things
Archetypes—Idealism..................High Self and Solar Angel
Moral Codes and Judgments........Conscious Thoughtforms
Creativity—Music and Color........Programming re: Self
Reflective Ether............................ Devotion and Spiritual Pride........Unconscious Patterns
Light Ether .... Glamours and Illusions
Life Ether..................................... Appetites and Sexual Agitations
Chemical Ether ....Wishes and Fantasies
Gases
Liquids
Solids

Fig. 21. Before Transformation. The personality has developed three clearly defined vehicles through which it expresses. It embraces transformation in order to give birth to the True Self which already exists only in potentiality.

On the following diagram, note that the fourth level of the emotional nature, *devotion,* merges with the densest level of the mental body. Until the emotional and mental natures surrender to more than personal delusions and desires, they serve only basic drives. The astral body, which served to drive instincts, unfinished patterns, and programmed thoughtforms, now partners with lower levels of mind. New capabilities emerge; what conscious mind energizes will bear fruit. Due to previous purification work, *energy follows thought* with less restriction and *mind power* is magnified. On figure 23, we see our focus lifts from devotion to aspiration, then toward guidance. As consciousness expands in the mental nature, we progress from unconscious to conscious. Spiritual practices guide us toward our true nature (manas).

PHYSICAL	TRANSMUTATION OF THE ASTRAL AND LOWER MENTAL	MENTAL (ABSTRACT)

Divine Contemplation
Inspiration—Holiness
Cloud of Knowable Things

Identification with Solar Angel and High Self..

Ability to Perceive Personal Part of the Plan.....................................

Ability to Express the Image of the Self..

Reflective Ether Desires...Ability to Be Devoted to a Particular Pattern.....................................

Light Ether Illumines.......Ability to Appraise Clearly

Life Ether Enlivens...........Ability to Energize Creations

Chemical Ether Conveys...Ability to Create Through Imagination

Gases

Liquids

Solids

Fig. 22. Transmutation Occurs. The blended energies of the astral and lower mental natures (no longer two, now one) bring about "thinking in the heart." The higher mental (abstract), sensitive to solar angel's influence and soul qualities, stimulates the intuitive body now developing. The purified ethers of the physical welcome and reflect the changes: better health, increased sensitivity.

Humanity utilizes undifferentiated (disorganized) mental energy — mindstuff, as it is known in the East — to form its advancing levels of mind. Mindstuff is attracted by the magnetized consciousness created through seed-thought meditation and contemplation. As each more subtle level is organized and integrated, so is advancement achieved on the path of initiation. *Abstract mind, formed by more refined mindstuff, accepts droplets of soul's wisdom as they flow together, permeating the subtle frequencies with higher wisdom. These abstract-information levels easily blend, vibrating as they do at the same frequencies. Called the Cloud of Knowable Things, from here man(as) begins to perceive what soul knows. This blending or saturation of the mind with soul knowledge (wisdom) facilitates soul infusion (third initiation) — the prime objective of working "as if" to build the new identity: *I am the Soul*.

Working "as if" activates the consciousness threads to bring an increased awareness of subtle inner life to outer mind. As soul awareness grows, wisdom held in higher planes adjusts personality to more perfectly harmonize the game of life with the higher plan.

*Becoming responsive to
higher frequencies is a major goal
for those practicing meditation.*

Here in the midlevels of the mental body (levels 5, 4, and 3) is created the interface where spirit struggles with conscious mind. In this battlefield of human experience, we confront desires and express free will. Where shall we direct our allegiance: to the dense world of personality or to higher purposes for which the inner nature longs?

Solar angel, making its home on mind's subtlest levels, guides us for centuries as soul's anchor. Solar angel projects its influence toward conscious mind, flooding the lower levels with its guiding

RANGE OF VIBRATIONS	ASTRAL NATURE	MENTAL PLANE	INTUITIVE PLANE
↑			
Etheric			Cloud of Knowable Things, from which droplets precipitate
		Home of the Solar Angel	
		1.	
		2.	◊
		3.	◊◊
	guidance	4 ☆ interface ☆	◊◊
	^aspiration	5 conscious mind	
	^creativity	6 programming	
	^devotion	7 instinctual, past-life memories	
	delusions		
	desires		
↓	wishes		

Fig. 23. Subtle Levels of the Mental Plane receive impressions flowing from the Cloud of Knowable Things. Droplets of *straight knowledge are realized. Now the higher chakras (receptors) attuned to subtler levels receive impressions and learn to translate them.

influence. The stimulated High Self (activated by passive meditation) contacts the resident point of solar angel, sparking a new consciousness. As this Divine-Within matures, the Self experiences the second initiation, and solar angel ascends to a higher level of mind to continue its guidance, encouraging further expansion of consciousness. Soul and personality join in coworking relationship as third initiation, soul infusion, is realized.

Who Is Solar Angel?

A significant mystery, solar angel lives out of sight, just beyond our comprehension. It is believed this agent of soul is anchored in the *pineal gland of the etheric body to help its charge evolve. To know our angel is one of our most ardent desires. Although difficult to understand its function and the challenges it presents, the principal responsibility of solar angel is to be ever vigilant of the Plan on our behalf. As it contemplates its true work, it vibrates the Plan at the edge of our minds for each of us to perceive.

This companion, helper, and guide assists the soul in stepping its energy down into the denser atmosphere of human consciousness. This representative of soul is often known as "guardian angel," "guardian of the way," and appears in teaching myths as the age-old companion of our journey. This guardian prompts experiences until we realize its presence and respond.

> At the time the physical body is to be formed, the Solar Angel spins the Sutratma and creates a coil or etheric body in accordance with the records stored in the *permanent seed atoms. This etheric body, or coil, is woven of energy threads as a web, and for the average person is mostly constructed of buddhic substance.
> —Torkom Saraydarian, *The Science of Becoming Oneself*

Solar angel is a separate entity — not our own nature but a guide to help the integrated personality develop into a human soul that can stand on its own power. Later, this soul will give way to the *monad, the immortal spirit. Think this way: personality is the industrious child, soul is the vivacious youth, and monad is the wise elder. Solar angel is the guardian of personality until we know ourselves as souls. As soul matures and becomes conscious, it will embrace its divinity, the monad.

Solar angels are not of the angelic kingdom; the name is given them because they are messengers *of the *solar deity to this realm.* Billions of years ago, they evolved in another system, and achieved mastery there. When the call came for aid for humanity, they responded. Their relationship to us is similar to parent and child or teacher and student.

A synopsis of the story of solar angel, according to ancient wisdom teachings, relates that as humanity struggled to free itself from animal consciousness, it seemed trapped by a strong instinctual desire nature. *Sanat Kumara, or Melchizedek, asked God to send help to humanity. Responding in three immense waves, the first *kumaras found humanity unready; when impacted by solar angel energy, humans died. On the second wave, the kumaras touched them, and although they died, the solar angels were able to plant a seed in the developing form. The third wave of angels took residence within the higher frequencies of the mental sheath of each human being, forming a *bud* from which they stepped down the energy of the Creator measuredly, as a transformer, knowing in time each maturing human seed could handle soul's powerful energy unassisted.

Once solar angel's attention is captured, it guides our steps and responds whenever invoked. It has always nurtured and assisted from afar — our inner source of wisdom, goodness, beauty, courage — until we build a consciousness that seeks to know the true soul. The evolving nature absorbs energy in higher and higher frequencies, like richer and richer food. In the light of solar angel, personality acquires soul qualities, or virtues, the goal from the birth of Self.

Negative energies — doubt, despair, hatred, resentment, fear, and so on — create barriers between our conscious mind and the angel's bright light. So we repeatedly clear these, invoking beauty, practicing positive emotions, words, and actions, as we learn to stay open to love and sensitivity. As we rejoice in the inspiration that comes like nectar from on high, we truly *become* our spiritual self. Personality realizes at least part of what soul knows at this wiser level.

Solar angel lives in deep meditation, telepathically stepping down its awareness of the Plan for life and humanity through noble thoughts. As soon as we begin to meditate, we are seeking the light of our inner teacher. As we persist in our practice, a sensitive becomes increasingly aware of the great truths held by Wise Ones and of symbols charged with the dynamic energy of the Cloud of Knowable Things. When we encounter illusions, thoughtforms, and nontruths that permeate the unpurified mental atmosphere, solar angel seeks to guard and guide by directing corrective impressions and holy thoughts to our developing mind as best it can. With perseverance, we increase our ability to discern the light and follow it to higher realities.

MENTAL PLANE

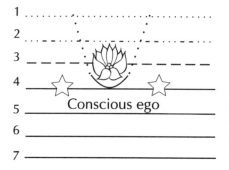

Fig. 24. Meditation Constructs the Chalice. We begin by "building the cup" as we learn to calm the mind and open to the light of the soulstar. Working "as if," we direct our attention toward more subtle levels. Each initiation expands the chalice.

As Saraydarian states in *The Science of Becoming Oneself:*

> The chalice is built primarily of the substance of solar angel. The human soul makes itself ready to wear it as "the robe of glory." When this . . . "robe of glory" is . . . woven, the emotional sea disappears and the astral body disintegrates. Thus [we enter] into direct communication with the intuitional plane. Here lies the source of true and direct knowledge.

Over aeons of time, solar angel has passively emanated its presence to an unawakened personality. As stirring begins, our diligent caretaker becomes more active in directing to us what we need to keep progressing as we consciously search. Awakened, we become aware of *synchronicities that prompt and encourage us, when we have "ears with which to hear" and "eyes with which to see." When we begin to comprehend these synchronicities beyond our usual rational intellect, we affirm our inner awareness. The Self continues its advance into more abstract, forming the subtler planes of the mental body.

Now the maturing Self must reconcile all differences between itself and solar angel, as well as adapt to the power (agapé) it contacts. As more progress is made, the fourth initiation is realized. The chalice — the container woven of the blended energy of solar angel and transmuted properties of personality — breaks, and solar angel goes free. Now the initiate must stand alone, proving s/he can handle the powerful connection to agapé, the soul force.

From the beginning, solar angel encourages us to practice "right conduct" — spiritually synchronizing our action with insights from our meditation. The degree of our ability to align to solar angel depends upon our own spiritual maturity, but a major step is realized as we recognize a guardian is watching over us. We learn to appreciate its assistance in aligning our nature to the great solar lord — Christ, to Christians — who watches over all planetary life.

In the battlefield of human experience, spirit struggles with conscious mind, we confront desires, and express free will.

We also need to recognize that humanity functions as solar angel to the *elementals of the physical, astral, and mental bodies as they adapt to the shifting energies of the evolving process. Just as holy ones are guides to humanity as it awakens, we are guides and guardians of the minute intelligences (through the devas) — first, within our own body, emotional nature, and mind; then in interaction with the world of nature: animals, plants, and minerals. As Genesis 2.15 (KJV) relates, *And the Lord God took the [hu]man, and put him into the garden of Eden to dress it and to keep it.*

Recognizing the Christ is called differently in other religions and traditions, esoteric Christians always desire to be respectful. Known as *Maitreya by Buddhists, *Hunab K'u by the Maya, Lord *Krishna by Hindus, and Horus to the Egyptians, esotericists think of the Christ as head of Hierarchy and teacher of angels and of humanity. As solar deity, the Lord of Lords (all masters are Lords — El Morya/Mary El) guides us into an all-encompassing planetary experience; being both spirit and matter, we are to relate to higher vibrating worlds, as well as all Earth kingdoms.

The Lord Christ, planetary sun being and solar angel of our planet, serves to guide all planetary life, the true reason it is recorded in John 14.6 that *No [one] comes to my Father except by me*. Eastern and Western ideas are reconciled by acceptance that holy consciousness is being acknowledged, not a personality. An enlightened consciousness makes each a son or daughter of the Most High, and toward this we strive.

A source of inspiration, beauty, and goodness, our solar angel responds. The power of this call, known as the science of *invocation, dawns eventually. As we penetrate the Cloud of Knowable Things, we receive and perceive our guidance, our part, and our work. Seed-thought meditation particularly prepares us to access what is held there. Bit by bit, we become increasingly attuned to this guiding frequency — solar angel — the one the ancients call the inner teacher.

In *The Science of Becoming Oneself* we read:

> In esoteric literature, heaven is the mental plane where the chalice is found. The treasure is in the chalice. It was symbolized as the Holy Grail sought by the Knights of the Round Table. It is in the chalice that our true Guide exists, but He cannot express Himself until the permanent atoms or seeds are cleansed, purified, and the chalice is in full bloom, filled with the elixir of life. The purifying process is the result of the contemplation of the Solar Angel within us. Solar Angel vibrates in higher octaves and these notes act as purifying streams of energy which throw out all that does not fit into the plan of the human soul. The act of meditation is a process of conscious assimilation of these energies.[3]

Opening the Heart Center

The term "opening the heart center" is heard frequently today. Its meaning and its results are understood differently at different times and levels of development. As aspirants working consciously with the light of soul, we purposely draw energy from our soulstar down to the solar plexus first and then the heart. This gentle but persistent invoking prepares us to express creatively under inspiration. We continuously exercise love, wisdom, and will to transform the outer life. It takes will to initiate each new step, to *walk our talk*. All religions — whose very purpose is to align us with holy influences — prescribe commandments, dogma, or behavioral direction to require practitioners to exercise will and to respect certain protective boundaries. Will promotes change within personalities and aligns us with the "cause" rather than "effect" side of the *Hermetic principle of karma.

As soulstar energy sensitizes the heart, we blend head (knowledge) and heart (caring), learning to relate to each other as souls. As groups within humanity open their collective heart centers, they will radiate a true kind of love of which many are not yet capable. Today, we reference this as humanitarian love; on a more personal level, let us embrace *acceptance* — thereby emanating a kinder reality to the world.

As we grasp the four kinds of love (refer to figure 26 on p. 98), we realize two are personal and two are impersonal; self-love is the bridge over which we move from eros and philias to humanitarian and then agapé. We hear, as we love ourselves, we will become capable of loving others, but rarely do we grasp why it is so.

Humanitarian love witnesses to unconditional acceptance that acknowledges equality of soul and diversity of purpose. With this new perspective, true love can flow through personality. Previous loves — sexual attraction (eros) and tribal or blood ties (philias) — pale by comparison to a heart-centered (humanitarian) outpouring. Now the rightful pattern within each is honored; we give freedom in order to get it, thus we advance toward what we are meant to be.

Caring ones seek to alleviate suffering, not just to ease another's pain but because each knows there is no separation: yes, we *are* the keepers of our sisters and brothers. We become one through humanitarian love. The Great Commandment, the challenge of the Christian tradition, charges us to love others. Humanity will gain a new perspective as this consciousness is realized collectively. As the heart center is sensitized to a higher natural order, healing energies flow unrestricted. Look again at these words:

> *Love the Lord your God with all your heart and with all your soul and with all your might and with all your mind. This is the greatest and the first commandment.*

And the second is like to it, Love your neighbor as yourself. On these two commandments hang the law and the prophets.

Matthew 22.37–40

Now we recall the seven major chakras of the etheric body, each relating to a specific body, or vehicle. For example, the chakra, or energy center, at the base of the spine relates to the tangible form, through which flows life force to animate the physical body.

The second center correlates to the astral body, involving sensation, vibrating to the range of feelings created by humanity. This astral energy is a major concern to awakened ones seeking to cleanse emotions and the instinctual consciousness that has sunk below the levels of our conscious mind. Here we experience astral reality through the dimensions of instincts and feeling.

The third chakra relates to both the lower mental body and rational mind. Here we experience our alliance to ego. The solar plexus retains issues of ego power and control, as well as aiding us with issues of the outer world. Clearly, we relate to third dimensional reality through the realm of rational mind. As we become wiser and this level is more integrated, we exercise our capabilities more easily. We also recognize subtly disguised values, personal opinions of others, and/or their need to explore in ways we may not feel necessary. As sensitivity to others begins, we may find rigid rules are not to be taken quite so literally — as the avant-garde often demonstrates. Also, here we may begin to have "gut feelings" as our psychic faculty awakens and begins to communicate.

The fourth dimension is affiliated with the heart chakra. Two important themes beckon awakened ones: 1) opening the heart so as to realize our relationship to one another and 2) activating intuitive energies from which we build the fourth-dimension *light body*. The good news is that the two are connected. As either is focused upon, both are enhanced. Thus we clear away blockages to soul influence coming from abstract mind and the intuitive plane. The heart center opens naturally through a series of steps.

1. Allow our feelings to flow, rather than suppress or restrict them. As we liberate emotion, expression becomes freer and more comfortable.

2. Acknowledge and even name feelings that surface—owning each. We take responsibility for both positive and negative emotions.

3. Clear old hostilities. We use psychological or psychospiritual technologies to discern, heal, and release emotions long held and no longer appropriate. We do the nightly review, and make amends whenever possible.

4. Encourage thoughts and feelings of a positive nature; magnify love-caring. Express positive emotions: gratitude, respect, impersonal love, forgiveness, and release.

5. Yield to even subtler feelings while practicing quiet time. Exercise detachment. Remember, all consciousness elevates with the addition and nurturance of beauty: music, color, nature. This is where we often break through to our interconnectedness.

Dimensional body five, the atmic, is beyond the comprehension of most but may be imagined as our part of the collective soul. Flashes of this high state may register in holy moments. This fifth body integrates into the mystical body of Christ. As we study building the light body (fourth dimensional, personal aspect of soul), we recall Oneness. The fifth dimensional vehicle is the group body for the collective, one human soul. Vehicles six and seven are potentials not yet built, except for a few highly enlightened Wise Ones.

So, we encourage our heart to open as best we can. We stretch to greater love, and each higher frequency energizes the corresponding potential. Remember, each body — physical, emotional, mental, and spiritual — is to be fed, exercised, and cleansed regularly. As energy flows, each body develops, coming to life a bit at a time. As positive emotion moves within us, we nurture the maturing forms. As we release old residue and process current issues, we continue to create our "bodies-in-process." As new chakra centers function, we build corresponding forms.

As we progress toward opening the heart (the majority of awakened humanity is here), we ask: What knowledge and tools will help us advance toward this important step? We love and we care, as we remember the song, "We Are All One Body."

Personal therapies provide tools for releasing old pain and finding new perspectives. Numerous psychospiritual techniques are available today, and resistance to seeing a therapist is dissipating. Good approaches are: *gestalt, Jungian analysis, inner-child work, Psychography (a form of past-life therapy taught at Sancta Sophia), and family reconstruction as designed by Virginia Satir, author of *Conjoint Family Therapy,*[4] often referred to as the family therapist's "bible." There are others.

People rebel when pain becomes too intense. Most struggles are battles with ourselves, but few recognize this. Fewer still solicit a mentor to guide and support them. Modern inner-child work and twelve-step programs are splendid procedures to heal the past and prepare for spiritual birth. Group work, wherein true empathy exists, achieves much. In *Discipleship in the New Age II,* Alice Bailey says of the heart center:

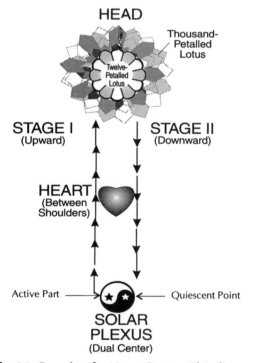

Only from the heart centre can stream, in reality, those lines of energy which link and bind together. For this reason, I shall give you for your *group meditation* a form which will stimulate the heart into action, linking the heart centre (between the shoulder blades) to the head centre through the medium of the heart centre which is found within the head centre (the thousand-petalled lotus). This heart centre, when adequately radiatory and magnetic, will relate you afresh to each other and to all the world. This again — when connected by an act of the spiritual will to the solar plexus centre — will help to produce that telepathic interplay which is so much to be desired and which is so constructively useful to the spiritual Hierarchy — provided it is established within a group of pledged disciples, dedicated to the service of humanity. They can then be trusted. This practice directs the building of the creative thread.

Fig. 25. Opening the Heart Center. This diagram illustrates the procedure I suggest. In lesson 6, Weaving the Antahkarana, we will study how this occurs.

Bailey continues:

> The activity of the heart centre *never* demonstrates in
> connection with individuals. This is a basic fact. What
> devastates most disciples is the solar plexus ability
> (when purified and consecrated) to identify itself with
> individuals. The heart centre cannot react, except
> under group impetus, group happiness or unhappi-
> ness, and other group relations.[5]

As you review this diagram, be mindful that, if you are
following the seed-thought procedure in these lessons and the "I
am the Soul" meditation, your daily practice is calming the solar
plexus, linking heart and soul energies through the soulstar, and
aligning lower mind to soul. You are constructing a pattern for
personal growth. When meditating with a group, the group energy,
as well as your own, builds and blends experience by experience.

It is especially important as we move toward the Aquarian
age — an age of group work — to identify with a group of our
choice. Try to meditate together; if you cannot, project yourself.
Join them and work "as if" you are physically present. The group
effect is exponential, like logarithms, hastening humanity's enlightenment and your own. Recall the words of the Master in
Matthew 18.20, *For wherever two or three are gathered in my name,
I am there among them.* Even as we draw into alignment with one
another, we are also aligned to the Christ. Though we retain our
individuality at personality level, we prepare for Oneness.

The opening of the heart center by three in a group distributes
humanitarian love to all members. No longer alone, each discovers
the inner connection with life — not just oneness with human
beings but also with new awareness for fourth dimension realities
of Lots Of Vital Energy. We begin to experience the next step in
evolution. When the group heart truly opens, we "know" the Great
Life of which we are each but a fragment. When we perceive with
our *intuition, we realize even more. Here greater energies of the
will of the soul express with its bounty of love and wisdom.

Love of nature, music, and color often is a first step for the
receptive seeker of higher sensitivity — a less threatening affinity
than loving a person. Each step enriches life, adding new dimensions to be integrated. In the expansion process, natural spiritual

senses emerge as the sensitive mechanism releases trauma, caring increases, and the mind releases prejudices and expectations. We redirect freed energies into what we perceive as our purpose while intent and motivation are carefully observed.

As we cultivate a detached, less emotional heart-centered acceptance to daily living, we clarify our true self as a continuing pattern of growth unfolds. Unconditional love brings healing and the freedom to change and grow. Love, freedom, beauty, and joy invoke grace to our pathway. Buddha taught detachment, disassociation, and dispassion as preparatory tools for those seeking enlightenment. All of these help free us for the purpose for incarnation.

When humanity achieves love of all life (humanitarian — the love of which we are all capable and for which we long), only one more advancement in the love process waits to be achieved. The biblical word *agapé* is often construed as God's love for humanity, or Christ-like love. We could redefine it as *cosmic love.* This is not technically correct, but it gives us an inkling of agapé's dynamic power.

More precisely, agapé is the fiery love of the higher nature; (fifth dimensional, intuitive, and atmic planes) descending toward a greatly expanded consciousness. This is the Creator's love — oneness — flowing through open channels. Think how we feel when we step back and admire our handiwork — how we love our painting, how we identify with music we have composed, or books we have written, or businesses into which we have invested such effort. The activity of creating requires pouring life force into whatever we wish to bring to life. Now we experience the love expressed by *God, who so loved the world.* The Creator has invested Lots-Of-Vital-Energy, yet most of creation slumber unaware.

Learning to embrace these powerful energies of creation challenges us, so solar angel, agent of soul, guides the energies as we move through

---

LOVE REDEFINED

In reviewing the Four Manifestations of Love, we recognize them as levels of love, reflecting human evolutionary advancement. Think of humanity moving up a staircase step by step, with self-love as a landing.

AGAPÉ. Cosmic in nature; power of divine fire flowing.

HUMANITARIAN. Group soul outpouring. Unconditional acceptance and impersonal Lots-Of-Vital-Energy for one and all.

> **SELF-LOVE** bridges to humanitarian love. Love self to love another.

PHILIAS. Personal identity established, personality caring, neighborly, brotherly, familial, tribal.

EROS. Animal desire. Instinctual, sexual, easily unconscious, self-centered.

Fig. 26. Love Redefined.

changes in consciousness necessary to align and become capable of using them. Acting as a transformer, solar angel bequeaths to us only as much soul energy as we can manage at any given time.

Integration, as well as shifting consciousness from level to level and point to point, is the journey to high consciousness — the path of initiation — consummation of a wondrous *transfiguration that moves us from ego consciousness with its self-satisfying incentives to soul infusion, soul-conscious agapé. When this is achieved, fourth initiation is realized, and solar angel goes free. Remember, however, current humanity's goal is the third initiation, or soul infusion. This is why we use techniques of active meditation and strive to remember *I am the soul* with such dedication.

We must not presume, however, that our more subtle soul vehicles are developed. The intuitive vehicle is only beginning in most people and the atmic partially unfolded in a minute few. Expressing qualities of the monad is most limited because, for most, those vehicles as of yet remain merely a part of divine potential.

This Self-Within integrates with personality, building the consciousness threads that step down awareness. The root system is in effect the *antahkarana anchored through the physical nature, grounding capabilities to our physical life. As we experience soul maturity, we realize wisdom and adjust our outer

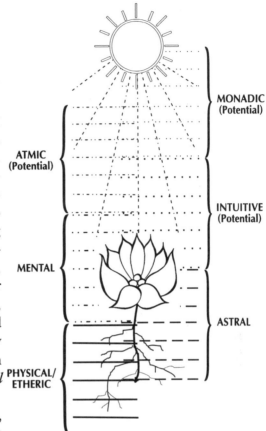

Fig. 27. The Chalice and the Self. Here we see the physical world represented as mud/earth/body. Astral dimension supplies the water/feelings. Mental nature brings focus/self-consciousness and will, as soul shines like the sun on the newly born (bud) self to bring it to fulfillment. Due to its likeness to nature, the lotus was chosen by ancient Wise Ones of the East to represent evolution of the True Self.

life to reflect what the soul knows. This wisdom must be demonstrated in the game of life to walk the path of initiation.

Known as wisdom, Sophia, gnosis, or Daath, this high consciousness, commonly called wisdom of the heart, is once again emerging. Insights to Sophia are better preserved by Eastern orthodox Christianity than Western. We can best understand if we think of Sophia as the Holy Spirit, or as the feminine nature of God, Divine Mother, or even read Proverbs 9 where Sophia/Wisdom was the companion of God while creation occurred. In this way Scripture acknowledges the long-neglected feminine aspect of creation. Proverbs and the Song of Solomon have the most to say about wisdom/Sophia.

Currently, much effort is being made by many to help us reclaim straight knowing, high consciousness, as both love and wisdom. ChristoSophia is our way of acknowledging the "Word made manifest" as the love principle (Christ) and the wisdom behind the word (Sophia). Saint Joachim of Fiore, a twelfth century mystic, stated the Arian age was the age of the Father (or Law), the Piscean age the era of the Son (or Gospel), and the following era was to be the time of the Mother (or Holy Spirit). We see such in the renewed understanding of Father-Mother God with the re-emergence of the divine feminine and her mysteries. Sophia is her name.

Assignment

> ### Seed Thought: REVERENCE

Our first seed thought for this lesson is *reverence,* the virtue assigned to the Libran influence.

> Let knowledge grow from more to more,
> But more of reverence in us dwell;
> That mind and soul, according well,
> May make one music as before.
>
> —Alfred, Lord Tennyson

Reverence-solemnity. Solemnity, an old word, seems ponderous, heavy, but if we think of it as expressing an ever-increased reverence for all life, we grasp its truer meaning. Reverence for divinity manifests as respect and appreciation for others, their gifts, and the Plan unfolding. Inwardly, we develop a special kind of reverence for divinity, however we may perceive it.

Veneration of the Masters is natural respect for the light they carry, while reverence also reflects the awe and solemnity of holy moments experienced in meditation or in prayer when we contact soul. At those moments, we are flooded with joy and reverence, qualities of deep solemnity and awe.

Seed Thought: TRANSFORMATION

The second seed thought for this lesson is *transformation,* the virtue assigned to the Scorpio influence.

> For a conscious being, to exist is to change, to change is to mature, to mature is to go on creating oneself endlessly.
>
> —Henri Bergson

Transformation may seem remote, but it is not a distant process. It is going on within us daily, here and now. As cells in the body of the planetary Logos, we strive and evolve with Earth as she undergoes her tests, or initiations. The transformation of Earth spells change for us all, just as our change signals change for Earth. These processes (within and without) acknowledge the innate wisdom of each cell of matter, whatever its form. As inner wisdom becomes increasingly conscious, we experience transformation, transmutation, and transfiguration (see vol. 1, lesson 7, for complete discussion).

Envisioning humanity as an enlightened species may seem impossible, but such changes become more real as we discover more of our inner potential. Transformation as a goal is not to escape human limitations but to awaken us to the divine potential awaiting each of us.

Constantly advancing in evolution, humanity transforms a bit at a time — each day and unconsciously. However, the spiritually awakened embrace transformation, willing it, hastening it. Disciples are consciously *transmuting* their nature in order to become ever more responsive to the subtle influences from within. As we realize soul infusion, our very nature *transfigures*. Transformation, the birth of the Christ-Within, the first initiation on the esoteric path of Christianity, is in itself a seed thought of significant value.

In the Light of the Soul

Truth has no authority, no value in personality,
until it authenticates itself,
until the mind leaps up and sees it is true,
and accepts it, not because its truth
is imposed or its refusal dreaded,
but because it is seen to be true.
—Dr. Leslie D. Weatherhead
The Christian Agnostic

F or centuries the pyramid, as a sacred symbol, has preserved esoteric concepts. First, its four-sided base represents the four directions and Earth's four elements (earth, water, fire, and air), acknowledging the foundation of material life. Each side, a triangle (physical, emotional, mental), rises to the apex of high consciousness and union. Multiplying four times three gives us twelve, representing the celestial influences that silently watch over human life. Twelve reduced (1+2) to 3 reminds us of the trinity within our own nature and the power of its creativity. Consider the triads of sun, moon, and ascendant in *astrology, or soul urge, quiescent self, and expression in *numerology. Primarily we acknowledge love, wisdom, and will, God's reflections in the human kingdom. *Made in the image* (Gen. 1.26), we too are creators, challenged to come into the fullness of divine nature. *Remember, you are gods* (Psalm 82.6 and John 10.34).

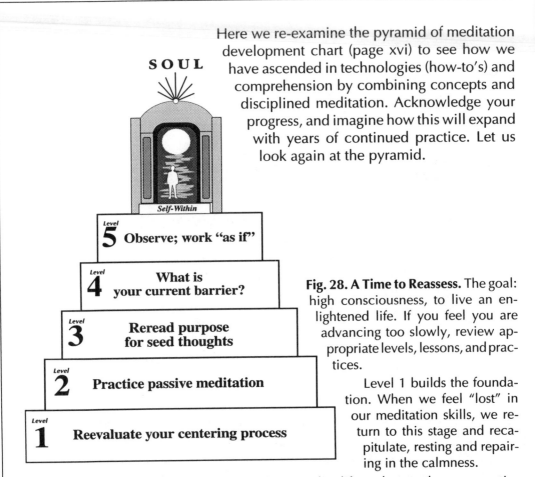

Here we re-examine the pyramid of meditation development chart (page xvi) to see how we have ascended in technologies (how-to's) and comprehension by combining concepts and disciplined meditation. Acknowledge your progress, and imagine how this will expand with years of continued practice. Let us look again at the pyramid.

SOUL

Self-Within

Level 5 Observe; work "as if"

Level 4 What is your current barrier?

Level 3 Reread purpose for seed thoughts

Level 2 Practice passive meditation

Level 1 Reevaluate your centering process

Fig. 28. A Time to Reassess. The goal: high consciousness, to live an enlightened life. If you feel you are advancing too slowly, review appropriate levels, lessons, and practices.

Level 1 builds the foundation. When we feel "lost" in our meditation skills, we return to this stage and recapitulate, resting and repairing in the calmness.

Level 2 helps us understand issues of personality life and strengthens perceptive abilities. Use a mentor or spiritual guide as needed.

Level 3 opens the mind. The magnetized consciousness attracts insights of a particular nature, according to the choice of our seed thought, keynote, or phrase. Utilize the assistance of mentors, therapists, and inner-child work.

Level 4 provides ways and means to clear fog and miasma from personality so the light of soul shines more clearly into our prepared and focused nature. The Twenty-Third Psalm can be a noble reminder.

At Level 5 we practice right remembrance. The soul-alignment technique at the end of lesson 7 will help us align with *what the soul knows*. This wash of goodness and radiance clears personality, and we advance toward becoming the *possible human* we only vaguely conceive.

As we grow, each of us ascends the pyramid for the view at the summit, which is Oneness. Our inner work helps us observe life from a broader perspective, and we take our places as wise ones — a great need for our society and humanity as a collective.

> Let there be light! So the dawn shall rise over heaven and the Earth. There can be no glory, no splendor, until the human being exists as the fully developed person.
> —*The Popol Vuh* (sacred text of the Maya)

Ancient wisdom records the story of humanity's long struggle. Rhythms and cycles provided challenges, opportunities, precise energies, and the environment for natural progress. Evolution produced instinctual procreation and tribal consciousness, levels of knowing less conscious than our awareness today. Collective tribal behavior was challenged, and free will expanded as independence was achieved. The ego emerged with its ability to differentiate, individuals emerged from the collective — individuation, it is called. With each new state of mind, we identified new choices and differences, and conflict arose, not just between self and others but within self as well.

Conflicting emotions, pretense, cover-ups, and mixed messages occur naturally as ego, the "I" of personality,

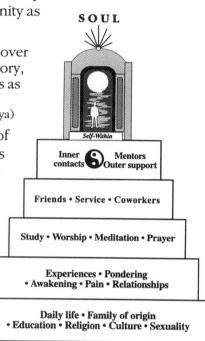

SOUL

Self-Within

Inner contacts • Mentors Outer support

Friends • Service • Coworkers

Study • Worship • Meditation • Prayer

Experiences • Pondering • Awakening • Pain • Relationships

Daily life • Family of origin • Education • Religion • Culture • Sexuality

Fig. 29. Unconscious but Natural Evolution. Each aspect contributes to humanity's awakening. When we focus at a particular level, the others contribute unconsciously. Awakened ones seek to be conscious about as many aspects as possible. Disciples are called to be "conscious" to the Plan and to *thy Self.*

flounders through one experience after another. Experiences build more points of identity, and the nonself grows increasingly aware of its strengths and weaknesses. As expressed by kabalist Perle Epstein, "Confronting each level of his soul in succession, [the mystic] discovered that what he had initially considered his 'identity' was really a ladder of smaller selves, with the 'divine soul,' or 'intelligence,' at the top."[1]

Kept alive through *shamanism, secret societies, and folk wisdom, old truths are passed from one knowledgeable person to another. Ancient wisdom, indeed *ageless,* emerges here and there for those who are ready, then once more submerges. From time to time, *mystery schools surface and train initiates, leaving imprints upon each continent. With each successive high point, some become more aware of humanity's lofty promise: illumination, enlightenment, self-actualization.

Today, sacred writings from East and West are readily available to those who quest. Ethical guidelines provide boundaries for personal passions and cause awakening ones to pit their will against less worthy desires. Practices fan the higher nature, burning away lower impurities. Meditation provides energy and insight to keep the process vibrant. Bright minds discover accessible teachings to point direction, requiring only clarity and contemplation to discern distortion or to release confusions.

To the Westerner, the laws of Moses may be the best known of ancient guidelines. The Ten Commandments laid a foundation for socialization of the various Hebrew tribes. Obedient to these directives, the tribes matured to magnificence. These laws continue to influence behavior through both Jewish and Christian cultures.

The Ways of Buddha

Before the time of the Christ, Lord Buddha, called the Blessed One by the East, emerged from the Hindu system to enable humanity to attain a next step on the pyramid of high consciousness. His path required mind development, the art of contemplation, and right use of will. Emphasis on wisdom directs attention to refining the mind. Buddha sought to move us from information gained only through sensory experience to rational knowledge and self-discipline, as he prepared humanity to go beyond the emotionalism so strongly expressed in Hinduism. According to esoteric teachings, Buddha anchored the wisdom principle upon the planet for humanity and created a preparatory path for the love principle the Christ would bring to Earth five hundred years later.

Buddha encouraged humanity to choose the light, to discern which direction leads to light and which to darkness. He offered directives using will and mindfulness to free oneself from the wheel of rebirth. Once we embrace the path of high consciousness, no longer is it a choice between good and bad; the disciple has made that choice. Now options become subtler; they are between "good" and "good." What serves the *higher* good? What is the more appropriate response at this time? Discretion is to be developed.

Along with individual meditation as the most significant practice, Buddha defined a succeeding element of the path as *wisdom*. His teachings, the *Four Noble Truths and the *Eight-fold Path, are often called the "middle-road path."

His Eight-fold Path, consisting of simple rules, provides guidelines for disciples. Allegiance to the Eight-fold Path requires right-belief, right-thought, right-speech, right-action, right-means of livelihood, right-endeavor, right-remembrance, and right-meditation/concentration. These rules of ethical living are totally voluntary, embraced because their wisdom is recognized and the disciple desires to advance spiritually.

Again we have obvious exoteric statements with more obscure, or esoteric, meanings. For example, "right memory" can mean, esoterically, we are to remember each of us is a soul and here for a reason, and we are to contemplate our reason for being. "Right thought" reminds us to think before we act. To change our actions, we must first change our thoughts.

Siddhartha, the Buddha, renounced the life of excess he had led. Then, living as an extreme ascetic, he found no enlightenment in the abuse of body or emotions, or in mind*less*ness. He finally adopted a middle way, practiced meditation and contemplation, and achieved enlightenment. In this holy state he defined a new path: *the use of mind to offset the power of instinct and emotion.*

Volumes have been written on these revelations. The challenge for disciples is to learn to live the truths of their path in daily existence.[2]

As we have seen, humanity's collective experience continually advances to new heights of awareness. Moses defined a system of spiritual laws (right use of will), opening the way so humanity might *choose* alignment to higher worlds. Buddha provided guidelines for mindfulness. Meditation centers, balances, and initiates our contact with High Self and higher mind. Contemplation then organizes personal insights into purposely workable patterns.

Even as it empowers, choice allows us to accept, resist, or refuse. As lower mind opens to higher mind, more awareness is accessible. Techniques and results differ, but mystics through the ages testify to the existence of higher dimensions. Experiences of light flood humanity with information, direction, and wonder. Bathed in the light of soul, we ascend the pyramid. Step by step, the journey to enlightenment moves from unconscious prompting of basic self to love-wisdom of soul; in time, we advance to the cosmic properties of the monad.

The Coming of the Christ

Further guidelines for evolving humanity were provided by the Christ, who gave specific instructions — but again, hard-to-understand. These commandments structure the preparatory path so we may delineate the love process. Every path requires disciplines because will is necessary for transformation. While we may not always be sure of his exact words, we pursue meanings in meditation and contemplation.

The love principle anchored by the Christ brought new opportunities to humanity. Love now begins to pour from the intuitive and atmic planes, creating a bridge by which human consciousness, the prodigal child, may return to its Source. As we practice meditation, we build the essential mechanism to ascend to higher consciousness, *to know what the Knower knows.* While challenges exist, so do the means to meet them. We place ourselves in posture, meditate regularly, discover inner contacts, dissolve barriers, and release limitations.

> *We advance toward becoming*
> *the possible human*
> *we only vaguely conceive.*

Spiritual maturity evolves as a correct blend of energies facilitates inner changes. Just as we experience puberty naturally — without a consciously known formula, but because we are so encoded — our divine potential just *is: Christ in you, the hope of glory.*

As we dissolve barriers and continue our seed-thought meditation, we are freed from personality's unfinished business. Determining areas of challenge is the important first step. Invoking positive thoughts and seeking guidance as we build virtues produce sweeping changes in our perspective. The combination of self-discipline (personality training), dissolving barriers (astral scrubbing), and seed-thought work (building the spiritual eye) brings a personality-centered life to a higher focus.

The word "spiritual" does not mean allegiance to a religion or even discipleship. It means we live in such a way we do not forget, ignore, or omit recognition of the true nature of Self in our day-to-day existence. To be spiritual is to remember our Oneness, both inner and outer. We strive to bring right-relationship into our work, our play, our attitudes, our business deals, our romances, our friendships — yes, even our arguments, our alienations, discipline of our children — every decision. No matter which area of life challenges us, we resolve to remember our true nature.

From this higher self, we seek to create the most appropriate responses possible, considering spiritual laws as we know them. Over time, our perspectives change, and we should be prepared for that. As we clear the haze from our psychological nature, the light shines more clearly, and we are better able to stop, look, and listen before jumping to conclusions (personality's gambit). Humanity's spiritual nature is evolving slowly toward an exquisite compassion. If we fuel the process as conscious participants, we move faster. We may expect "spiritual efforts" to make it easier for us; not so. Spiritual efforts hasten the journey, allowing us to serve as we grow, providing leadership, love, and encouragement for those who follow.

We are training to be cosmic astronauts. We know that to be futuristic we must relinquish all that restricts. We

The Rabbi's Dream

In the kabalistic tradition is an insightful story of a scholarly rabbi who overhears an ignorant cowherder praying to God in a quite improper manner. He promptly apprises the simple man of the importance of praying correctly.

That evening, the rabbi dreams he has stolen something very important to God, and God is offended. He is told to persuade the simple man to pray as he once had, for God values the heartfelt love and prayers the cowherder offered so freely. The rabbi is told he will be punished severely if he cannot return to God that which is God's. Rushing to find the cowherder, the rabbi implores him to disregard his instructions, to go on praying and loving God in his own sincere way.

The significance of the story is, of course, that many formal creeds and procedures do not speak to or from the sincerity of the individual. For our spirituality to flow, our prayer and practice must embody our own essence. That is the genuine gift we have to offer our Creator.

Fig. 30. The Rabbi's Dream.

dare to become the god-being we have glimpsed. So we train strenuously for that journey into space — in this case, inner space. We commit to meditation because we choose clarity, knowledge, and wisdom. We choose expansion of consciousness, new perception, more awareness of our potential in the *now*. We build levels of mind to transform our nature and our comprehension. We *will* to be made new and whole.

People of high consciousness have been chosen in the past to lead kingdoms, projects, expeditions, and many frontiers of human endeavor. Egypt's pharaohs were trained in mystery schools in order to assume their roles. The feats of the Greeks in both the arts and sports required mystery school preparation. Thinkers of ages past bequeathed their wisdom to those gathered about them. We are told in the perennial wisdom teachings, humanity is emerging from the *kali yuga,* "the iron age," a time of darkness and ignorance; the new era is to take us from the limitations of materialism into an awareness of the veiled Plan and Purpose. Those of expanded awareness have roles to play in the shift to free humanity from bondage.

In *Journal of Transpersonal Psychology,* Vol. 1, No. 2, 1969, Lawrence LeShan,[3] well known researcher of our time, told of taking sixty-two statements of how the world works — half from serious mystics and half from modern theoretical physicists. After removing identifying names, he scrambled them, and no one tested was able to separate quotations successfully by their identifying groups — physics, mysticism, or neither.

Mystics and physicists, then, independently concluded that there are ways to perceive "dimensions beyond the physical." Furthermore, when describing this transcendent reality, all agreed on four major points, according to LeShan. These metaphysical concepts acquire new depth as we become less fixed in our perception of life.

- There is a better way to know the mystery of life than with just the five physical senses.
- There is a fundamental unity, a oneness to all things.
- Time is illusion.
- Evil is mere appearance.

110

Mystics speak of life flowing — moving like a river, as water to drink, or as "living water." Water symbolizes motion, emotion, movement, change. We ask ourselves: Can we allow our reality to be fluid, shifting, transforming, or do we fear or resist this? If so, we must explore why. Albert Einstein said, "The highest form of insight is mysticism."

Ego's resistance to the higher subsides as we open our consciousness to higher thought. As each surrender occurs, more barriers fall. This is the experience of mysticism — a force for change. To become aware of new dimensions or expanded reality, we must release many old concepts — outer and inner — and dualistic attitudes natural to physical reality. Only we can dissolve the veils that separate us from one another.

Personalities may be veils, as may emotions, prejudices, and concepts. Whatever we cannot penetrate becomes a veil, restricting us to an accustomed level of comprehension. Veils block the higher world of causes from computing in our brain mechanism. Veils screen our windows of perception, preventing realizations; simply put, they obstruct the light. Yet in one flash they may be penetrated, and we are then born into a new reality or world view.

Veils that form between levels of consciousness, it is said, serve specific purposes. The eternal cycle of expansion and rest resounds again and again. Those who would ascend to subtler areas are cautioned to proceed prudently; this is no place for fearful or weak minds. Spiritual law teaches, those who seek a more perfect state must first deal with their imperfections in order to advance cleansed and pure. If we allow negative attitudes — perimeters of darkness — to crystallize, veils become firmer and denser.

Veils obscure each level for our protection. The chick must peck its way out of the shell by its own strength if it is to survive; the seed must burst its hull if it is to sprout. We must struggle free from one level to be ready for the next. Experience propels us to master the components in order to ascend.

As we expand in consciousness, our new developing skills help us connect with whatever awaits us at each level. As we discover the hidden life of each new plane, it nourishes us for the next level; but until our personality and higher nature blend, we cannot digest what is given. We hear tales of the Halls of Learning and Hall of Wisdom, but little is comprehended rationally because our minds cannot handle much of this hidden reality as of yet.

Respected teachers write much concerning veils that separate us from our Source. Formed by humanity's collective thoughts and attitudes, the veils of maya, glamour, and illusion have congealed over the ages. Aspirants must struggle through these veils, then open to the next level by resisting ages-old influences that strive to thwart us. As we break through patterns of personality and mental concepts that blind, we finally sense an inner guide and come to trust.

As trust builds, we follow our know-ingness deeper into our inner nature, the Self. We discover the *Halls of Learning,* and we are encouraged to explore. The *Hall of Wisdom* teaches discrimination and the power of free will. We advance into the *Hall of Concentration* for the development of mind powers. Upon graduation, we pass to the *Hall of Choice,* from which those who have finished earthly work may choose their next service. Only holy ones — Masters and *Cho-hans — pass through to the even more remote *Hall of Blinded Ones* (the light is too powerful for others). Initiates are led by this beacon. When humanity stands with massed intent to serve its higher nature, aligning its collective will to higher will, the last veil will be rent, the *Veil of Aspiration* [4] dissolved by the wisdom of the Buddha and the love of the Christ. The

Christ, the World Teacher

Veil of Aspiration

Hall of Blinded Ones

Receive Christed Energies

Veil of Separation

Hall of Choice

Experience more light of saints, sages, and Masters

Veil of Distortion

Hall of Concentration

Experience the inner teacher

Veil of Impulsion

Hall of Wisdom

Discover your inner hidden resources

Veil of Impulsion

Human Initiatory Path & Halls of Learning

Probationary efforts—birth of the Christ-Within

Fig. 31. Humanity's Inner Halls and Veils. Different systems apply different names to veils and halls, but the same principles apply. I have used names from *Christ the Avatar of Sacrificial Love* by Torkom Saraydarian. The first two veils are known by the same name.

cosmic pattern is to ascend, with the wiser assisting the less aware, or the "little ones."

Gaining love and wisdom, we now comprehend the true meaning of *love one another, serve one another.* In the bigger picture we know that helping another truly benefits the server. When one enhances the life of another, the individual, the group, and the consciousness of the world advance.

The law of nature is to aspire to serve something more highly evolved — a respected project, an honored cause — and then to work diligently. We observe our service to ascertain wherein lie our good intentions and our selfish. We discover mixed motivation, and over- or under-used qualities. In giving our allegiance to something significant, we are stretched. We discover new and unrecognized abilities, and our weaker areas are strengthened. In such a way, we realize our uniqueness.

Fig. 32. One Reason to Serve. When our cup is full, nothing more can be poured into it until we share some of our bounty.

As awakened ones, we choose to be in harmony with the One "in whom we live and move and have our being." Our dedication to serve something greater than ourselves prompts the effort to ascend. Thus striving, we surrender our life energy into the Great Plan.

As we learn to serve truly, we note the flow that travels through the heart (no longer controlled by solar plexus) and we experience a sense of openness. As we share, we expand our understanding of relationship and how we contribute to group consciousness. We move from creating merely an emotional response to gaining a broader grasp of what is truly good for the whole. We shift allegiance from self-centered ego to advocate humanity's effort to align its will to higher will, its mind to higher mind, its heart to the great heart, in a process best known as metamorphosis.

> Service is the first real effect, evidenced upon the physical plane, that the soul is beginning to manifest itself.
>
> —Alice Bailey teachings[5]

113

Wise Ones of East and West have sought to guide humanity beyond restriction and suffering, from bouncing between pain and ecstasy. As we study and do the practices, our levels of comprehension advance and our nature transforms. What we value in our mind and what we know in our heart, as well as how we perceive events of life, must then be integrated in our outer life.

Before we experience additional changes, we are tested to see if our perspective is solid. Transformation requires endurance. All of this blends within the psychological nature, so bodies change and adapt as well; our emotional and mental natures are in continual flux as we bring spirituality into daily life. Through tenacious practice of meditation and regular alignment, vehicles of expression are redesigned to sustain our true natures: both physical and celestial. We become wise on the physical plane, and out of sight we become capable *inner-plane workers.

Humanity's spiritual nature is evolving toward an exquisite compassion.

Self-discipline guided by self-love is vital as we ascend toward the Great Life. Realizing our temperament and persistently seeking more light, gentle practices constitute a bona fide spiritual path. We need not be sanctimonious or theatrical as we fine-tune our personality-in-distress. *Divine discontent is nature's way of prompting us. As we undergo spiritual puberty, higher energies create a more vibrant etheric field. As we learn how to be this more sensitive, more spontaneous spirit, we patiently release self-condemnation. We truly do learn to love ourselves.

Our ongoing task is day-by-day integration of the puzzle pieces. The truly simple person is a profound unit — not divided against him- or herself. To create such an integration, we must be flexible in multiple circumstances, and this means building many new perspectives. We adapt wisely to diverse situations, no matter the mood of personality. This synthesis, upon which the principle of simplicity is based, is a complexity free of complications. We are a kaleidoscope responding to the panorama of outer life. Awareness helps us adjust smoothly from within the *psyche. Each facet we build achieves a more concentrated unity.

Our contact with the Cloud of Knowable Things in meditation produces new ideas, symbols, and outpourings — perceived in bits and pieces. While our mechanism is only now being assembled, the more we use the seed-thought method, the more we gain. Insights from this level are inspired, a wisdom stream that often comes in a rush: words, thoughts, images, realizations.

For some, contact brings a flow musical in nature; for others, poetic. For me, words often come in lines or short paragraphs expressed rhythmically. Do not fix expectations; just allow yourself to experience. After using this technique for a while, you may find, "I know when it happens. It feels a certain way." Experience builds trust — an important stage of growth for those developing skills of expanded consciousness.

Ascending the pyramid, we gather what we need for our own growth and for the good of humanity. To experience holy moments, to grow wise, we often follow the path of those who have preceded us in love and service, returning to everyday tasks with perseverance to do our whole duty and lay the gift of our lives at the feet of the Christ.

Mantra of World Servers [6]

*May the power of the one life pour through the group
of all true servers.
May the love of the one Soul characterize the lives
of all who seek to aid the Great Ones.
May I fulfill my part in the one work through
self-forgetfulness, harmlessness, and right speech.*

Contradictions among Techniques of Meditation

Contradictions in meditation practices are not disagreements so much as differences based upon individual suitability. Several techniques, especially those involving breath control, require more guidance by a qualified teacher. Others entail levels of abstraction for which many may not be ready. Some may need a method more mentally tangible. At different stages of development, certain methods fit our needs better than others. Two or three months of consistent practice may reveal that a particular method is not beneficial at this time. Ordinarily a considerably longer trial period would be better since easily recognized signs of "success" — i.e., peace of mind, less stress — are not primary goals of meditation for serious spiritual students. Important contributions, usually quite subtle, emerge after proper, extended practice.

When we engage in a specific system of study, it is wise to follow its suggestions to the best of our abilities. When we complete a certain stage, we are in a better position to judge whether or not we wish to continue. However, just as it is important to stay with an approach for a time to see if it really serves us, occasionally we need to try a new technique just for the experience. Certainly, the occurrence of frequent headaches after a new meditation practice needs to be addressed with an advisor or tutor, as do any energy disorders.

In recent years, conditions labeled "spiritual emergencies" are being addressed. Certain experiences seem likely to precipitate distress hard to reconcile with our rational order of things. These particular events frequently create spiritual emergencies in daily life (though these are not the only ones):

- spontaneous psychic happenings
- kundalini experiences (static energy in the body)
- visitations from discarnates
- near-death experiences
- UFO, extra-terrestrial encounters

Should you meet with such experiences, allow others to assist. I refer you to the excellent work of Emma Bragdon, Ph.D., *A Sourcebook for Helping People with Spiritual Problems,*[7] and Stanislav Grof, M.D., and Christina Grof, *Spiritual Emergency — When Personal Transformation Becomes a Crisis.*[8]

Differences in Vocabulary

We may resolve certain differences by noting that various terms mean the same thing; therefore, little or no contradiction exists — e.g., *samadhi* of yoga literature is *satori in *Zen Buddhism.

As we examine various systems, we find each has degrees of completeness, with an ultimate condition of final absorption within the Absolute. But levels are portrayed differently, and paths to the summit are not the same. We might reconcile this with some variation of the *Higher Third technique (see lesson 8). Perhaps different ways of talking about satori and samadhi are inadequate descriptions of the one reality, but we do not need to decide which is "correct."

To advance, we repeatedly put ourselves in posture and just do the work — turn within, meditate, learn to wait on the Lord. The intention works, and interaction follows. Is this not the ultimate mystery? We feel intense hunger for an embrace, and when it occurs, it is beyond words. Intent ignites the experience, and the interaction is profound. Imagine the Great Magnet at work. We position ourselves — relaxed, yet magnetized. Responding to the pull, the magnet within leaps toward the Great Heart. Experiencing a shift in consciousness, we rejoice in a lighter, higher moment of freedom. Gently we return to outer awareness, with or without new thoughts to contemplate.

We have introduced a few paradoxes you may encounter and possible ways to treat them. Some contradictions will not be resolved; some irreconcilable differences may prevail. We each must choose our way. Do not assume you need to be

Fig. 33. Many Paths, One Goal.

stuck with your decision or limit yourself for ultimate progress. Stay alert for possible fallacies in your own decisions or for changes in your development that indicate a new approach is in order.

Studies in esoteric thought and ancient wisdom may cause questions or perplexities that need to be addressed. In the meditation area alone, we read and hear statements that do not seem to compute rationally. In order to retain a degree of clarity of thought and purpose regarding the total meditation experience, it is important to develop ways to deal with discrepancies or paradoxes. The more we read and hear about meditation, the greater our confusion can become unless we work with constructive ideas. So many conflicting theories float about, it is easy to wonder which might be the "right" way.

We have discussed common differences in procedures and purposes. These are not all, but they illustrate useful methods to resolve dilemmas. It is not possible to cover the myriad differences and paradoxes or summarize all that can be said. If particular statements seem inconsistent or obscure, consider contacting the meditation tutors for further assistance.

Confusing Views about Meditation

While we acquire ideas about meditation from reading, perhaps we receive the most impact from what others say. Someone whom we feel is an authority or spiritually advanced may make a statement in a lecture or in conversation that impresses us as truth. If we hear a conflicting idea from another respected source, we have a dilemma. We feel we must reject one concept or the other to determine which authority is right. A frequent source of contradictory ideas is informal discussion. Often, as a viewpoint is discussed, we tend to accept it. Later, we recall what was said by another or read a disagreeing opinion, and confusion resurfaces.

Assuredly, for one view to be right does not mean another must be wrong. Wanting black or white answers is natural for rational thinking, but meditation is not a rational procedure. Expansion of consciousness or the creative exploration of reality does not fit the dualistic mode of the analytic process.

Contradictory ideas usually involve four aspects of meditation. There may be, first, differences in procedure; second, differences in expectations; and third, variations in ultimate purpose. This most important aspect of meditation determines to a large degree the procedures and happenings. A fourth area comprises purification activities which clear the way for successful meditation. Some systems ignore the necessity for right action, required cleansing, and so on, as a proper context for meditation. Others insist they are necessary preparation. We find overlapping conflicts even among these four aspects.

Procedures

A simple difference in methods lies in the use of objects for concentration. Some teachers discourage concentration in the form of gazing, such as at a candle flame. They see this as an unintelligent, mechanical process that could result in a black-out of rational consciousness, a trance-building exercise. Others advocate beginning with gazing at a candle flame. These examples illustrate the diverse fundamental approaches of teachers. Different instructions are acceptable within each proposed system. Most astral or psychic approaches use points of concentration involving visualization or other senses, while mental techniques encourage using an idea upon which to focus, i.e., seed thoughts. As individuals, we may find an affinity to one or another at different stages in our development.

The wisdom principle: the use of mind to offset the power of instinct and emotion.

Many who practice psychic development techniques feel the pull of higher consciousness and simply progress from one level of interest to the next. The biblical "gifts of spirit" provide models for distinct talents. As human cognizance evolves regarding ways these aptitudes work, so do methods that assist in unfolding extended senses. Most children have open psychic senses, and many retain this sensitivity into adulthood. Often when individuals demonstrate psychic abilities and ethical, spiritual lifestyles, they inspire others to awaken to their psychic nature and spiritual awareness — either or both.

Yet, meditation remains a "beyond-words experience." While we seek to expand into the vast mind of God and become one with it, we realize it is an experience of wonder and subtle power. We are stirred by the profundity, and we struggle to adequately describe our experience of inner reality.

Taken step by step, every effort performed is a unique part of the necessary endeavor to move from one level of mind to another. Suitable tools vary somewhat for each person, as do anticipated goals, physical condition of the practitioner, and his or her degree of experience. Realizing the power of meditation to affect outer life, the ancients would never teach even simple techniques to novices until they were committed to change. This suggests working with a mentor is prudent. Many changes — possible and probable — await the dedicated seeker.

Conflict surrounds the term "meditation." Some insist the term refers to techniques for spiritual growth, and others argue for self-improvement. Having explored active and passive procedures, we know both are useful. And although different purposes may create disagreement over techniques, we find the same approaches may be used to achieve unlike goals.

Active meditation may be compared to going to the bank to withdraw riches — in this case, themes with which to align and virtues to build. We contact love, wisdom, faith, courage, benevolence, and more. Tapping into divine mind may only be achieved by concentrating mind and emotions in a focused intentional activity. Many feel this active way of meditating is more apropos to Western traditions. Some see the Eastern emphasis of passive *silence* as not tapping into available wisdom we might unearth at soul level.

While the meditation style of the eminent teacher *Yogananda appears to be primarily passive, with initial activity designed to quiet the mind, it develops into an alert awareness within a stillness achieved by coming into one-pointedness. By giving the mind a chosen focus, we avoid chains of chatty, scattered rational thought. With preparation and purification, experienced meditators often move easily into stillness. If we consider holding a tight mental focus as active — the dynamic needed to penetrate the next level of mind — we reconcile the differences. While we may express ourselves differently, great similarity exists.

In passive meditation, if a thought intrudes, imagine it to be a log, floating on a clear, still lake; push it to one side, and return to a sense of calm water, or inner clarity. Each intrusion may be dealt with in such a way. Visualization keeps us alert and clear. In active meditation we deal with intrusive thoughts by remaining objective about them, by restating the seed thought, magnifying it, and tightening the focus. We reinforce mental acuity as we practice single-mindedness, returning to the seed thought whenever the mind wanders. We restate the seed thought and focus on *the thought behind the thought*.

While some teachers enumerate steps, as we have done — centering and relaxing, focusing within, allowing chatter to go on without response, using seed thoughts, discovering new concepts and direction — most feel an overall approach to spiritual life should be in place for advanced techniques to be taught or beneficial. At Sancta Sophia Seminary we seek to offer a transformational program: education, meditation, daily disciplines, love, and service. Such a combination of effort has a profound effect in any life. Under guidance of a personal mentor, the proper attitude and hidden talents *of the disciple* emerge.

What to Do with What Happens in Meditation

A principal area of disagreement exists here. Some, especially Eastern paths, say we should do nothing with thoughts, feelings, insights, images, and realizations that arise during meditation. The goal is to go beyond them to stillness — not an empty mind but a point often called "the void." At an earlier time in the evolution of humanity, this was indeed the goal; however, since the rapid evolution of the neocortex — especially the last three hundred years — we may now cross that point and enter the Cloud of Knowable Things, the Vast Mind.

As consciousness evolves, new levels of mind are achieved. At one time, human beings could not think abstractly; now conceptual approaches abound — witness innovations of sciences, mathematics, philosophy. The higher energy makes itself felt in this abstract level of mind. Using the seed thought as a key, we penetrate higher mind and magnetically attract resonating thoughts. Our modern goal is to be wise, not blissful. The seed-thought process invites mind power to interface higher frequencies and contact wisdom at the Source. We focus upon and energize the key words, attracting ideas related to the seed thought. When adequate magnetism creates enough pull, the outpouring begins, and new insights rain forth.

Some examples of powerful seed thoughts:

- *The Great Life exhibits wisdom and synthesizes all truths.*
- *The higher nature guides through life experiences.*
- *Dwelling in purity, the holy Self within conceives a life of peace.*

When meditation is linked with concentration, we hold only one thought in mind. Many exercises facilitate concentration — focusing on a candle flame or a mandala, or observing our breath without attempting to control it. Internal visualization may be a method of practicing concentration. Techniques include holding an image steady or creating a mental picture as clearly as possible after a period of observation. In a more difficult exercise we visualize something formless — a color, or a quality, such as joy, compassion, balance, grace, even utter darkness or space.[9]

Concentration, one-pointedness, can take a much broader form. Next we learn to focus on ideas in phrases, penetrating the essential source of the idea (whether symbols or words) to discern relationships with the Ultimate Source. This one-pointed focus — more dynamic than that of visualization — is in the mental body, rather than the astral.

In a different way, a *mantra not only fills the mind with its sounds, it so saturates the mind as to lead us inward. Seed-thought meditation helps us develop skills leading to mindfulness, a goal long held before East and West as the mark of wisdom. As a goal, mindfulness is a state of self-observation, not unlike witness consciousness.

Implicit in: *I am not the body, I am not . . . , etc. I am the Soul,* mindfulness pervades our spirituality, providing a platform of observation from which awakened ones move dynamically toward enlightenment. Consistent practice of mindfulness expands consciousness significantly, yielding new awareness. Watching the breath stills the mind and leads to a level of peace. Therefore, it is not easy to limit these and like procedures to centering, one reason many different methods are viewed as meditation techniques.

A similar resolution can be adopted in the "results, no results" dichotomy. Active meditation stresses the need for improvement in everyday life, harmonious and creative living, sharing, caring action — relaxed and nonattached. To be real, meditation results in character changes, new revelations, and increased, inspired power to think, love, and act.

The "no results" camp continues to stress moving into stillness — a state of consciousness beyond thought, while remaining alert and aware. Here is emphasized the value of an ineffable experience, one which defies words or action. The most important point to emphasize is that to dissolve ego barriers, we must experience and recognize the nonself or we cannot shift to become the Self that is one with God.

The Orphic, the Occultist, the Mystic

In these processes we are reminded of the differences of three basic paths: the *orphic,[10] the *occultist, and the mystic. The orphic experiences God through *feelings,* and the occultist aspires to *know* God, especially seeking to comprehend and act within the laws of life. The mystic *blends* the two and experiences some of both.

Basically then, people approach spirituality from emotions (orphic), mind (occult), or some combination of the two (mystic). The person of feeling may dance, sing, act, paint, or merge with nature, sensing God in the forest or under a splendorous sky. Occultists use mind power, longing to know God through profound realization, to perceive the will or the way of God by inner knowing. Each conducts searches with distinct approaches, perhaps believing theirs to be the only way; with persistence, all bear fruit. Mystics long for the embrace of God through personal experience and with great acceptance, however it occurs.

Meditation and contemplation are resourceful practices for the one who would know with the mind — the occultist. Since this book emphasizes "knowing" God, it would be considered occult in nature.

The **occult** is that which is hidden and must be studied to be understood. In Latin, "to conceal," formed with the prefix *oc* meaning "opposite, against," is the opposite of "cult" because its philosophy teaches each to do his/her own thinking. The word may be used to correlate to the study of universal phenomena, but true occultism seeks to penetrate the causal mysteries of being.[11]

The **orphic** might lie upon the ground, look into the clouds, and experience psychic reality. Another ancient way was to gaze at the water of the lake or flames of a fire in order to "skry" — receive a clairvoyant impression. The orphic may dance in joy or in pain to transcend separateness, seeking Oneness through feeling, experiencing God through the senses. *Tantra techniques fit here.

The **mystic** truly is one who testifies to other dimensions, often exhibiting great fervor. Such experiences may be induced by intensity of devotion or focus. Particular seed thoughts or ardent

Fig. 34. Caduceus. In human nature, one stream of consciousness is mental, the other emotional (or we could say masculine and feminine). At the points of the crossover exists the true experience of the mystic, one which synthesizes heart and mind.

fixation, on Jesus in prayer or sitting beside us, for example, has this effect on certain people. Blending mind and emotion, the mystic is a combination of the preceding two approaches. The caduceus illustrates this beautifully.

Humanity's different approaches remind us that behind emotion is feeling — kinetic, deep, and inner; behind intellect is knowing — innate, profound truth. To penetrate to abstract mind, we bypass the intellectual level and come to an intuitive knowing. We distinguish this as *moving from intellect to intuition*. Similarly, before we can comprehend true compassion, we must cease emotionalism and sentimentality. Then we break through into a little-suspected clarity of feeling.

The contemplative system of meditating has been described as using intellect to transcend itself. Starting at ordinary levels of intellectual activity — discursive, verbal, and dealing with dichotomies (good/bad, black/white) — it continues until all thought energy leads to a new state of knowingness.

Questions Within the Process

As we meditate, happenings can paradoxically become non-happenings within the process itself. Using a seed thought, *we are aware of mental activity.* Thoughts are directed consciously, at least initially. We attempt to move the flow of thought toward a specific level and purpose, finding the truer — more esoteric or hidden — meaning of the word or phrase as held in higher mind. On occasion or in time, conscious effort may be supplanted by a self-generating flow which elevates awareness even higher.

Another method in vogue, one of "free thinking,"[12] aims at increasing the mind's flexibility and fluidity. This involves approaching a subject with an open, unbiased mind and pursuing an idea to its furthest logical conclusion, wherever it leads — similar to a seed-thought procedure except no effort is made to direct or focus mental energy to another level. It involves looking at any idea that enters the mind and referring its ramifications to inner judgment. We also call this creative thinking. Whatever comes to mind is accepted as truth but available for revision as we remain open and flexible. This approach resembles Krishnamurti's "choiceless awareness," which rejects most of what we usually consider meditation.[13] This is similar to the popular management practice of brainstorming. As students of meditation, it is valuable to acknowledge a wide variety of methods and practices do exist.

Approaches for Resolving Contradictions and Paradoxes

Ample evidence reveals different ways of meditating have led a host of people to exceptional states of awareness and being. Patterns for resolving dilemmas or paradoxes are not mutually exclusive and may be used simultaneously or in sequence.

We learn to match the goal and the type of meditation we choose. The time of day makes a difference. In early morning, using an active seed-thought approach awakens, stimulates, and stretches the mind, putting us in touch with the cosmos. By late afternoon or early evening, we often need a passive, restful, contemplative time — perhaps a simple visualization or relaxation exercise. We then feel relaxed and refreshed for several more hours. Should we become distressed, the soul alignment technique in lesson 7, p. 173, offers wise assistance.

Levels of Consciousness

In summary, the depth of consciousness we achieve is not limited. When we are focused and centered, our consciousness is not the same as when we are engaged actively in visualizations and other sensory expansion experiences.

In passive meditation particularly, we may reconnect to the energy (quality) of love that fills heart and mind until it is hard to remain conscious. As we experience this blissful state, sometimes it seems only ecstasy; at other times we return full of knowingness. Whatever we focus upon is magnified. Should this be love/agapé, the state of joy may continue for some period after the conscious experience ends. We call this "filled," "glowing," or "rejuvenated." Thus, we examine wisely the avowed intent of any meditation process.

In seed-thought work, as we penetrate the meanings behind words, we initiate perspectives and insights apart from ordinary intellectual activity. We move into heightened creative and intuitive functioning, as illustrated by truly eloquent language of inspired speaking or writing, a common experience even for those who do not see themselves as creative. Feelings seem to acquire a refinement atypical of our usual emotions — not just because violent, negative reactions are absent but because quality of feeling differs. Closely allied with this higher level is awareness of solutions to everyday problems and relationships, insights or aha's that reconcile differing perspectives.

It is possible to move even further beyond mental activity and known emotions. It may be the bliss/light described in yoga literature, a universal awareness, or an indescribable experience from which we emerge with a positive knowing of having touched into the ultimate Source. Meditation experiences can thus have common denominators with the near-death experience, about which you may read in *Messengers of Hope* [14] and *The New Age Handbook on Death and Dying.* [15] Experiences of the Light occur in meditation spontaneously as well. For more depth, read *Cosmic Consciousness* by Bucke. [16]

Assignment

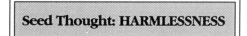

Seed Thought: HARMLESSNESS

Our first seed thought is *harmlessness, or nonviolence,* the virtue assigned to the influence of Sagittarius.

> *Do all things without murmurings and disputings, That ye may be blameless and harmless, the [children] of God, without rebuke, in the midst of a crooked and perverse generation, among whom ye shine as lights in the world.*
>
> Phil. 2.14-15 KJV

Most acts of harm, violent or subtle, are easily recognized; spiritual students must also realize the damage caused by careless speech, gossip, negativity, pettiness, and vengeful thoughts. Even our unintentional acts and our "sins of omission" are recorded in the immense story of life. As awakened ones, we learn to monitor our thoughts and perceive the pollution or beauty they create in non-physical realms. For those who want a truly spiritual life, "It is no longer enough to cease to do evil, we must do good," Lord Buddha taught.

As we expand the concept of harmlessness, consider our relationship with the world of nature. Teachings say, when we are truly harmless, we can pass unharmed by the beasts of the forest and the insects about us. Since they know they have nothing to fear, they will not attack. We desire to be truly harmless, for we know we are one with the All.

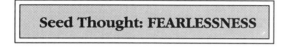

Seed Thought: FEARLESSNESS

The second seed thought is *fearlessness,* the virtue assigned to the Capricorn influence.

> Heroism is the brilliant triumph of the soul over the flesh — that is to say, over fear: fear of poverty, of suffering, of calumny, of sickness, of isolation, and of death. There is no serious piety without heroism. Heroism is the dazzling and glorious concentration of courage.
>
> —Henri Frederic Amiel

We become fearless by building courage. First, we must identify consciously with spirit, the divine Self. We fear loss as long as we identify with possessions and position. If we identify with life, no matter what happens, we realize there is no reason for fear, for we *know* life continues. This deep knowing undergirds all trials and all adventures — our entire experience of life.

With fear, we do not sacrifice. People are reluctant to serve if they are afraid to lose several hours or something of measurable value. When we do not fear loss, we can surrender all. We become a fearless, heroic example. Now we assume identification with the spirit Self, and we willingly relinquish all that we are not.

Thus, free of fear, we develop the ability to penetrate cosmic mysteries. Only when fearless might we dare to enter the vibrations of Great Ones. We achieve the archetype: hero/heroine. Fearlessness is mastered.

Weaving the Antahkarana

To get into the core of God at his greatest,
one must first get into the core of himself at his least,
for no one can know God who has not first known himself.
—Meister Eckhart

The ascent to high consciousness leads to new reference points, many of which seem strange to those who find it difficult to move beyond rational thinking into the fluidity of other realities. We all experience dreams that seem "so real," so similar to our waking state, we react to them as to an outer event. At such times, we see how indistinct is the line where one reality begins and another ends. Such wondrously real inner thought shapes meditators' world views. The same is true of myths, story telling, legends, and many archetypal tools. The muse is a generic term often used as an archetype of divine inspiration. Subtleties may or may not be thoroughly ascertained, but their impact is felt, for they are authentic in our perception of life.

We continue to uncover new inner contacts, inner life, new realities, and the parts they play in expansion of consciousness. As we establish our own pathways, we share this reality with others who have found similar, more clearly marked avenues to higher realms. We seek to stay midstream in the flow of love-wisdom coming from Wise Ones who have gone ahead of us, checking our reality against their guidelines while maintaining our stability on the physical level.

*Pythagoras taught that those who venture to explore inner reality need to study either a physical science or mathematics to insure equal development of both the rational and the intuitive faculties. Today we might say, "equal access to the right and left hemispheres of the brain."

Students of esoteric systems traverse paths cut by predecessors who guide through oral teaching and example. Students are encouraged and reassured by thoughtforms created and maintained in the inner world for aeons which now serve as luminaries on a path others have blazed.

For example, because Kabalah has been taught for several thousand years, the temples of the *sephiroth now exist in radiant colors on the astral plane, their symbols often seen and brought back by their beholders. Those who experience the inner assure us: yes, this reality exists and may be experienced by others as well. Shared events often make something *real.* It is not the only way an experience gains value, but an important way. Sharing empowers the one having the experience and the path to which it witnesses. However, the value of mystical moments is in the change in awareness they yield.

While marked paths exist, we must take care not to surrender our own perceptions too readily because our meditation work validates our experiences, insights, and journeys in consciousness. Each creates her or his own path as a personal work, quite important to the quest as we see a bit later. Being true to our insights has value and is not to be surrendered lightly.

In Marion Zimmer Bradley's *The Mists of Avalon,* in a theological discussion with the priests, Merlin said, "I am dedicated to the belief that it is God's will that all men should strive for wisdom in themselves, not look to it from some other. Babes, perhaps, must have their food chewed for them by a nurse, but men may drink and eat of wisdom for themselves."

A Closer Look at the Astral Dimension

We have mentioned High Self in context of a ball of knowledge which always "feels like us"; indeed it is constructed of our experiences on the journey. Solar plexus consciousness, one of our first ways of knowing, registers this quite readily. We may call it "gut feeling" or "flying by the seat of our pants." This ball of knowledge is usually quite close at hand, and under duress, we connect with it with little effort.

The journey to connect to soul (solar angel, soul's representative) is quite different. To achieve soul infusion, we move through a progression of levels — much like locks of a dam. On the way, we experience various realities. As we pass beyond the usual boundary of rational mind, we discover astral dimensions of fantasy and imagination, a dreamlike realm of subtle ethers corresponding to physical reality and reflecting the emotional and lower mental realms of collective human experience, as well as our own. A chronicle of past events (known as *akashic records) is held in both individual and group memory. Particular attention is paid to the astral realm early on. It holds little charm for the more mature spiritual seeker, for it is but a reflection of the past combined with hopes, dreams, and wishes created by still-energized thoughtforms; it is not the home of soul.

The astral, also called the nonphysical, shelters *discarnates with little aspiration. It is a meeting place for those in the physical and those deceased as well, that they may come together briefly in particular times of need. While we are in physical body, we awaken first to the astral realm and then develop a consciousness to transcend it. Those less in touch with their feeling nature may never be so "psychic" but much more in tune through intuition. Here exist telepathic impressions in a more mental, though less dramatic, medium.

> "Enlightenment," when defined as the rational acquisition of knowledge, deals with only a very limited aspect of human transformation. I follow the teachings of the ancients in proposing that the notion of enlightenment is meant to be taken much more literally: the process involves seeing more clearly, both internally and externally, so that there is more lucid awareness,

Adventure in Meditation, Vol. III

a feeling of the light and warmth of love in the heart—ultimately a complete immersion in the ocean of light called God, Being, or Spirit. This aspect of self-transformation is actually a process of moving from darkness to more and more light.

—Ralph Metzner, *Opening to Inner Light*

The Cosmic Being

As we grow in comprehension of human potential, we realize we are individual and one simultaneously. We know any segment of a hologram contains the whole design and that our brain mechanism is truly holographic. Correspondingly, as a part of creation, we contain within our mysterious nature the entire Great Plan. Depending upon how our brain mechanism is animated and how mind is harmonized to brain, we may perceive a limited physical reality, many levels of ourselves, or a cosmic consciousness.

The ability to shift mentally from point to point, to discover new avenues to explore, and to tap into the cosmic wholeness has forever been the quest of those who seek to know. Our conscious self — the ego most recently developed — can enjoy its power, but we need not be restricted to its limitations. We need only examine the power of words, stories of self-healing, and inner and outer imaging to become convinced we have resources yet untapped.

The brain mechanism serves the mind. The mind is not contained in the brain but incorporates a whole vibratory field of mental stuff, a part of which we have individually attracted and integrated into our mental body. Remember, each of us is but a brain cell in the consciousness of planetary life. Analogously, the planetary being plugs in to the wholeness of the solar system, the solar system in to the universe, and the universe in to the cosmos. Expansion of consciousness is realized level by level, and then we integrate this new awareness into constructs useful to the view of wholeness we have gained.

Life is God's gift to us;
what we do with it is our gift to God.

Spiritualized, integrated hearts and minds of humanity comprise a mystical oneness. There is but one soul for humanity. To some this is the *mystical body of Christ wherein we all are one. The mystery held before us in religious thought is but a simple way to say that a group mind of holy ones is motivating the consciousness of all humanity. As it becomes increasingly clear and potent, a higher degree of awareness dawns for the human group soul of which every person is a part. *Kabalists know this divine being as the "heavenly (hu)man," *Adam Kadmon. Just as our own brain receives from our more spacious mind, our consciousness develops subtler levels of the mental plane. As we contact corresponding realities, we learn to register these different realities as our own.

Contemplating such wonder, we realize cultivating our own mental mechanism is our doorway to the cosmos. The brain mechanism of humanity is evolving — yes, individually and for all. The mind leads the way toward fulfillment of divine potential, individually and collectively. Accordingly, we function at a rational level, at an imaginative level, and ultimately at a soul-conscious level. Through various practices, we expand day by day to encompass the blessings of each reality.

As *Sri Aurobindo explains, "Life evolves out of Matter, Mind out of Life, because they are already involved there: Matter is a form of veiled Life, Life a form of veiled Mind. May not Mind be a form and veil of a higher power, the Spirit, which would be supramental in its nature? [Our] highest aspiration would then only indicate the gradual unveiling of the Spirit within, the preparation of a higher life upon earth."[1]

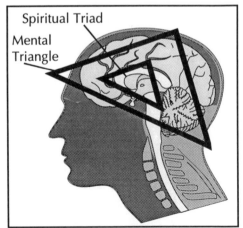

Spiritual Triad

Mental Triangle

The soul energies and awareness of the intuitive plane enable self-actualization and soul awareness. The *spiritual triad — reflection of the divine trinity within the human being: will, intuition, and oneness — develops within and the head centers synthesize into a triad of great significance.

As the spiritual triad develops, long-sought abilities emerge: creative solutions; straight knowing; love — impersonal enough to accept challenges generated by the masses — with a perception of patterns, occurrences, cycles of events and their

Fig. 35. The Spiritual Triad involves the three head centers and synthesizes them into one harmonious whole to guide the perfected human. This spiritual triad, not the brow center, is the true third eye. *If the eye be single, the whole body be filled with light.*

consequences, as well as an awareness of cause and effect and what links what together. With our spiritual eye, we see the Plan at work as we comprehend the reverberation of happenings more clearly.

In a perfected human, energy flows through well-coordinated chakras. *Perfected human* does not mean "perfect," which is a judgment, but the state of beingness for which we strive — a reference to the desired state for expressing our capabilities to a high degree of excellence. Just as a perfect rose cannot be compared to a perfect lily, we refine our nature in light of our individuality. "Perfect," as a judgment, measures us against a thoughtform built over the ages by societies of less awakened ones. A perfected human has mastered him- or herself and flawlessly reflects qualities of that particular soul, for impediments have been eliminated.

> Once the Antahkarana is nearly built, some inner cleansing also takes place; some purification processes begin also. Many, many blind commands, complexes and dark urges accumulated throughout ages in the inner levels slowly come out to burn and disappear, giving . . . great psychological and spiritual release.
> —Torkom Saraydarian, *The Science of Becoming Oneself*

Ultimately we surrender in allegiance to divine patterns we discover. With increased clarity, we perceive our path one step at a time and align to higher reality. Exceptional trust is required — difficult, because while we *know with our Knower,* rational mind may not understand or personality's temperament may complicate matters.

Challenges are most often met in the millisecond between experience and response. Inner auto-pilots execute our unconscious patterns, energizing thoughtforms we have created, ways we have visualized responding, and fears we fight. Instantaneous dialogue takes place in our heads, though we often are unaware of these old patterns, and we question why we respond as we do. Examining the problem, as we are now, encourages us to recognize our programming, to self-correct through examination and visualization, and learn to choose a desired response.

Remember: to live in the now, we must learn how to be present in the immediate experience, not responding from automatic pilots, unaware and reactive. Jean-Jacques Rousseau said it well: *The moment passed is no longer; the future may never be; the present is all of which [we are] the master.* By focusing intentionally, we energize and discover, then release deep restrictive factors. We discover the tricks of personality by self-study—how to best use our talents and when to tread carefully.

Consciousness Threads:
Weaving the Antahkarana/Rainbow Bridge

To Helena *Blavatsky is attributed, "Like pearls on a thread, so is the long series of human lives strung together on the *sutratma." Life by life, we gain experience. We could add: experience by experience, living in the now, we hasten progress by using each experience to form a pearl.

On the path of initiation, many changes occur in the consciousness which once identified itself as an average human being. As the journey to higher awareness progresses, we weave connecting threads between a number of specific points in the etheric body. Our consciousness becomes less and less restricted as these threads develop and connect to points sensitive to soul influence.

An electrical harness connecting electrical valves would be analogous to the three threads which link spirit forces through the triad to the stimulated and evolving forces rising up from within matter (as energies of kundalini).

This connecting of threads —called in the East the weaving of the antahkarana and in the West, most commonly, the *rainbow bridge — consists of the develop-

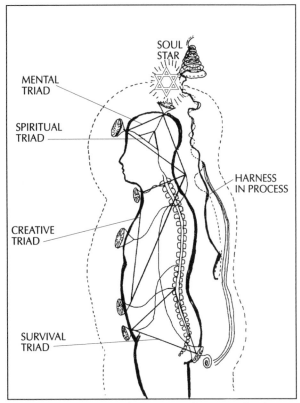

Fig. 36. Entire Body Chakras are shown with etheric column and harness in place. The electrical harness is built as the threads are woven; our connection to Earth and soulstar is established.

SOUL STAR

MENTAL TRIAD

SPIRITUAL TRIAD

HARNESS IN PROCESS

CREATIVE TRIAD

SURVIVAL TRIAD

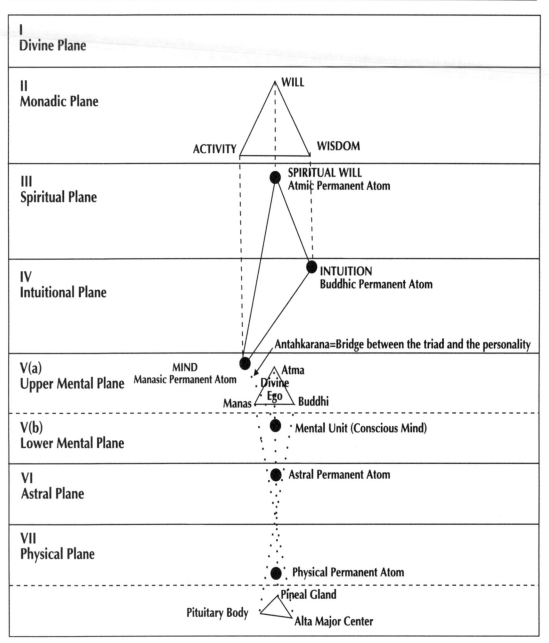

Fig. 37. The Six Permanent Atoms• of a Human Incarnation. The atoms are connected with thin strands of spirilla; when open, these spirilla allow energy to flow between the permanent atoms and different planes of consciousness. Integration of attributes is required in order to open these spirilla, thereby allowing a continuous flow of energy between them . . . *"continuity of consciousness," *Master Djwhal Khul said, was the object of evolution at this time.[3]

ment and integration of three parts (called threads). The first is called the sutratma, or life thread, and comes from the monad. The second, called the antahkarana, or consciousness thread, comes from soul itself. And the third is known as the creative thread; it evolves from our human experience and self-mastery.

As we examine these new terms, *sutratma* means "...the thread of spirit; the immortal Ego, the Individuality which incarnates in [us] one life after the other, and upon which are strung, like beads on a string, countless Personalities."[2] Similarly, we need to know *antah* (prior) plus *karana* (passage way) means "bridge." The Sanskrit name of the third thread seems to be unknown. Commonly it is called the creative thread and is that which we weave as we move through experience after experience, seeking to become wise. It is indeed woven by the path we take as we consciously lift our human nature to intertwine with the divine.

In Western tradition, the first two are often called life thread (anchored in the heart) and consciousness thread (anchored in the brain). When the life thread between soul and body breaks, physical life is over. When the consciousness thread snaps, the mind is gone; the brain can no longer accept information from higher levels of self. When people have this experience, they lose the use of most of their conscious mental capabilities. The frayed thread picks up astral experiences, or old memories emerge which

---

Two Clues

In *The Rosicrucian Cosmo Conception* Max Heindel relates that "the *silver cord grows anew in each life" during the uterine period. The three major threads — usually called the life thread, the consciousness thread, and the creative thread — are brought forward for the task of continuing to weave the antahkarana into the bridge over which soul can travel.

"The seed atom fastened at the heart contains a greater amount of *reflective ethers than any other atom of the body." Here we reflect upon any issue to see what we truly think and feel in our heart. Heindel continues, the seed atom of the heart "sets the keynote for all the atoms of the body." Here reside "all records of previous life cycles back to the very beginning." Here we vibrate to our truth as comprehended at a spiritual level and in so doing often suffer as the outer life is not brought into alignment. This is especially so when our programming and rational mind are quite disparate from our inner knowing.[4]

Fig. 38. Two Clues

seem real to the disabled person. While we may not realize the cause of trouble, we probably have observed just such a situation. If a temporary condition of fraying exists, it can heal, but if the consciousness thread snaps, there is no repair or getting well; it is not mental illness but a permanent condition, just as death is the result of a broken life thread. At the time the physical body is formed, solar angel spins the sutratma (life thread) creating the etheric body in accordance to records stored in the permanent seed atoms. Often these three threads are referenced as one, just plain "the antahkarana."

Permanent seed atoms are small force centers around which the bodies (physical, emotional, mental, and spiritual) of an individual are built. These centers form parts of personality, each of which distributes a certain type of force and responds to a particular vibration. Each seed atom is a reservoir of data encoded to preserve information regarding each individual's evolutionary pattern on a specific level of expression.

The third thread, the creative thread, is the real work performed by each of us on our journey to higher awareness. *The weaving of the creative thread **is** the path.* Thus, it is said, we each walk a unique path. We spin this thread from the seed atoms where each record awaits. The first segment of the creative thread emerges from the life thread at the heart, and in time it links to the spleen (after we dissolve the lock between heart and solar plexus). Will — self-discipline — is needed to develop this segment; our practices gradually link the organ of caring with the spleen, the organ of vitality. As we subjugate selfishness to higher values, we give our personal power to what our awareness treasures, surrendering to the highest we can perceive. *We will our will to higher will.*

Concurrently, the quiescent point at the solar plexus begins to form a vine-like segment growing toward the heart. Our ability to love ourselves and others is necessary for this to occur. We would be wise to remember that often Native Americans called themselves "the real human beings" because they knew their rare ability to love (humanitarian love-wisdom) set them apart. As we practice love — first personal love, then impersonal and unconditional — overcoming prejudices and concepts that judge, grudge, and separate, segments of the creative thread anchored in the seed planted so long ago now grow.

Legends provide many references to the bridge between lower world and the heavens. We are told it is built of light substance and only the perfected sons and daughters of God may travel across it. See the important truth held here: Those who are capable of great dedication bring their nature into harmony with higher plane energy. The astral and mental begin to merge — transmutation — the work continues, and the evolved vehicle is ready to build another bridge, this time to the soul.

Muslims speak of this bridge as being "thinner than a hair and sharper than a sword." The king's and queen's chambers of the Great Pyramid are believed to symbolize the narrow approach to secret places within ourselves to which we must ascend. In India those in service to Brahma wear a sacred cord consisting of three threads braided into one, reminding us of both the antahkarana and the Trinity, three in one. Think of this as will, love, light — as in the three sets of Mysteries of the rosary: Joyful (will energy), Sorrowful (love-wisdom), and Glorious (active intelligence or light energy).

The third segment of the creative thread begins at the forehead (brow) center and goes toward the crown center. Each segment grows in proportion to the developing "petals of the lotus of high consciousness." The petals can be defined as three qualities of divinity necessary to function in higher mental realms. Areas to strengthen are love, knowledge, and sacrificial will. The lotus is anchored in abstract mind. The third segment of the creative thread completes the developing thread and connects the petals.

The segments called the creative thread are built by disciples' conscious work as they interweave will, love, and knowledge with discernment. Utilizing the two foundational threads (life and consciousness), experience builds the creative thread as integration of daily life and high consciousness is achieved. Establishing its means of expression in the physical plane is soul's work. Once built, this creative thread can "speak the word" or express the unique flair of the Self.

The rainbow bridge has three parts:

1. **Sutratma/Life thread**
2. **Antahkarana/Consciousness thread**
3. **Creative thread: built by human experience**

The creative thread, shown as the dotted line, is an extension of the life thread. It is developed in three parts:

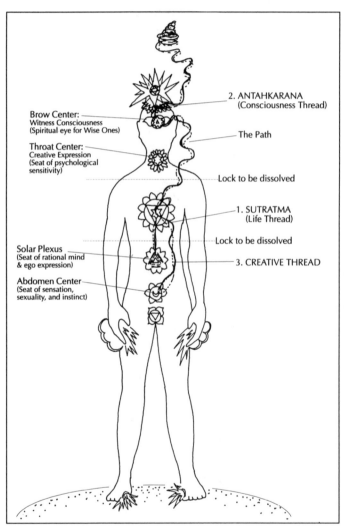

- Heart to spleen correlates to sacrificial petals (utilizes will)
- Solar plexus to heart — love petals (utilizes love)
- Brow to crown, builds witness consciousness — knowledge petals (utilizes light).

Thus the rainbow bridge comes into being.

Now the creative thread picks up the first segment at the heart and goes to the brow center while intertwining with other threads.

The weaving of the creative cord and the unfolding of petals of the lotus of high consciousness (also known as the egoic lotus) occur simultaneously.

Labels on figure:

2. ANTAHKARANA (Consciousness Thread)

Brow Center: Witness Consciousness (Spiritual eye for Wise Ones)

The Path

Throat Center: Creative Expression (Seat of psychological sensitivity)

Lock to be dissolved

1. SUTRATMA (Life Thread)

Lock to be dissolved

Solar Plexus (Seat of rational mind & ego expression)

3. CREATIVE THREAD

Abdomen Center (Seat of sensation, sexuality, and instinct)

Fig. 39. Summary: Weaving the Antahkarana/Rainbow Bridge. In proportion to our degree of expression of goodness, beauty, and light of soul, we become the Self. As the rainbow bridge is built, energy centers of the hands and feet develop to allow each to distribute the higher vibrations earthward to the world of matter.

These three invisible, spiritual threads put down by soul come to life through simple activities: worship or invocations; inviting spirit into one's life is a call, or invitation, to the higher currents — life forces — to enter and stimulate the sleeping spirit awaiting within matter to come forth. The threads gradually weave themselves into the so-called harness in order to distribute their higher-vibrating energies. In very simple acts we begin the work of alchemy, not realizing that in so doing, the sleeping spiritual energies resting at the base of the spinal column will awaken kundalini: *ida, *pingala, and *sushumna. Sushumna is considered the middle column, with ida (feminine) and pingala (masculine) on either side. Each flow is important to the evolution process. Think of this as the trinity within, or the three columns of the kabalistic Tree of Life. As inner stirring begins, consciousness refines matter, ascending from the lower world of vibrations to the higher.

Kundalini is the igniting, evolving, and uniting of these embodied spiritual forces. When awakened, kundalini energy, little understood, is often felt as vibration, either hot or cold. A battle between spirit and matter ensues as they struggle toward reconciliation — the smoother and gentler the better, we are told, for our delicate modern nature. The Tibetan Master Djwhal Khul says, "These three paths of life are channels for electric fire, solar fire, and fire by friction."[5]

Kundalini, called the coiled serpent, is recognized as a potent and powerful agent of transformation, a spiritual potential that transforms consciousness from average to superior. When aroused, kundalini begins its climb from the base of the spine toward its goal, the crown chakra. It may seem to sleep, but as we remove barriers and meditate steadily, we encourage its ascent and its consciousness-changing effects.

These age-old energies, waiting in matter to be redeemed, are activated by meditation, the principal practice of any spiritual tradition. As the rainbow bridge forms, the sleeping serpent starts to rise, and the center of consciousness of those in training begins to shift. Those unawakened, centered at the lower abdomen, live in sensation; the creative, psychologically sensitive person lives at the throat center; and in due time, the wise one emerges at the witness center (brow) to watch the Plan unfold through human life. When a breakthrough occurs and the current surges, a new pinnacle is achieved. As the energy recedes, purifying fire descends

141

through the chakras, the perspective of each chakra clearing somewhat. Continued washes — meditative moments — hasten the clearing of restrictions and bring new light to each level.

This process of change is the work of the path of initiation. Significant stages are:

> development of the chakras,
>
> then their opening to function,
>
> the integration of astral and mental natures,
>
> the construction work of the creative thread,
>
> the gradual coming to life of the kundalini,
>
> the solidifying of the spiritual triad, and
>
> the flowering of the lotus of high consciousness.

Building the antahkarana/rainbow bridge is the transformational process humanity bears from the onset of the probationary path to third initiation. By then, the antahkarana is completely built. At the culmination of the process, the spiritual triad — made up of active pituitary, pineal, and alta major centers — focuses the light, love, and power of soul through the real spiritual eye. *If the eye be single, the whole body is filled with light.* With the evolved, proficient wiring mechanism in place, personality can handle the ebb and flow of spiritual fires.

> The inner work is no less fiery than the outer. I want to immerse myself in that fire—new images, finer tuning.
> —Marion Woodman

Continuity of consciousness is an advanced capability linked to the active crown chakra, when consciousness can expand in and out of the physical body without losing awareness of where we are and what we are experiencing, often recognizing two simultaneous levels of life. The development of the spiritual triad allows us to see with the eye of the soul.

The mental body is a vibrating field of light around the head and body. When fully developed, it has seven frequencies — levels — of

Rainbow Bridge II[6] helps dissolve karmic hindrances awaiting ignition. This technique uses soul's wholeness to dissolve barriers to enlightenment, known and unknown, without bringing them to consciousness or fruition. The work is done by soul power and requires only that personality persist. Rainbow Bridge complements seed-thought meditation.

Seed-thought work expands consciousness and prepares us to be taught by the inner world. It would have us *know what the soul knows.* Although the goals are quite different, the two procedures are compatible and may be used concurrently. Discuss with tutors if you desire. Both prepare world servers to assist in human and planetary initiations.

Fig. 40. Rainbow Bridge II.

registration. This expansion of mind is the present human endeavor, with approximately three frequencies (levels) completed and others only begun. While meditation is the principal means of attracting mental energy, contemplation is the primary work for stabilizing these frequencies into levels.

Simultaneously, as the rainbow bridge is being created, changes are occurring within personality. Each time "light" registers upon the consciousness, there is a reaction. The "stuff" of emotional (glamours) and mental (illusions) frequencies is being burned away. Old limiting emotions and false truths that entrap are being cleared. The nonself is changing as charges of soul energy traverse the bridge into the lower nature; each sheath is affected and adjusts to the charges. These charges of soul energy prepare us for soul infusion. Though not yet smoothly operating threads of connection, the bridge carries charges to the disciple-in-process.

A delicate web is said to hold the various body vehicles together (or apart, as is sometimes said). As emotional and mental natures integrate, the web separating the bodies dissolves, and a more refined human species results. In the masses this process happens naturally through evolution, but disciples choose to hasten it. They encourage spiritual growth and expanded consciousness by invoking subtle energy, primarily through meditation and other disciplines of body, emotion, and mind. They consciously confront age-old hindrances as they emerge from storage in the permanent seed atoms. Invoked energies of the higher dimensions burn the residue, and the captive is set free.

Thus, we see, as we practice meditation, we call into play the out-of-sight, sleeping kundalini energy. As we weave threads of the rainbow bridge through our psychospiritual work, we also dissolve barriers that restrict the awaiting Divine-Within.

The weaving of the creative thread is the path.

The vocabularies of differing traditions produce confusion. As steps for the advancement of humanity are given, goals differ according to needs of the times. Since meditation assists both individual disciples and evolution of the species, not all disciples of any one era need the same experiences. Some have already

In a wonderful explanation of cosmic consciousness, M.C. Nanjunda Rao helps us discern these changes as they happen within our bodies, which then eases our adaption to the "next stage" human being.

The Inherent Perfect Nature

It is interesting to note that the great father of Yoga philosophy, Patanjali, who lived several centuries ago, has not only mentioned this attainment of supra-consciousness but has clearly explained that such an attainment is nothing more than the manifestation of one's own inherent perfect nature, ordinarily hidden by veils of ignorance, and that these accumulations of concepts and their fusion with moral elements, leading to the establishment of an intuitional mind, or attainment of supra-consciousness, as stated above, are only so many processes whereby the veils of ignorance, or obstacles, are removed one after the other and the inherent inner light of perfection is allowed to manifest itself.

This pure manifestation of one's own perfect[ed] nature is called Realization or Liberation. The two aphorisms by which Patanjali explains this subject run as follows:

1. The change into another species is by the filling in of nature; i.e. by the accumulation of concepts.

2. Good and bad deeds (representing here the effects produced by the accumulation of concepts) are not the direct causes in the transformation of nature, but they act as breakers of obstacles to the evolution of nature: as the farmer removes the obstacles to the course of water, which then runs down by its own nature.

Swami Vivekananda, giving a running commentary on the last aphorism, says:

The water for irrigation of the fields is already in the canal, only shut in by gates; the farmer opens these gates, and the water flows in by itself, by the law of gravitation.

So, all progress and power are already in every man; perfection is man's nature, only it is barred in and prevented from taking its proper course. If anyone can take the bar off, in rushes nature. Then the man attains the powers which are his already. Those we call wicked become saints as soon as the bar is broken and nature rushes in. It is nature that is driving us toward perfection, and eventually she will bring everyone there. All these practices and struggles to become religious and attain perfection are only negative work, to take off the bars, and open the doors to that perfection which is our birthright, our nature.

The great ancient evolutionist, Patanjali, declares that the true secret of evolution is the manifestation of the perfection which is already in a potential condition in every being; that this perfection has been barred, and the infinite tide behind is struggling to express itself. These struggles and competitions are but the results of our ignorance because we do not know the proper way to unlock the gate and let the water in. This infinite tide behind must express itself; it is the cause of all manifestation. In the animal the man was suppressed; but as soon as the door was opened, out rushed man. So in man there is the potential god, kept in by the locks and bars of ignorance. When knowledge breaks these bars the god becomes manifest.[7]

Fig. 41. The Inherent Perfect Nature

moved ahead in consciousness; others are just awakening to the Godself and are in the earlier stages of *conscious* evolution.

Since we are apt to hear some dreadful kundalini stories, we must consider, is kundalini a blessing or a curse? (We recall the same question being asked about puberty.) The answer: It is natural to be built into the human "god," and, as conditions beyond our grasp are met, kundalini awakens.

In our modern quest, we find two distinct attitudes concerning kundalini: one fearful, with dire warning against doing practices to arouse it; the other (best personified by kundalini yoga) inspired, with the entire life structured to bring it into play.

I believe a third approach is the most prudent: teach and practice natural spiritual procedures, and trust the innate to awaken gently and in a timely fashion. Arousal will come naturally, as gentle and regular spiritual practices are established — middle-of-the-road style — and the mind prepared for its arrival.

Kundalini *is* a natural process, even if not well understood. It is a part of coming to the full consciousness of which we are capable. It does not need to be feared; in fact, as we have learned, fear is detrimental to spiritual life. To be fearful of kundalini implies the Creator did not know what s/he was doing when such power was placed within humanity. Believing these forces are to be respected, not feared, I encourage embracing your spiritual life without reservation and trusting the process. We should not force the process for indeed it deserves respect. After all, it is fire, and fire — inner or outer — demands healthy procedures for its judicious use.

Tricia Nickel, M.A., MFCC, presents an interesting and comprehensive view of menopause and the moon cycles in her article "Wisdom Moons" in *Welcome to Planet Earth*.[8]

> Women in their forties and fifties are now addressing another taboo . . . menopause, the potent blood cycle bridging us into the wisdom phase of life. As I vision it, the first two blood mysteries are focusing on opening the three lower chakras. . . . Tasks of opening to our sensuality/sexuality, childbirth, creativity and relationship are primary issues being awakened in us. Empowerment and self-esteem as well as struggles

with blocks to our power are issues of the 3rd chakra. At both the first and second blood mysteries, our female bodies are making a commitment to "be here" as spiritual beings in and through the physical body.

While approaching the gate of the 3rd blood mystery, most women experience the phenomena of hot flashes. The first two blood mysteries, with finished and unfinished tasks, now move us into the alchemical chamber of the heart and 4th chakra. . . . One client smiles as she flushes with a hot flash and says, "I am swampy again!" There is something fierce and sweet, akin to orgasm, as the heat signals the Goddess opening the heart and head centers (the 5th, 6th and 7th chakras).

. . . The hot flashes of peri-menopause now tell us that our birthings will come through the heart and mind. We are asked to speak our truth, 5th chakra, and express the intuitive wisdom of the 6th chakra . . . as well as knowing mystical moments of unitive consciousness of the 7th chakra.

. . . . The 7 chakras at menopause can now glow with a lifetime of the wisdom we have acquired. . . . This fire is personal as well as archetypal.

Hunbatz Men, Mayan daykeeper, says the word *Ku* reminds us that kundalini energy comes from Hunab Ku, the Mayan name for "Creator of Movement and Measure." *Ku* is the "power of God," and *kundalini,* a Hindi word, translates "the god coiled within matter." Hunbatz maintains the Maya gave the word to the Hindus. Kundalini is recognized as the latent intelligence within the body that holds a blueprint of humanity's divine potential.

In *The Astrology of Personality,*[9] Dane Rudhyar says that the one (in whom kundalini is active) has realized the mystical marriage where indeed male and female are unified, but even more for herein we have reconciliation of "individual (ego) and collective (the generic self in the solar plexus)." True individuals do not stand against the collective, opposing generic energies with will, or human drive, he says. "The true individual is the flowering and the fruition of the collective, which finds itself fulfilled in and through (the individual)." Having assimilated the wholeness of its being, s/he becomes the perfect specimen of its potential — "collectivity become conscious and significant."

When we realize inner energies are stirring, our lifestyle may require adjustment to accommodate them, but if we are following meditation practices and doing reasonable purification — dieting, exercising, psychological work, and opening to the love of life — we are indeed providing the path for the kundalini's ascent and preparing our bodies for its movement through their domains. Negative attitudes, impure thoughts, or sexual desires without outlet or balance may create problems. These are areas to address; indeed, we must desire to do so if we are to see true spiritual growth. These are the obstacles to high consciousness we have been examining in our lessons on dissolving barriers. We will confront other areas of unfinished business one by one as we become aware of them and make way for the coming of the Lord.

Remember, through meditation you have been stirring psychic ("of the soul") forces already. Even the most ordinary, disinterested-in-these-matters person, by the mere act of thinking, directs energy. Energy follows thought, and focused thought fuels awakening. Meditation may not be conscious, but the more focused and intent the mind is, the more likely the arousal of the kundalini.

> Think not that only the religious devotee or mystic, or the [one] imbued with what we call higher teaching, is the exponent of the powers attained by meditation. All great capitalists, and the supreme heads of finance or organized business, are the exponents of similar powers. . . . the personifications of one-pointed adherence to one line of thought, and their evolution parallels that of the mystic and occultists. . . . Supreme concentrated attention to the matter in hand, makes them what they are, and in many respects they attain greater results than many a student of meditation.[10]

Spontaneous kundalini experiences will and do occur. As spiritual awakening occurs, the spiritual gifts of the spirit appear. Kundalini can and often is compared to the Holy Spirit. While there is a relationship, do not attempt to equate the two exactly.

Body changes, headaches, unidentifiable aches and pains that spontaneously appear and disappear, unusual sounds in the head, all kinds of physical and psychical manifestations may indicate kundalini. When these occur, the least disturbance it causes in life, the better. If it becomes increasingly difficult, discussion with a spiritual teacher is advised. Meditation and other stimulating spiritual practices may need to be modified, grounding techniques used, even the reading of inspiring material may need to be regulated. The issues are individual so no blanket guidance can be given, and those having such experiences need a private advisor. When traveling unfamiliar territory, it is wise to have a guide.

The most common manifestation related to kundalini is the result of static energy affecting the physical. Jerky movements or uncomfortable physical sensations are attempting to clear the path for an easy passage of the rising force. This is a spiritual rebirth; the whole nature is involved. The entire makeup of personality is being prepared for the "queen" — indeed, kundalini is considered feminine (shakti) — traveling to the crown to meet the king (shiva), pure consciousness that is cosmic.

We caution aspirants: No one should experiment with kundalini or attempt to force premature awakening. Learning to relax, praying, meditating, loving and caring, chanting, and exercising build healthy boundaries for personal expression, encouraging higher consciousness and bringing the inner nature into play. As we do all of these, plus dissolve known barriers, we create pathways within each level of our nature which allow energy to move freely.

Most naturally psychic people are born with a degree of this energy flowing through the body, the etheric, and the astral nature. Many children have this flow, but our do's and don't's inhibit their spontaneity and erect boundaries. We do this for social well-being, but to do so by causing fear means those fears ultimately must be dissolved for the living spirit to be free once again.

As we, as a species, become wiser, healthier ways to guide come into vogue. The psychology movement of the last century in our society is the result of activity in the collective psyche pushing all toward high consciousness. This is because enough individuals have reached a new level of consciousness to be effective — whether or not it is called spiritual. This is natural evolution at work.

Let us trace simple, healthy steps that assist us to provide a clear path for the ascent of kundalini.

- Caring for the body (dietary practices, exercise, healthy habits) respectfully.
- Minimizing poisons (toxins) to the body and emotions
- Indulging only in healthy sex—in loving, positive situations
- Purifying our nature of negativity, dissolving barriers
- Living our practices daily, as clearly as possible
- Aspiring to high consciousness
- Becoming aware of psychic impressions and intuitive occurrences
- Strengthening our goodness: love-caring, service, appreciation of others, gratitude
- Meditating — the principal spiritual tool
- Allowing our creativity to express
- Aligning our will to higher will, as we best perceive it

These practices open energy centers, dissolve seeds of karma, and allow sexual, creative, and spiritual forces the freedom to lift us toward our potential. We thus establish patterns to invite high consciousness. Encouragement from a mentor and trust in the Creator guide us as we transform.

Virtues Used as Seed Thoughts

With this lesson we complete our examination of the twelve virtues being built within humanity through the assistance of the celestial hierarchies. Even if we contemplate these only as archetypes, we magnetically attract these essences.

Our true nature develops these twelve aspects of Self as we evolve. Each of us has a personal relationship with three of these virtues as life-long assignments — the virtues associated with our personal astrological sun, moon, and ascendant. Conscious effort of our ability to express these virtues more clearly and meditating upon them hasten the process; thus, we gather precious droplets.

Many teachers provide an annual list of seed thoughts appropriately selected for astrological influences to help continue the cycle of growth you have begun.[12] In addition, you might use the seed-thought technique to explore many intriguing thoughts or words. We all have favorite ideas we like to explore to discover deeper meanings.

To access soul awareness, the rule is to focus upon a high ideal, a virtue, or an impersonal phrase. Since seed thoughts are to lift us from personality level to higher awareness, we concentrate upon inspiring, motivating thoughts, words, and phrases to become increasingly attuned to soul energy. Such impersonal inspiration elevates us above lesser self and its distortions into the light of soul where we can perceive with superior clarity. In meditation language: *we press our mind against divine mind.*

"Meditation is essentially a science of light primarily intended to

- increase sensitivity to higher energies;
- build the first half of the antahkarana, connecting personality and soul;
- produce an eventual continuity of consciousness from the lower vehicles through the spiritual triad."[11]

Fig. 42. Meditation Is a Science of Light.

Many virtues and pertinent concepts have not been touched upon in this text, of course. A few that come to mind are: honesty, sanctity, healing, communication, self-image, holiness, innocence, obedience, balance, vision, sacrifice, reality — and many others you may wish to explore on your own.

We further suggest you use the seed-thought method with ideas, phrases, or sentences, in addition to single words:

- *The mystical body of Christ.*
- *I and the Father are One.*
- *Greater things than these shall you do.*

As you advance in this way (yes, try it), you will create your own meaningful commentaries.

Assignment

> **Seed Thought: HUMILITY**

The first seed thought for this lesson is *humility,* the virtue assigned to the Aquarian influence.

> *What doth the Lord require of thee, but to do justly, and to love mercy, and to walk humbly with thy God?*
>
> Micah 6.8

Humility is the realization of who we really are in the deepest sense of our spiritual nature. We realize our inner nature and separate what is glamour and illusion. Humility comes from constantly reidentifying with our true Self as we are able to release qualities not true to it.

When we have acquired humility, we may more readily realize and surrender to our part of the divine Plan. Humility is a state of identification with that which we perceive as more noble. When personality acquiesces to the purposes of the higher nature, we experience humility. In deep humility, we bow to higher will.

> Lord, help me be precisely the person
> I actually am before God.
> Aware that since no two people are alike, if I can
> have the humility to be myself
> I will not be like anyone else
> n the Whole universe.
>
> —Thomas Merton

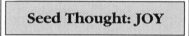

Seed Thought: JOY

The second seed thought for this lesson is *joy,* the virtue assigned to the Piscean influence.

> Land of Heart's Desire . . . where beauty has no ebb, decay no flood, but joy is wisdom, time an endless song.
>
> —William Butler Yeats

Happiness and joy often are mistaken as synonymous. Happiness is a condition of personality when it is pleased temporarily. Joy is a charge of energy — bliss or samadhi — which results from contact with soul, or the Christ-Within. When personality thus connects, strong rushes of energy are received, and we experience joy, or bliss, a truly spiritual condition.

This joy is nectar which nourishes us. When life becomes difficult, when life ricochets painfully, we are sustained by the grace of inner joy. This sustaining force nurtures our inner nature and gives us faith to continue.

The Dweller and
the Angel Interface

*From earliest times, humanity has struggled with the problem of evil.
The dark mysteries of life . . . . have become polarities, turned into "good"
and "bad." Religions have helped us to struggle with these oppositions . . .
all the while reinforcing the dualistic perception of our world. Worldwide,
the artists, storytellers, priests, priestesses, and healers have always
reflected these great themes back to us, challenging us to bring our
struggle with the unknown into awareness, to acknowledge and
confront the forces in life that give us the most trouble.*

—Jeremiah Abrams

On its way to enlightenment, humanity struggles, held on a line of tension between the inner drive for freedom and the outer life of ego's structure. From this contest have sprung all spiritual traditions of history. Religions define general guidelines and rules, rather than individual or select guidance; therefore, for those who awaken to be spiritually fulfilled, each tradition embodies a philosophy whose essence must be penetrated for the disciple to experience initiation.

*Strait is the gate, and narrow is the way, which leadeth
unto life, and few there be that find it.*

Matt. 7.14, KJV

An Eastern perspective related by Swami Venkatesananda[1] gives us insights into the familiar concept of high consciousness as an inner kingdom.

Gurudev Swami Sivananda used to sing, "When you get knocks and blows in the daily battle of life, then

Fig. 43. The Mandala, as noted by Carl Jung, "is an archetypal image whose occurrence is attested throughout the ages. It signifies the *wholeness of self.*"[2]

your mind is duly turned towards the spiritual path." . . . BUT it does not happen to everybody. . . . It needs an inner awakening to bring about an inner awakening. So the master, Vasishtha, suggests a few hints. He says: "Inner awakening, enlightenment, liberation or moksha, nirvana — whatever you wish to call it — is regarded as a kingdom. There are four gate-keepers or sentinels guarding its four entrances. . . . Try to make friends with them and they let you in." They will strip you of the ego and then let you enter.

These four are the enemies of this ego-sense. . . . It is very difficult to translate them, so I will give the dictionary meanings and then we will look into them. Sama is *tranquility,* self-control or control of mind. Vichara is usually translated as *enquiry* but it is a lot more. It implies a mind that is constantly observed. Santosha may be taken as *contentment,* the total absence of craving. And . . . the fourth, is satsanga — *company of the wise,* the enlightened, the good. Every factor which contributed to the formation of the ego-sense is negated by or destroyed by these four. . . . The Master adds: "If you cannot make friends with all four, then cultivate the friendship of at least one of these and you will realise that all the rest accompany this one." One leads to the other, one involves the other, one embraces the other, one is the same as the other. You cannot have peace of mind if your mind is not restrained or controlled. You cannot have peace of mind if you are not contented. You cannot have peace of mind if the mind is not being observed all the time. And that mind itself is good company. If you have peace within, that is the best company in the world. (italics added)

The validity of any tao (way) may be found by how adequately it fills the cup of its practitioner. Seekers may advance into unknown, sometimes dangerous territory. Myths and fairy tales warn of dangers and dark forests, conceding they must be faced to reach the destination — the kingdom, the beautiful sleeping princess, the white knight, or the good fairy.

Today we frequently use the word *initiation* — both personal and planetary — but rarely do we question what it means beyond "to begin anew." To grow in wisdom and to advance on the path of initiation we commit to the necessary work. We all know this, but we are not quite sure just how to proceed. Esoteric teachings suggest each body, or level of our being, contains a multitude of tiny points of matter evolving in consciousness. The physical body, for example, is made up of sparks of intelligent matter — cellular consciousness, we call it.

At the etheric level, tiny sparks of consciousness are easily charged with basic emotion and thought, sweeping us first one way, then another. Such minute intelligences await organization. The work of those who would evolve is to stabilize and train these "baby" consciousnesses. In time, they will congeal into obedient servants.

Similarly, the thoughts we create impact the evolving sparks sensitive to mind vibration. Filled with minute points of consciousness, mind-stuff resonates to emotional and mental frequencies; it is, in fact, in training. We frequently see great distress, our own or others', as we ricochet between emotions and mind, first one way, then the other. Rarely are we of one mind. The greater the inner conflict, the greater the indication that both aspects of our nature — mental and emotional — are strengthening.

> *The validity of any tao (way)*
> *may be found by how adequately*
> *it fills the cup of its practitioner.*

This struggle primarily is addressed by social programming or religious training, our "rules of the game." Collectives have long provided guidance for training the human nature. At some point, however, we evolve enough to take the initiative to steer ourselves through our maze of less-developed elemental influences. Using will as our tool, we begin to develop. Self-discipline may lead us first one direction, then another in pursuit. We enjoy short periods of happiness. Then life heats up, tests come; we collect all the self-awareness we can muster. Thus personalities acquire experience and do what we so often call "character building."

The human body, we find, is subject to a variety of influences, levels of consciousness, conflicts, and basic desires, and works hard to satisfy their commands. What we think of as "changing" consists of teaching these components of basic self to obey our will. The lesser learns to conform to the chain of command. We talk to ourselves and call this "programming." We command the body to obey. We teach it new patterns, we promise, and we struggle. We learn to communicate with the autonomic level of mind, often not realizing the implications of our efforts and our achievements.

Most of humanity take for granted or ignore the innate intelligence of the body and do not think of their own vehicle as a *miniature universe* commanded by a central headquarters or great mind. Learning to communicate with, understand, and correct confused signals encourages central headquarters to manage an efficient, peaceful enterprise.

We also can integrate into this chain of command a perception of elementals and organ devas. Elementals can be presented here for our purposes as the indwelling intelligence of each cell. As individual cells group in function to form an organ, the deva becomes the oversight intelligence for the organ, guiding the work of the elementals. We rarely are aware that commands to the body can reach and affect both organ intelligence and the very basic cellular level.

As the aspirant begins the process of disciplining the lives within each level, conflict, confusion, and mixed messages fade, and a greater single-mindedness reigns. We are advancing on the path to self-mastery, and each level of our universe is gaining momentum to help us on the way. The degree of cooperative alignment within levels is measured and locked in at each initiation. We never lose the progress we have made, and we ever strive for greater light (intelligence), love (energy), and will (focus).

Think of this lengthy process as an astronaut marshaling his or her forces or as a ballerina in training. The weaknesses of each level — body, emotions, mind — must be recognized and the devotion to fulfill our desires must be elevated to aspiration. We aspire to achieve a particular quality or goal. We strive.

Thus, for the well-being of the subconscious intelligence and its command over cells and organs, we learn to watch remarks, to say what we mean and mean what we say. Subconscious intelligence learns to call for what is needed and to resist avoidable negatives and assaults. We learn to control desires that could pull us off course and to escort the force of personality into desired areas, rather than be whipped about by the mighty desire-nature. We realize we are powerful life-builders and that each word, each action, and each visualization effects a sphere of experience with infinitely more impact than the unconscious individual may think.

Thoughts are powerful creators. As we become increasingly aware of what we think and how it comes to pass, eventually we learn to produce the powerful words that form *joy, goodness, beauty,* and other such desired qualities. We see the process of karma at work in daily life and realize the power we wield. Now taking mind in check, we cease strengthening the darkness within, no longer choosing to criticize, blame, hold grudges, gossip, find fault. We align our discriminating mind to training for higher consciousness.

So, disciples organize their lesser lives to be at their beck and call to do the work that is needed in each level of the personality so they can strive upward, defeating temptations and resisting setting into motion new detours of experience when it can be avoided.

We gradually respond to the prompt of spirit or to the tug of higher self. Divine discontent continues to stir, and we invoke stronger will with which to enter a probationary path. The more we live receptive to this gnosis — sophia, straight-knowing, the intuitive feminine, known in Christianity as the work of the Holy Spirit — the more we eagerly embrace spirituality and being nurtured toward wholeness. We depend less and less on the rational level of mind *alone* as we grow into a relationship with the Illuminator.

As we seek to reconcile duality, Sophia, wisdom, is our guide. Built of heart and mind, this love-wisdom is utilized through the witness consciousness as it seeks to see the Way. Remember, the Holy Spirit is called the Comforter. We use the term "paraclete" as well, which, correctly translated, becomes "advocate."

To proceed we must broaden and deepen our perception of two significant participants on our journey: the Dweller on the Threshold and the Angel of the Presence. Built through many experiences, the time comes to face these mighty ones. In this lesson, we will develop our understanding of both.

For now, let us define "Dweller" as, *symbolically, the collection of unique imperfections (old selves) with which each of us struggles. The sum of all that personality holds and its unlived and denied potencies (physical, emotional, and mental) which, underdeveloped or distorted, limit the expression of soul.*

A way to think of the "Angel of the Presence" is *an imagined picture of oneself as all goodness and light, that saintly self we wish we truly were. Again, each individual and each collective develops an archetypal outpicturing for itself—perfect, as it would wish to be perfect.*

Alice Bailey[3] explains these personifications in this way.

> *The Dweller on the Threshold.* A thoughtform universally available to human experience, triggered into conscious awareness by two types of events: a readiness for initiation; and the approach of death. The Dweller is the sum total of all the forces of the lower nature. . . . within the psyche of the individual. It also represents similar accumulations within the collective psyche of humanity.
>
> *The Angel of the Presence.* An angel thoughtform who mediates the glory of the Divine Presence for human consciousness. It is a powerful presentiment of the glory of the Oneness, Deity, and Eternal Life that waits beyond the threshold and step down the divinity to us as we best perceive it.

This is the challenge. As we mature spiritually, we develop a *witness consciousness,* observe, and build no attachment either to good (as society defines it) or to bad (again, as in glamours and illusions). From this position, when wise, we negotiate between the two poles.

Facing the strait gate

Fig. 44. The Dweller on the Threshold.

Fig. 45. The Angel of the Presence.

In Esoteric Christianity, two powerful concepts help us identify the Dweller on the Threshold and the Angel of the Presence, often characterized as the bad angel on one shoulder and the good on the other. These are certainly over-simplified, but when we remember divine revelations must be stepped down for us to comprehend, they serve their purposes.

Gradually, the Dweller on the Threshold and the Angel of the Presence have solidified into two great force-fields to be confronted on our way to enlightenment/salvation/initiation. Candidates for initiation realize a deep inner struggle as they cease to identify with the values of outer world and build an allegiance to the inner. Rarely are we of one mind. As we learn to observe from a witness consciousness, both sides of our nature present great challenges.

The words "Dweller" and "Angel" imply vast differences. Each term contains an auto-pilot that brings instant reactions to stimuli. To progress, the initiated Self must learn to forestall the automatic-response mechanisms and elevate them from automatic to chosen conscious responses. The interaction of perceived glimpses of good and bad becomes entwined with glamours and illusions and is energized by maya. Complex consciousness at either extreme awaits dismantling as we spiritually mature. In time, we must face distortions too subtle to be discerned earlier.

Facing the Dweller, according to Bailey, seems to be triggered by such events as a readiness for initiation or the approach of death. I would suggest the term "born again" applies to such moments — not to emotional experiences sometimes so labeled, but to true moments of life-threatening experiences or initiation. Esoterically understood, that rush of power is designed to end the life we have known so a new life can begin.

At such critical change points — dynamic tests we could call them — personality may become conscious of the Dweller and the Angel. Since these archetypes have both a personal and a collective meaning, they contain the power to challenge or obscure the higher reality toward which the divine within would move. Such powerful moments allow a glimpse of the higher glory awaiting.

Djwhal Khul advises: The way for the disciple to pass this point is to go directly to the center. Do not deviate toward either side.

Esoteric teachings describe guardians (solar angels) who watch over us as the true Self matures. These wise ones, members of the Hierarchy, serve as keepers of the Plan for each evolving quiescent self. As they patiently observe, the Dweller and the Angel come to power. They are to be acknowledged. Tests must be met; consciousness must expand. The Self-Within/the inner Christ navigates its course through many experiences from which the true Self learns. As soul matures, the mystical Christ-Within is empowered to direct the life. Choice, free will, initiation — all are part of this process.

So many names, titles, and descriptions make it seem as if any number of entities are evolving and separate. While only one evolving human soul is in-process, various aspects of the whole are identified by names appropriate to their function. So we struggle to define, comprehend, and integrate. To proceed is not for the faint-hearted.

"Beware these words do not ignite the wrath of God in your soul," Jacob Boehme warns, for "this little book [information] belongs only to those who wish eagerly to repent, and who have a desire to begin."

A warning given to students newly introduced to Kabalah, the mystical Jewish tradition, is often discomfiting, but it demonstrates the regard with which kabalists commit to serious spiritual study. The warning states that one out of four who enters the study reaches enlightenment; of the other three, one turns back, one loses his mind, and one dies. Approach with respect.

Jesus told his disciples: *I have yet many things to say unto you, but ye cannot bear them now* (John 16.12), meaning they could not yet shoulder what would later be revealed. Such warnings are designed for those considering the path of initiation: spiritual training opens Pandora's box and is not mere entertainment, or a temporary assuaging of emotional or intellectual desires, or even a means of obtaining God's mercy. True wisdom teachings serve as a ladder — *Jacob's, to be sure — between the worlds of differing vibrations. We have work at each level: purification, testing, and integration. The energy of each level ignites more experience, thus more learning.

Energy — feeling and mental — imprints upon the minute evolving points of consciousness determining the pools or patterns into which the points will be drawn. Remember, on the nonphysical, like attracts like, so buildup is easy. Similar experiences with far-reaching effects upon the personality can build upon themselves to reinforce the distorted complex dual consciousness.

Dedicated disciples can withstand only so much at a time or at a certain stage. Offered too much too soon, they often oppose the revelation: spiritual illumination conveyed from higher to lower beings. If too charged, the Dweller takes on the "overage" and is energized into battle (providing a very good reason not to push esoteric teachings on the unready). These dualistic points now have to cope with the seeds that have become energized.

Indeed, Djwhal Khul adds that the Dweller on the Threshold must be dissolved by the fourth initiation. Think of this as, our karma must be neutralized by this stage of development, we must have learned to use wisely all available energies, and we must have discharged all indebtedness. Indeed, I say, "We must give back to the human experience, for it has given to us." Every time we expand consciousness (remember, consciousness does not develop, it expands), we begin anew. In Matthew 13.12, *For to him who has, shall be given and it shall increase to him; but to him who has not, even that which he has shall be taken away from him.* We must realize each time we encounter a greater truth, other Dweller aspects emerge. The astral and lower mental are filled with the debris of unfinished lessons. We learn by doing or by insight.

Think of the Dweller as the sum total of the unfinished business of the less-wise human which continues to exist as powerful charges in the lower nature — *dugpas*[4] in Eastern literature. These must be neutralized before the Dweller is dissolved. Imagine all the excess "bubbles" combining to form a force-field or entity unto itself. This complex makes itself felt as an "inferior self."

Because we are part of the human collective, the human condition, it is wise to recall that in this glimpse of the lower nature experienced *prior* to illumination, death, or initiation, we perceive the Dweller carrying humanity's accumulated darkness and the Angel as a figure of extreme, unattainable light. Could this be why, as recorded, Master Jesus himself wept over Jerusalem? over the human condition?

When initiates are faced by intense testing times, fearlessness and courage are necessary to complete karma and to hasten maturity, *for fear sustains the Dweller.* We are taught that at the fourth initiation we must prove we can stand in the light of the soul and handle the forces provided. We must be able to confront the Dweller, releasing personality's forces of limitation: shame, guilt, and fearlessness.

Helena Roerich, Agni Yoga tradition, says:

> A most hopeless situation is shown to them, and one waits to see what solution will be chosen by the tested one. Very few will think, what is there to be afraid of since the *Brotherhood stands behind us? Precisely such a premise liberates one from fear and brings to light a free, beneficial decision.[5]

The Angel, that aspect of self which identifies with glorified good, helps us confront the darkness. However, as we struggle toward the light, we define and redefine good and bad. This Angel self contains unrealistic concepts of good. As we create a model by which to measure ourselves, we energize and distort it by glamourizing or denying parts of our nature we do not admire.

The Angel often represents angelic good, the Presence of God in a non-human way. It can be so idealized that it may incite trepidation in us, making us feel unworthy before it. The archetype represents all that has been identified as good when perhaps we have been severely damaged by exposure to abusive religious approaches, such as fear of God, hell, or damnation. In these moments of testing, we may feel unworthy or identify as a sinner. We recoil, and the Angel becomes the Angel of Judgment.

Before the Christ-Within can stand as the *adept, this fourth-degree initiate has many experiences begun in ignorance and needing to be resolved. Situations arise as the incarnated person encounters indelible past records, ruminants of old selves, and outstanding accounts to balance. The accumulation of such unfinished pieces awaits our attention in the shadowy domain of the Dweller. Our unrealistic ideas of non-human goodness, the Angel or excessive perfection, also await disintegration.

"Nothing great was ever achieved without enthusiasm," wrote Ralph Waldo Emerson. Esoteric training teaches that enthusiasm combines will and love energy. Used correctly, it easily accumulates psychic energy, which heals, enlightens, and animates the Plan and the purpose — to be achieved with enthusiasm through the assistance of the God-Within.

In *The Coming of the Cosmic Christ* Matthew Fox says, "The Cosmic Christ leads us to explore suffering and new levels of truth and honesty instead of covering it up. . . . Our capacity

---

What Is the Dweller on the Threshold?

Has the Dweller on the Threshold a certain intelligence, or does it act unconsciously, automatically? Can it so influence a person that he will yield to his passions?
The Dweller on the Threshold is the entitized product of all the past evil thinking and acting a person has done through all the lives which he has lived. In the purgatorial state between lives, all the coarse portions of the desire body and the thoughts which vibrate to evil, sensuality, etc. are torn out by the force of repulsion. But they are not destroyed; they merely are torn out. These torn-out evil portions, or their essences, coalesce and are added together life after life. They constitute the composite entity which we know as the Dweller on the Threshold. All these various evil thought forms and desire forms await transmutation after a person has reached the stage where he is ready to enter the invisible planes consciously. Before he can enter there, he must first face and master the Dweller on the Threshold. If he is able to do this, he is free to go on into the invisible worlds and take up higher development there. Then there devolves upon him the duty of transmuting the Dweller into good. He created this entity in the past, and now he must reform it. He cannot progress beyond a certain point in his work on the invisible planes until the Dweller has been completely transmuted.

The Dweller has a sort of intelligence and acts in a semi-conscious manner for the reason that it is composed of the essence of thought forms and desire forms. People are partly protected from its influence during Earth life by the insulation which the physical body affords. However, if a person takes up negative psychic development, he is likely to break down this insulation, and the Dweller then might appear to him prematurely and might force him to yield to his passions. But a person will not be unduly influenced by the Dweller unless the latter has appeared to him.[6]

Figure 46. What Is the Dweller on the Threshold?

for the universe is both divine and demonic, both positive and negative, both glory and shadow. . . . the letter to the Hebrews develops the cosmic suffering that Jesus underwent in His wrestling with the Cosmic Christ yearning to be born fully in him. . . . creation mystics all invite us to explore the dark, to taste the pain, to make the deep journey into the underworld of grief, anger and pain — the Cosmic Christ is there and accompanies us on our journeys. We are in pain together."[7]

Exposure to the light during meditation prepares the etheric and physical (the slower-vibrating levels of consciousness) to receive the high-powered charge of inner contact. Were it not so, lesser beings would be overwhelmed by the extraordinary light of initiation. The Christ revelation continues to strengthen modern disciples today, just as it assisted the apostles to bear all that illumination delivered two thousand years ago. Remember, the greater the light we experience, the more clearly we see the unfinished and the raw within ourselves.

Disciples, or initiates, prepare themselves to receive *sophia,* wisdom that is the result of high consciousness. Perceived in numerous ways, now the mystery is revealed, which may be felt (ecstasy) or known (sophia). It washes into the emotional or the mental nature, illuminating either or both, registering wherever possible. This down-pouring reveals, fills, lifts — words used by mystics to describe the experience. Spirit embraces matter, and matter meets the embrace.

How does this fit with the Dweller on the Threshold and the Angel of the Presence? Over aeons of time, clumps — patterns — of emotions have formed; our minds have established fixed attitudes. Experiences of the lives we have led slumber, deeply ingrained in the unconscious. Sometimes rough and crude, sometimes graceful and sensitive, auto-pilots have been put in place. Memory, tool of the mind, in each cell, or spark, holds fast to our story. We re-create old mannerisms over and over until will is invoked and we consciously seek to eliminate them. Now we refine our understanding once again.

Unconsciously evolving, we have become instilled with the maya of our cultures and the glamours of our emotions; our illusions are reinforced. The basic nature, with its minute intelligences, awaits correction and liberation.

Maslow's Hierarchy of Needs (lesson 1) again comes to mind as the unconscious evolutionary path. Those who choose to invoke will or who are fortunate enough to receive disciplinary or spiritual training hasten ahead. Creativity is another means of invoking High Self. Imagination, the image-making ability, calls us to use our inherent "made in the image and likeness" capability, and we open to inner prompting, inspiration. Inspire: *to breathe in spirit.*

During the long period of evolution, both our Dweller and our Angel have amassed power. These complex force-fields have become ensouled, often crystallized, and need to break free of the rigidity of old habits of consciousness. The temperament we carry responds in style, mannerisms, vices, and virtues, each making strong contributions to the personality that will awaken to a nonphysical awareness, long called "metaphysical." *There is more to life than meets the eye;* now we seek higher consciousness.

Human beings are illumined to the degree the soul purpose is revealed. In the esoteric tradition the story of the angel warning Joseph to flee into Egypt with infant Jesus exemplifies our own struggle between dark and light. Herod announced he would kill infant males; he died, but his son Archelaus carried out his plan. In the same manner, even though we think we have ego (Herod) in hand, its offspring still lives and will kill the Christ-Within if it gets the chance. Having given birth to the inner self, we dwell in darkness, awaiting that which can lead us out of isolation (Egypt) and into the land of spiritual vision and insight, the land of plenty. Ego identity would keep us in darkness.

We must recognize we need not cast out or deny underdeveloped aspects, nor even slay the Dweller. Here we add good psychology to spiritual comprehension, knowing the nature of creation contains light and dark, male and female, and so on. *Contain* is the key. Accepting that we have darkness — under-equipped, unilluminated, unexpressed aspects of potential and overly idealized hopes, dreams, and false pictures of our nature — we do not seek to obliterate these but to live increasingly consciously, that these distorted aspects gradually will dissipate.

Both the Dweller and the Angel contain energy patterns and psychic energy generated by the unconscious as an impulse to carry us forward. This is so we can be tested or complete a lesson the inner nature now believes we are able to face. Trials occur all the time, and personality must cope with situations through which wisdom is offered. Just when it seems we will be torn apart, help comes — if we stay the course between the two poles of opposites.

Thus we see humanity lives in a world of distinct and conspicuous duality. Today, spirituality is emerging into broad new areas of human endeavor; at the same time, crime, violence, and addictions explode before our very eyes. As we accumulate more light (higher consciousness), we see more clearly the shadows of ignorance and wasted potential within and about us, as well as within the groups of which we are a part. This should not be disheartening, but should encourage us to make corrections that can move human evolution forward between these collective poles of duality. This is reconciliation, the work of the moment — balancing and maintaining right-relationship. We could call this the healing work of our time.

This may be the place to recall the old adage: there is a bit of good in the worst of us and a bit of bad in the best. This fits the reconciliation consciousness that helps us dissolve the duality necessary to proceed.

A helpful way to think about a high ideal is as a concept or principle that lives well on a higher level and is charged with a magnetic force. When we touch it, we receive a charge. The challenge we face is to become like it; as we stretch toward it, we do so. If we cannot and attempt to pull it down to our level, we distort the image (becoming hypocrites). This distorted energy then becomes part of what we must dissolve later. Should we be elevated in our stretch toward a pure expression of the ideal, the true Self grows.

Parallels in Esoteric and Exoteric Psychotherapy

Now let us take our spiritual study of the Dweller and Angel to a modern psychological perspective. In psychology the shadow contains that which is undesirable to the conscious personality, e.g., the "devil" aspect of self, unacceptable to the spiritual student.

Here we find suppressed impulses, painful memories, guilt, or intentions inappropriate to our honored role of ethical thinker, as well as raw material and undeveloped capabilities. Much that we have experienced in our evolutionary journey will not be appropriate to our self of today. We have little desire to recall experiences wherein we have held ill intent or have been the abuse giver. We may suppress these memories in guilt or pain, thereby increasing the power of the shadow.

Similarly, we choose to give more conscious attention to the Angel of the Presence, or to our "nice self." We enjoy affirming our goodness, applauding our successes, conforming — at least on the surface — to the societal code, thinking of ourselves as "good." Remember, the Christ said, *There is no one who is good except the one God* (Matt. 19.18). This admonishment is not to cause us to think poorly of ourselves but to avoid the dangers of glamourizing good which further complicates the unfinished business to be faced.

> Build a plan in yourself where you can live with your shadow and your divinity together from a position of observation.
>
> —Carl Jung

The late Carl Jung, renowned Swiss psychiatrist, acknowledged the spiritual work that occurs within the framework of psychology and psychotherapy. His open recognition of the inner nature and the creation of tools to help access it gave birth to a revelationary Jungian school of thought and the training of Jungian analysts who so ably assist those ready to move toward self-actualization.

In comparing esoteric wisdom — the tool of confessors, spiritual teachers, and wise ones — to contemporary, more scientific exoteric psychology, we reflect upon the mystics of many traditions who sought assistance from spiritual directors. We recall the dream wizards of the Bible and of Delphi and the wise men and women of myriad tribes and clans who have counseled their people with spontaneous and profound wisdom and traditional mysteries, to contemporary, more scientific exoteric psychology. We realize, many psychologists do not relate to the spiritual, but any work which diminishes barriers to high consciousness advances us toward our goal to soul infusion and the expression of the spirit within.

167

In modern spiritual thought we recognize the need to integrate and balance the feminine with our often over-developed masculine society. Many still speak in the code of the masculine path: up the ladder of success, head of the pack, fellow workers, king of the mountain, and so on. When productivity (measurable results) outweighs process (internal shifts), the irrational and intuitive are devalued, as excesses of masculine influence eclipse the feminine. Spiritual teachings call for the integration of our masculine and feminine natures. Represented by the strait gate, integration of polarities becomes the way to progress. Jung identified these internal forces as "animus" and "anima," acknowledging the need for reconciliation of our dualities. Androgyny is often suggested as the key to becoming a balanced being with access to the appropriate energy as needed.

Christianity, as well as other religions, has become enmeshed in extremist perspectives with such concepts as "heaven or hell." Such duality easily lends itself to the demonization of other perspectives, whether from an individual or group, a sect or religion.

> We know that the alchemists projected the problem of the light and the dark, the good and evil, upon matter. Modern man, so Jung found, is still struggling with this problem. No longer is it projected upon matter; usually it is projected upon other people, upon other nations.
> —E. A. Bennet, *What Jung Really Said*

In trying so hard to be true to our faith, we energize the image of the "good Christian" (the Angel), often viewing even minor infractions as bad, thus energizing the Dweller. We create guilt and repression when we cannot meet unrealistic standards we set. Occult sciences seek to help us understand the methods and means of growth which are integrative. While this may inflame those upholding rigid church doctrines, people with experience and inner awareness temper judgments, having caught glimpses of their own less-refined raw material.

We try to remember we must walk a mile in the moccasins of another before we can pass judgment; since this is impossible, judging is not an option. Every world religion instructs us to do unto others as we would have others do unto us. As we move into a more and more profound comprehension of the esoteric wisdom of the Bible, we begin to recognize subtler levels of truths. Similarly, when we understand ourselves better, we value each delicate effort we make, our intent and motivation, as well as the actual results. Again, *Know Thyself.*

We are reminded of Matthew 5.28: . . . *whoever looks at a woman with lust, has already committed adultery with her in his heart.* With such a challenge, we face our desire to be perfect, we overreach our target and energize the impossible angelic image of ourselves. Spiritual students dare not be smug about their studies because the danger of energizing the angel exists daily when we over-identify with such terms as "awakened," "initiation," "master of" such and such. We will be challenged repeatedly to neutralize our duality at any given stage. We "tack" one direction, then another. We must realize the Dweller, or dark side of our nature, contains all the unspent related energy and lessons to be mastered, currently held within the etheric body and waiting to be ignited, while our Angel stands on its pedestal for all the world to admire.

Before we leave this topic of opposites and their interpretation, let us review the familiar we/they attitude. Here again, as we become comfortable in one pole, the other is easily demonized. We claim our goodness and sacrifice others to the Dweller. We do this when we blame or shame ourselves, as well as others. Lacking forgiveness or compassion, we burden ourselves with unnecessary guilt, which often leads to depression, doubt, or despair. This self-destructive streak is related to our issues of Dweller versus Angel. Good counseling to help us reflect our way through difficult territory is often advisable.

"No one," says Jung, "can become conscious of the shadow without considerable moral effort."[8] The "shadow," Jungian terminology, is the "incomplete, less refined, and ineptly expressed potential within each of us. . . . our dreams reveal our shadows — aspects of ourselves we do not realize in our awakened state."[9]

In astrology the concept of the hidden helper is often neglected or overlooked. It suggests that the energy of the sign opposite our sun sign helps us in ways little understood. We might think in this way: "in opposition" means from this perspective things seem quite contradictory. When we see one perspective clearly, we can then look for and focus from the opposite. Astrology recognizes the power of this opposition as a clearly defined dual action which helps us navigate (or integrate) in a given area.

Respect for the power of the full moon is always present in teachings regarding growth and meditation, partially because the moon in opposition to the sun at that time increases the intensity with which humanity is bathed. Our ability or inability to remain grounded or to respond positively to the bombardment reveals our inner condition. Our personal relationship to the influence in power is assisted by the opposite sign working out of sight.

> *The Dweller contains all the unspent related energy or lessons to be mastered, currently held within the etheric body and waiting to be ignited.*

Let us use this example: an Aquarian can be assisted by understanding or invoking the hidden traits of Leo. Self-love is necessary before one can love others. The Leo's self-love lifts us to a degree of confidence whereby we can become aware of the needs of another. For more insight to this hidden-helper concept, explore *The Book of Rituals—Personal and Planetary Transformation.* [10]

Similarly, in numerology we total the numbers assigned to the vowels of a name, then to the consonants. Prior to totalling the numbers, we label and define the work of each in order to discover the work we are to do. Again, dual perspectives must come together for wholeness to be realized. When the sums of the vowels and the consonants are totalled, we discover the expression through which we may achieve our goal.

Prior to a mature stage of integration we vacillate from perspective to perspective as our moods dictate. As our higher nature is established and more stable, we are better able to apply the benefit of experience.

According to the theory of reincarnation, we would have developed a particular set of traits in one past life, a somewhat opposite set another life, and now we must balance them. Through our male lives we build masculine traits of strength, force, rational mind, and strategic planning; our female lives introduce diametric qualities, such as nurturing, receptivity, loving gentility, intuition, and sensitivity.

Remember the basic self with the reservoir of male or female qualities it brings at incarnation. With its available resources and temperament from birth, our basic self has accumulated a certain nature through which to "work out" its salvation (enlightenment). Too often this is thought of as "outer work," rather than resources upon which we call as our inner nature matures. Each of us is, of course, to realize our real work is to create within our nature the equal-armed cross: *Pick up your cross and follow me,* he said.

Human beings are illumined to the degree their soul purpose is revealed. As we move from intellect to intuition, we strive to find ways to move more comfortably from inner to outer, from heart to mind, from duality to oneness. We cultivate listening inwardly because we want to hear. An eagerness sets in, drawing us into closer relationship with the inner nature, even when hard to understand. We begin to hunger and thirst for righteousness, even when we cannot grasp what or why.

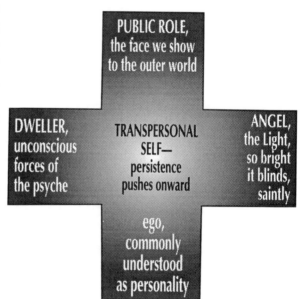

In wisdom teachings we learn that humanity had much more clearly defined roles in its earliest stages. Anthropologists confirm this. As we advance on a spiral of evolution, the points move closer to each other, refining previous energies and allowing each set of qualities to clarify. The breadth of swing between the

Figure 47. The Evolving Transpersonal Self learns to navigate among its many aspects, and, in fact, each higher initiation brings more integration, until we reach fully human and fully divine.

points of duality, or what I call the line of tension, is lessened — like the swinging pendulum moving closer and closer to centerpoint.

To hasten our progress we may look at an issue from two clearly defined perspectives. To find the truth of the matter then, we choose an imaginary point a bit higher and midway between the two. As we energize this point we seek to lift our own consciousness and stay centered. Imagine at that chosen spot the yin-yang sign of integration. Fixing our mind at this point, we attempt to navigate between the two perspectives, the Dweller and the Angel, without an intense identity with either. Thus, we can advance through the strait gate to a higher level of reality.

Note how persistently the path to enlightenment returns to points of reconciliation. We first need to recognize the dual nature of the solar plexus: the scanning restless ego versus the quiescent self awaiting. We seek harmony to empower the light center which in turn awakens our psychic self. Acknowledging the soulstar, we invoke its light to nurture our developing personality and facilitate the building of connecting threads to the soul.

> *Human beings are*
> *illumined to the degree*
> *the soul purpose is revealed.*

In time, our contact with the High Self initiates a relationship with the solar angel. The two must work as a unit in order for the Christ-Within to be born. Later in our quest, we reconcile personality to soul energies for soul-infusion, or transfiguration, to occur. The two harmonized give birth to a new condition. In some vastly distant future and in a similar manner, the unit of soul and monad will comprise the two poles through which we travel to embrace monad. This mystery truly is not revealed, but the recurring pattern of the strait gate or two poles to be transcended appears repeatedly.

Look at the simple statements of how we are mirrors to one another. Yes, whether too good to be true or condemned as terrible, we do mirror that which we need to see. Males are said to seek out a female who will enact their astral self while females tend to seek a mate who will manifest her mental nature. Ann Ree Colton in *Kundalini West* [11] offers further interesting ideas on this subject. One additional thought she suggests is that, if we change mates, we need to study how different their characteristics are. The shift in what we "fall for" indicates the changes we have made within our own consciousness.

In a similar way, even in the nightly review we see how the same issues come up time and time again because we bump into our Dweller, those raw materials we are learning to use or unfinished business providing needed lessons. It is much more difficult to discover the Angel, but this is usually the pedestal we stand on when we are judging others. From this "holier than thou" perspective we see only our light and the distortion makes all else look dark.

SOUL ALIGNMENT TECHNIQUE

Since by now you are quite familiar with seed-thought work, we suggest while continuing that approach, you add the soul alignment technique presented here. Seed-thought practices provide access to the Cloud of Knowable Things and are designed to instruct, while soul alignment is much like a wash of encouragement, joy, and grace to hasten our growth, flooding our entire nature with soul energy. As this radiance emanates into the world around us, it also becomes service to the world.

Please note, several years of seed-thought work are advised before this next technique *alone* is adequate. We continue seed-thought work for its contribution to our perception and intuition, as well as the instruction it brings from the Higher. Now we add the alignment technique for its magnetic effect. At some point, you may wish to repeat some seed thoughts in this course. You will find that a few sessions spent on each will again yield new and penetrating insights, for you have matured since their last use. Persistent seed-thought work continues to prepare the outer mind to receive gnosis: inner knowing.

Our new alignment technique will hasten change in the mechanical nature (body/etheric centers), bringing the outer more readily under dominance of soul. It facilitates transfiguration but has little value until we approach soul infusion. However, after a number of years of working "as if" with seed-thought meditation, the time may be right for adding this simple but powerful technique. Please note, I suggest we *not* stop seed-thought practices; that work should be ongoing. This additional active technique works harmoniously with seed-thought work. Remember, subtler exercises are more powerful and need to be practiced for shorter periods of time.

As we prepare to use the soul-alignment technique, be mindful that:

- We are invoking light to strengthen soul at each level. We could think of this as grace to impact the personality more effectively.
- The individual does not do the work, for personality cannot will this. Become quiet, and ask soul to guide the process. Trust.
- Soul energy blesses, stimulates, and cleanses each of its points of contact. Thoughts are not needed to direct the activity because *It* knows. Soul directs the process.
- As the disciple is impacted, the whole of humanity receives the effects. There is no wasted effort in the universe.

This spiritual technique is beneficial to the individual, especially in troubled moments, as well as a service to the planetary consciousness performed frequently by dedicated world servers. Together we hasten our planet's sanctity.

Assignment

Soul-Alignment Meditation

The length of this soul-alignment technique should be less than ten minutes. It draws upon all our skills of working "as if." Since you are well experienced with the long version of the "I Am the Soul" mantra (expanded upon in vol. 1, lesson 9, and placed in the appendix of all three volumes), here it is appropriate to use the shortened version (which is not recommended for students who are in the early stages of seed-thought work).

I Am the Soul

I am the Soul.
I am the light divine.
I am love.
I am will.
I am fixed design.

Again, the format is explained step by step, and at the end of the outline, the technique reassembled.

Sit up straight, with your back not touching any surface. Become quiet now, and relax, taking three deep breaths. Let go of the awareness of the outer as you focus inward. Let us begin.

Align the energy centers in your own style. Move your attention upward to your crown center, and settle there for a moment.

Now bring your focus up higher to the soulstar. Hold your attention there for a few seconds.

Now take your attention back down to the crown center slowly and easily. Now

down to the brow center,
down to the throat, and swallow,
down to the heart,
down to the solar plexus (sense harmony between the
scanning ego and the quiescent self),
down to the abdomen center,
down to the base of the spine.

Now, from the base of your spine, bring the energy down your legs to your feet, and bless the Earth. Feel connected to the Earth itself. Feel the harness of Light which is your self sending energy to the Earth, and sense the matter that is your body balanced, grounded. Breathe; experience the connection.

Now let us lift the energy back up — gently, steadily:

from the base of the spine,
to the abdomen center,
up to the solar plexus,
up to the heart,
up to the throat,
up to the brow center, and
up to the crown. Let it settle for a few moments.

Now we return our attention to the soulstar. Here we will speak aloud the long version of "I Am the Soul."

I am the Soul,
and also love am I.
Above all else, I am
both will and fixed design.
My will is now to lift
the lower self into the Light Divine.
That Light am I.

Therefore, I must descend
to where that lower self awaits,
awaits my coming.
That which desires to lift
and that which cries for lifting
are now at one.
Such is my will.

Breathe. Again, bring your attention to the crown, the brow, the throat, and the heart. Hold the energy there to emanate through your heart as you go about your day.

Imagine a point of synthesis in front of you where the energy of the brow center and the energy of the heart center can merge. This is approximately in front of your mouth at about arm's length.

Now, work as if you are a soul-infused personality. Speak aloud the Great Invocation, sending forth the gift of your own creative energy, and sounding three *Oms* to serve the Plan on Earth.

The Great Invocation

From the point of Light within the Mind of God
Let light stream forth into the minds of men.
Let light descend on Earth.

From the point of Love within the Heart of God
Let love stream forth into the hearts of men.
May Christ return to Earth.

From the Center where the Will of God is known
Let purpose guide the little wills of men —
The purpose which the Masters know and serve.

From the center which we call the race of men
Let the Plan of Love and Light work out.
May it seal the door where evil dwells.

Let Light and Love and Power restore the Plan on Earth.

If you have comments or questions regarding the soul-alignment process, please correspond with the tutors. This technique should be restricted to advanced practitioners of meditation. If used before adequate work with seed-thought techniques is accomplished, its effectiveness is diminished.

Discover New Worlds

*You can talk about fundamentalism and reaction
and everything going backward,
or you can talk about new trends and things going forward.
You can talk about this trend to prove one thing;
you can point to that trend to prove another thing.
Each person selectively focuses on the data that his world view
attracts him to. . . . So every description is valid
to the degree that every description is a self-description.*
—William Irwin Thompson[1]

We have followed the trail of the generic human seed called quiescent self as it advances — to bloom under the care of High Self and then to merge with the Christ-Within where, under the care of solar angel, it matures into a soul-infused personality. Now soul becomes the ever-advancing agent which carries human history to divinity godliness. Destined to become fully human and fully divine, we become an authentic enlightened species that knows, *Ye are Gods,* and demonstrates it in daily life.

This luminous star is truly you with your personal light shining—in your own aura, emanating into your home, into your relationships, to friends and extended family. Your work place, profession or vocation, your citizenship, racial and religious affiliations, sexual identity, and social groups — all are touched. Whatever you come near experiences your presence. You vibrate your gift of self into each sphere, and your influence is felt, whether consciously or unconsciously.

It may come as an unwelcome realization how interwoven we all truly are; we like to think we are independent agents. Even when least aware, our emotions and thoughts wield more influence than we realize. Enveloped by a web of light, we attract and repulse individuals, circumstances, and experiences. Until we begin to think in terms of cause and effect and spiritual principles, the *how* of specific events is easily lost in the annals of time. We gradually realize the human "mind being" constantly creates thoughtforms in patterns with which we and our extended group identity must contend. Indeed, John Donne's *No one is an island* is an affirmation of inordinate truth.

> *The opening of hearts*
> *through group alignment is the*
> *true next step for humanity.*

Active meditation is an attribute of the dynamic power of thought. We are reminded of the archaic word, "fiery," used to describe higher-world energy. A good modern term is "intense." Our power of focus, or will, contributes to the intensity our mind can build. Surrounded by mere mindstuff, each of us is learning to attract and concentrate the "stuff," focusing it through the spiritual eye built by meditation and contemplation. In time, the fire ignites, providing the light to burn away the fog — glamours and illusions of distortion. We build the high consciousness necessary to see the truth we are capable of integrating. Thus, as the spiritual eye widens, so does our ability to know the truth that sets us free.

Our strong emphasis on seed-thought work is to liberate the mind from its limited education and experience. We are all to be free. No one is to control another's mind. Having first learned the benefit of obedience, we earn freedom. With the seed-thought technique, we attract that which our open mind can grasp. Then, working with others using the same seed, we compare streams of thought, testing to see if we draw from the same well. The outpouring makes its wisdom known and produces results which confirm the source.

> Nothing can be taught to the mind which is not already concealed as potential knowledge in the unfolding soul. All Teaching is revealing, all becoming is an unfolding.
>
> —Sri Aurobindo

As we come to accept karma and reincarnation as important principles, we begin to think in terms of far-reaching consequences. The good or not-so-good karma of our religion, nation, society, race, or sex becomes our concern as we grow wiser. We are either cleansing the clouds of negativity for each group identity or adding to them; we are either a curse or a blessing. We come to appreciate, "Let your light so shine."

Opening human hearts through group alignment is the true next step for humanity's evolution. A large segment of humanity is currently struggling to this end. We must determine our group identities, know where we find oneness, and build there. As we recognize the opportunity presented to us within this context, we consciously honor and appreciate our group, realizing the significance of networking. "Allowing" without judgment is more easily achieved when we link to one another as souls and let personality differences subside.

Level by level, the collective mind of humanity is building toward its divine expression. Just as we recognize the beneficence of becoming comfortably stable level by level, so too does our collective. Let us look at the steps for advancing the cause of humanity — our individual story, as well as the work of the collective. As we see the big picture more clearly, we may better ponder how we shift and change through our lessons and experiences.

Levels of Mind As Applied to Group Consciousness (from subtlest to densest)		
1	Oneness	Wholeness, holy
2	Vision/our personal role	Will-to-serve
3	Nonformed/chaos	Creative
4	Cooperative/locating like-mindedness	Love/caring
5	Competitive struggle: self/others	Rational
6	Tribal, clan, collective	Programming
7	InstinctuaL	Survival

Fig. 48. Levels of Mind As Applied to Group Consciousness.

Each level has a perspective to offer and bears its own gift — a way of seeing things. As we master and integrate each subtle point of consciousness, we advance to the next. Of course, these stages correlate appropriately to individual chakras.

From lower level to advanced, humanity encounters each stage of experience: *Instinctual* consciousness aids our survival, commonly observed in "fight or flight" tendencies. This includes all our earlier unconscious psychic awarenesses. For instance, the sense of smell helped us determine our mates. Unconscious autonomic and automatic reflexes, such as batting an eyelash to deflect a flying insect, still keep us from harm.

Tribal, or clan, consciousness abides within clearly designated guidelines observed as conventions, rules, dogma, boundaries, or taboos. We easily think of tribal customs of indigenous people, but we might also remember prohibitions of religions and races and of corporate practices that connect us to expectations and reassurances. This level is identified in spiritual teachings as *maya*.

Competitive consciousness immediately calls to mind the concept of "other," but indeed it is much more. Add to this the struggle between our own heart and mind, where we come to know strengths and weaknesses of our own nature, that a bit of "bad" is within even the "good" and vice versa. This uncomfortable level is defined by projection — blaming, shaming, and defaming others instead of recognizing our personal struggle making itself known. Intellect and emotion dominate this more subtle nature, and even they compete for prominence. Highly charged glamours and illusions certainly abide here. A competitive consciousness changes to one of cooperation a bit at a time — though it is more hope than reality at early stages.

Cooperative consciousness is briefly experienced by families or groups. Within this peaceful state, one senses a similarity of essence or goal. Generally a temporary like-mindedness aligns us into right-relationship. We achieve this awareness only at peaceful points when soul is felt. We might identify cooperative conscious-ness as our attraction to like-minded people. In Esoteric Christianity our sincerest dedication is to the Lord Christ; by coming into alignment with the great teacher of humanity, we align with one another at a heart-centered level. This consciousness builds bridges.

Nonformed, or chaos, is the level being energized by incoming Aquarian energies. We may call this stage creative or, better, individuated consciousness. Here, the powerful desire for freedom emerges, at times detrimentally — witness the teenager who refuses to conform to guidelines of home or school, or the renegade who accepts no statutes of law and order. Yet this is home to the innovative, the bohemian, the artist, and advanced thinker.

Appearing unordered, under scrutiny the law of *chaos displays subtle patterns leading to the new. Perturbations, which seem to be destroying all that has been built, disguise new, underlying patterns. Creative chaos will reorder gradually as will-to-serve converts the purified astral nature into the new consciousness meant to be. Our efforts at cleaner and clearer living lead toward a medley of expression and genuine fulfillment.

> Let diversity and creativity flow within the parameters of moral responsibility and committed love that we have seen celebrated in the Song of Songs and that truly reflect the moral laws the universe teaches us. Let new communities with new visions of living together be born — with a conscious and deliberate vow to create together, to sustain one another's creative powers, to stand in solidarity with other creators and co-creators in society and the cosmos. . . . The Cosmic Christ would be allowed freedom to dance, to play, to create anew.
> —Matthew Fox, *The Coming of the Cosmic Christ*

Vision, our personal role, brings the Spirit-Within to fulfill its purpose. Each one who leads humanity into its divine potential is a hero/heroine, charting the way for others. In *The Hero with a Thousand Faces,* Joseph Campbell identifies three distinct stages to the hero's journey: 1) departure or separation from one's former identity as a hero deserts the old for the new; 2) fulfillment, or initiation into a new consciousness (group, church, or tribal level) where unknown forces, experiences, or realizations are acquired and a decisive new awareness is won; and 3) the return — empowered now to bless and guide others — includes establishment of new parameters, or new renditions of old foundations.

In an article entitled "The New Religious Consciousness,"[2] Joseph M. Felser writes:

Visionary fulfillment occurs in essentially complete form by the midpoint of the hero's journey. What follows is development and elaboration of the vision into a form the community can use, but this is achieved by closing off the spirit of inquiry of the first stage of the journey. Thus, even though Abraham, Moses, the Buddha, Mohammed, and Jesus all rejected the religious status quo of their respective communities and embarked on visionary quests, each in turn gave birth to religious orders whose conservatism characteristically discouraged further individual inquiry of a heroic kind.

Each hero, in other words, breaks through to a high level and etches into human consciousness a new spiral — an advanced harmonic to the last — then sets guidelines to crystallize the spiral into a form solid enough that others can build upon its revelation. After a time, the new spiral of consciousness congeals, awaiting yet another hero who will bring the next advancing spiral.

> *Those who vibrate to Oneness*
> *set into motion*
> *currents that affect all others.*

Using this model, we see the "nonformed" as free-thinkers searching for ways to guide the collective's spiral toward transcendence. A unique mosaic of free-thinkers struggles to free itself without always realizing its significance. The throat chakra is often called the sexual center of the spiritually awakened because from this center we "speak the word" — conceiving, inventing, expressing, giving birth to higher creations. From this creative level, artists, scientists, and mystics serve humanity by breaking through to moments of unformed consciousness, vibrating to future reality, yet clothed in today's garments (thoughtforms).

Oneness, with respectful regard for individuality, is a goal humanity holds before itself. Glimpsed dimly, more and more people and the collective sense its value. At this consciousness point, we surrender our uniqueness to something greater than ourselves. A uniting vision provides a role for each of us. We are reminded we do not have to like each other, but the reason for coming together has a deep significance for each, and we are to assist the vision's manifestation and maintenance. The depth of commitment to the unifying work assists less-than-compatible personalities to persist and share their essence. Advancement to this level is witnessed as a serious depth of commitment to the creation. All individuals must love the work enough to resolve or tolerate personality differences for the higher good.

Unity with diversity requires contemplation of Oneness where a mandala of human interaction exists. As yet, only a few have experienced this Oneness. Guides of the human family recognize and value the point of Oneness amid diversity. Unique in background, practice, and journey, each guide — Masters, rishis, the enlightened — manifests an identifying factor which constitutes a wholeness. In the profundity of the grand vision, surrendering separation in order to be One is natural. Diversity is honored, appreciated, even encouraged — but *for* the Oneness, not apart from it. Thus the mystical body of Christ, or the Adam Kadmon (of Kabalah), is realized through high consciousness.

Hope sustains humanity on its quest. Although illusory, this world is a place of significant learning under soul's tutelage. Here, soul's unique complex of energies achieves clarity, purpose, and integration. We are challenged to bring into our current experience the flow of consciousness needed to assist us to transcend unreal limitations and behold potential otherwise hidden from view. Hope reveals and energizes possibilities.

The Purpose of Meditation Connections

While the guidance and work in this course are individual, most people have had some group experience. As beginners, group energy usually helps us loosen the tight grip we tend to have on the outer world. As we relax, chant, and become receptive in a group setting, the empowerment of a safe environment assists newcomers to move with the group energy. After some experience in a group setting, we more readily recognize the difference as we work alone in days that follow. A weekly group helps us establish rhythm, reassurance, and confidence. The guidance and encouragement of an experienced leader inspire beginners to continue until they find their own momentum.

From our very first private attempts at meditating until we undertake the more sophisticated practice of one core group attuning to another, often from distant places, we learn calm, clear group mind can hold an intent and focus its collective energy on a goal, a purpose, or a cause. Specific works evolve as disciples direct life energy to their projects. Many send the energy of their focus to support incubating seeds until they realize, "Eureka, this is mine to do!" Now the new leader emerges to coordinate impressions and insights with that of the larger work.

> The historical origin of any process can always be traced to a single seed, whether we are speaking of a tree, a human life, the life of a group, of a culture, of the whole world; or the course of a self-transformation.
> —Ralph Metzner, *Opening to Inner Light*

Our task then is to access impressions and step them down to register upon our rational mind as the part of the Plan we can grasp. We thus capture creative insights and use well the opportunities afforded us to touch into the intuitive level of mind.

Group alignment at the nonphysical level strengthens group focus and supplies energy for the etheric activity of each, forming connecting lines between participants. As thoughts and love flow, we create the resources for the unfolding work of the group. Think of this as personal and group enhancement, contributions we make to lives with which we link.

It has always been the custom of aware people to think of each other in times of need. Healing thoughts, positive and protective, flow to and fro. Blessings happen, and we are all revitalized. Today, scientists are researching and confirming significant effects. Studies in healing, telepathy, and remote viewing are increasing. Research affirms the powerful influence of a heart and mind with focused intent.

In *Healing Words*,[3] Dr. Larry Dossey, a friend to Sancta Sophia Seminary, presents breakthrough conclusions drawn from scientific experimentation which wonderfully support spiritual healing concepts. This exciting book inspires new effort on our part to link with others through prayer and meditation. Let us realize more clearly how blessed our connections are and how together we may affect conditions even more than we know. Let us increase our participation in meditations: in groups, in triangles, in whatever ways possible, grateful that we have access to such avenues for service.

Just as we defined the seven levels of the denser planes, we do similarly for the intuitive plane, also called the Buddhic consciousness or the Christ consciousness. Here we truly enter the realm of soul. The intuitive nature begins to develop at midpoint the mental plane — where personality and soul touch. Later, in the solar initiations soul will embrace the fiery light of the monad in much the same way.

ATMIC

Will to initiate

**REALM OF THE SOUL—
THE INTUITIVE PLANE**
**Soul empties into personality at the mental
level while it receives from the higher.**

Will to unify

Will to evolve

Will to harmonize

1 **Divine Will.** This level harmonizes to cosmic Will; it has no limitation or definition.

2 **Divine Compassion.** The divine heart of true love of the World Teacher.

Will to act

MENTAL 3 **Divine Intelligence.** The higher Plan of humanity is guided by the Wise Ones of Hierarchy.

Will to cause

4 **Illumination.** Direct knowing is the great light of illumination.

Will to express

5 **Blueprints.** Charged with power and purpose, impressions are beamed to humanity to reveal purpose, design, and objectives.

6 **Divine Archetypes.** Archetypes of intense energy are containers awaiting our contact.

7 **Divine Symbols.** Universal symbols seek to reveal as much as one can perceive at any given time.

Fig. 49. Levels of Intuitive Plane. Vague terminologies attempt to define this flow of consciousness; inspirational rather than rational, they do not lend themselves well to definition. However, each contact touches humanity with a profundity long recognized and valued.

The intuitive plane is soul's domain, and symbolism is its language. In meditation, archetypes descend as images and thoughts to energize our nature and animate our purpose. Divine symbols await our ability to perceive their gossamer but beneficent meanings. At each contact we seek to clarify what has been made known.

From Native American legends to *parables of the Christ, spiritual visions are imparted in images. Parables, dramas, and myths are teaching tools to guide the awareness of awakened ones. The unawakened await the comprehension of revelations or accept translations of those with perceptive skills.

Myths — profound truths formed with enough fluidity to be translated age after age — provide access to archetypes that nurture humanity. The term *myth* often is used erroneously as a term for "nontruth." However, a myth merely dons the cloak of the times and provides a new grasp of an ancient reality.

As humanity enters the new era, we move collectively into a new creative cycle and beyond many limitations of rational mind. While some will live their lives within the confines of old world views, the tide now turns; mind power with its offer of new realities is revealed everywhere. As visualizations, guided meditations, teaching dramas, and psychological discernment influence group life, we increasingly identify with our potential. The new mind gaining prominence lives in a larger mental room where imagination is alive and well. The *mind screen, active in a sufficient number of humans, is now ready for emerging revelations, pointing toward the future of the species.

> All the works of humanity have their origin in creative imagination. What right, then, have we to disparage fantasy? . . . Fantasy is not a sickness but a natural and vital activity which helps the seeds of psychic development to grow.
>
> — Carl Jung

Humanity's emerging capability to know its wholeness will be dedicated to healing the past and aligning with soul. As higher frequencies illumine our ability to know and integrate, we identify more with one another. Compare this to learning the workings of a computer step by step, needing hours of experience to master the fine points. Now humanity has built much of its enhanced equipment and must learn to use its truly vast capabilities. How do we advance? By repeatedly placing ourselves in posture for continued exposure to waves of illumination and revelation. Persist! Persist! Persist!

As personality integrates and intuitive mind unfolds, holistic senses advance. Remember, the brain is the mechanism, and mind is the consciousness expanding gradually through layers of experiences from which perceptions seek to flow into the brain. As mind improves its ability to anchor awareness, the impact of soul is felt. In esoteric understanding the practitioner's meditation and spiritual disciplines result in a more conscious use of spiritual senses. No longer do unconscious animal senses rule our emotional and mental natures; these natures, cleared and healed of barriers to high consciousness, welcome soul's energy as it radiates into and advances its claim upon personality.

Progress during this transitional stage is noted by disintegration of veils which once served to protect the formation of human ego and its essential rational mind. Bold seekers may access "a strange place," sometimes becoming fearful, reluctant to discuss their adventure. But with such experiences, change happens and effects accrue. The nature of the neocortex-centered individual is curiosity, so an experience cannot be held long without comparing, questioning, and discovering. The old rational mind weakens its hold when faced with very real inner experiences.

The new mind gaining prominence
lives in a larger mental room
where imagination is alive and well.

In the way of all nonverbal knowledge, the process germinates inwardly for a time. A knowing occurs but, without language to assist, it has no voice until a moment of readiness. Then, as one gives birth to words, others support disclosure. Drama, poetry, storytelling become wonderful tools with which to share spiritual adventures and discoveries. Some give credence; others receive new insights. All change.

Soul's task is to keep trickling down messages (dreams, impressions, symbols, and the energy with which to unfold) concerning our hidden inner-plane life. Ready members of humanity are nurtured under the guidance of solar angel until we blossom — alone and together.

Wisdom teachings remind us that hostile individuals live in a hostile world and happy people live in a happy world. Similarly, aware ones live in a world of synchronicity, sensing and seeing cause and effect at work in myriad ways, catching glimpses of new realities, of symbology and synchronicities. Indeed, the evolving human being discovers overlapping worlds and learns to participate wisely in each, carefully walking an ethical path.

Such wisdom draws disciples into closer comprehension of their part in the drama being created by freedom of choice. As we realize our soul's work, we make definitive effort to align personality's many traits and desires with the Plan. Similarly, as a group soul forms its part of the Plan, each individual surrenders to the group work. The real work is not merely in coming together as a compatible association but in protecting the group and its purpose.

Diversity is honored, appreciated, even encouraged, but it is for *the Oneness, not apart from it.*

We may think of a group as mosaic tiles fixed in place, but that projects an incorrect, immovable picture. A kaleidoscope is a better image, with its succession of symmetrical designs constantly changing patterns through the use of mirrors — alive, active, reflecting, vibrant. A spiritual group is dynamic because each member may have to fulfill any role, "taking up the slack" as needed. All must watch for defects, weaknesses, or dangerous aberrations which detract from the unifying purpose, being open to impressions of benefits to secure the vision that inspires the group.

Every piece of the kaleidoscope is joy-filled. Just to be participating, being a part in any way is better than not being a part. Guidance may move pieces about, sometimes out of sight, yet all note the patterns as they emerge. Group work challenges, for it means we must surrender some qualities of the strong ego that delivered this opportunity.

Alignment to a central keynote creates a group, and members contribute diverse characteristics to the whole. Each has the opportunity to refine her or his nature, to shine light, and to express wisdom. By doing so, each affects the entire group, sometimes consciously evoking a response. As we grow and transform, we may reevaluate and change groups, especially if we find we are without sufficient support or too much restrained.

Each awakening soul creates joy in the heart of the whole — not because of conversion, for ripeness develops from the inside out, but because humanity is maturing into its future and those who pierce the veil are finding the Way.

A truly heart-centered group consciousness is not possible on a personality level; it relates to soul. Personality/ego, a level of individuality, is as it is meant to be. However, as our interests rise above reactive self-interest, personal agendas, and judgment, we become increasingly capable of cooperating to determine what is most appropriate in given situations. Group intent and consciousness establish criteria which eventually determine success or failure of the work upon which disciples have embarked.

In every union, individuality must coalesce with the purpose for which persons have con-

Group Formation

This lovely story inspires me time and again with its glimpse of the power of a group at work. As the unity of humanity is realized, perhaps we will be as wise as geese.

The next time you see geese heading south for winter, consider what science has discovered about their **V** formation. As each bird flaps its wings, it creates an uplifting current, or draft, for the bird immediately following. By flying in a **V** formation, the flock adds at least seventy-one percent greater flying range than if each bird flew on its own.

When a goose drops out of formation, it immediately feels the drag and resistance of trying to go it alone and quickly returns to formation and to the lifting power of the bird in front.

When the lead goose tires, it rotates back in the wind and another goose flies point. The geese honk from behind, encouraging those up front to keep up to speed.

Finally, when one goose gets sick or is wounded by gunshot and falls out, two geese leave formation and follow their disabled comrade down to help and protect it, staying until it can fly or until it is dead. Then they launch out on their own or join another formation until they catch up with their original group.   —Source unknown

Fig. 50. Group Formation.

nected; otherwise, no unions would survive, whether marriage and family, business, or politics. Differences emerge because personalities exist, but reconciliation means embrace once more — wiser, and knowing the unit is more than the sum of its parts.

A spiritual group is not just a collective of individuals; it strives to become community, a state of consciousness wherein love flows in such a way as to sustain one another, through mutual respect, assistance, and trust. Without this love, community is lacking. A group may be just a number of people with interests, agendas, and goals; community happens when individuals create a state of consciousness which embraces the diverse interests, agendas, and goals, with spiritual appreciation and respect for each "soul" component of the collective.

In a spiritual sense, disciples become united in a specific endeavor by a unifying governing principle — a keynote — much like the cornerstone of a building. This unifying keynote needs to be identified early and clearly, for it is the rock upon which all work of the group is built stands or falls. Belief, goal, and perspective emerge from this keynote; relationships yet to be established depend on this common vision.

The dedicated meditator consistently seeks illumination and liberation. Oneness beckons, and moments of straight knowledge reassure the seeker of coworkers. Each new collective draws like-minded workers for the contribution they can make in this human life. Awakening ones create joy in the heart of the whole — not because of conversion, for ripeness develops from inside out, but because humanity is maturing into its future, and those who pierce the veil find the Way. For each one who reaches enlightenment, the heavens sing. Those who vibrate to Oneness set currents into motion, affecting all others. Vision and insight become gifts to those they touch. The disciple is a beacon guiding others into transcendent realities.

> There is no renaissance without a vast outburst of creativity—new images, new risk taking, new relationships, new dreams and visions. As Einstein put it, "the whole purpose of science *and art* is to awaken the cosmic religious feeling."
> —Matthew Fox, *The Coming of the Cosmic Christ*

By their fruits shall ye know them. The open heart aligns with the great heart in which we find agape, and agape rushes into action — healing, gifting, revealing right-relationship and right-formation to those so attuned. Knowing each soul is cloaked in its own karmic garb, having little-understood energy and experience, each brings her or his own configurations to the whole. Acquired discrimination provides a lasting key to help us discern coworkers.

Learning about Ascension

We need to determine just what *"ascension," a word often used today, implies. The Ascension of the Christ has caused many to assume it means transcendence or escape from the physical plane by building a spiritual vehicle and departing. To many, it may mean escaping karma, the wheel of death and rebirth. However, consider ascension as a movement into and through rather than away from. In recognizing the spiritual principle of cause and effect, a good guideline is: *when we love so much we feel we cannot release or when we dislike to a point of not being able to tolerate, we are bound—until we transcend, ascend, or dissolve the issue, the connection, or the attachment.*

Using this knowledge, ascension is the realization of a stage of growth wherein consciousness travels in an appropriate vehicle from level to level, to function at different dimensions as needed or desired. In fact, *Christ in you, the hope of glory,* and *the crown of glory that never fades away,* as well as, *Who shall transform our poor body to the likeness of his glorious body. . . .* (Col. 1.27, 1 Peter 5.4, and Phil. 3.21, respectively) present the concept of a glory body being constructed by the Christ-Within to fulfill its purpose. Using Jesus Christ as our model, ascension builds upon the concept that we too are capable of ascending, and participating in a higher reality.

The purpose of ascension is to construct a vehicle that can travel into higher vibrations, higher planes. In an earlier lesson we studied building the light (or glory) body and that as we do our daily practices we are creating a more refined vehicle to house our consciousness. Just as the physical body benefits from food and physical activity, the celestial body is nurtured by contacting energies of subtler planes. The vehicle of each strata — astral, mental, intuitive — is woven by contact with that which exists in each domain. Wise Ones tell us repeatedly that once the true point of identity is built, the higher world is much more real to us than this outer one.

Helena Roerich, among others, wrote that respect for our physical body is absolutely required. The body is far more than a mere, little-attended vehicle for expression on the physical plane. Spun of streams of energy, this creation is a subtle, intimate, and accurate mirror of present and past. This earthy cocoon directs our attention to imbalances we need to consider. Because it is a record, every component can impart valued information to us — each line in the hand, each bump on the head, even the shape and size of our ears and feet. We recall the biblical reference to "the temple of the living God," as well, 2 Corinthians 6.16.

Since the emotional nature is not so firmly fixed, always in flux, we are constantly bombarded by desire/emotional currents from present happenings, people, and events, as well as emotional residue from humanity's past. Personality presents a serious challenge with its propensity to attract old energies and to coalesce into repetitive patterns. We then undertake the effort necessary to purify our astral and mental natures.

Aware the collective mind of humanity contains an immense field of maya which awakening ones must navigate, a bold confrontation of the astral is required. Ego's intellect presents another acute hindrance; it thinks it does not need to share its control, abilities, or power with others. The spiritual-*warrior concept suggests that confronting and overcoming these fields of distortion require rigorous preparation and dedication. Work on one's own nature was begun by evolving disciples, modeling an identical process for the entire human family.

The Process of Ascension

Most have little concept of what it would be like to be free of the physical vehicle. The welcome contribution of a conscious out-of-body experience is that of truly knowing "we are not the body." The awareness that we can *think, feel,* and *be* outside the framework of our physicality is truly liberating. Now we can more easily shift allegiance to a spiritual view of life and begin to release many impediments. By persisting with meditation, we consciously and repeatedly expose personality to the inner knower.

Many who have had out-of-body experiences realize their less-dense form — shaped and recognizable as their personality — looks much like the physical. This astral, or "starry," body consists of an etheric form, some "stars," and usually a well-developed light at the solar plexus. Flecks of light move about and glow within this ether, much like distant stars in the heavens. Some say 144 minor centers exist in this celestial form and that it is the model for the Christmas tree. Ultimately, our Christed form will display all seven chakras vividly glowing and minor centers twinkling like stars in the night.

As we discover and experience new ways of knowing, better perceiving the process, we more readily trust impressions. First, we invoke the soulstar to use its light to cleanse and clear our being, to energize our thoughts, and to bless us with its peace. Should this happen regularly, we contribute to — out of sight and out of mind — the new sheath, the light body, a fourth-dimensional vehicle to serve us even as our third-dimensional one does in this physical reality.

As consciousness advances and our lower levels receive the more refined energies, the nature changes again and again. The purified feeling level begins to be fueled by soul qualities; freed from old emotional charges, we experience greater peace of mind. The lotus of high consciousness developing in the higher mental realm is assisted by solar angel who tends its charge, lending its properties to construct a chalice for inner-world use. The etheric body reflects the shifts in the subtle vibrating planes so its ethers are constantly refining. Indeed, the etheric body is a true servant of the inner nature. Similarly, we must acknowledge the restriction caused by negative thoughts, hostilities, and lack of forgiveness which might also be part of our nature. These dark clouds create *rings-pass-not which must be overcome.

The following is not new information to spiritual students, but we need to be reminded: spiritual people are healthier, they live longer and tend to be more attractive, their eyes shine more, and they typically respond with more compassion. As they evolve, they emanate inner goodness, as well as healing energies, and they become fonts of wisdom. Inner awareness — with its many properties — is stepped down to serve self and those with whom each interacts.

At an earlier time, personality had to integrate its emotional and mental natures in order to progress. Now, drawing the soulstar energy downward hastens personality's acquiescence to the soul nature. When the heart opens and unconditional love flows, the mind allows soul qualities to transform the mental working unit. Today, we know these steps as initiations and the new body we are forming as the light body, the radiant form Jesus the Christ revealed on the mountain during the transfiguration — *the glory body.*

Today many of us are aware of concepts of transformation and transmutation; we identify more with our inner essence. Building the light body indeed refers to the transmutation-transfiguration process and the importance of the nonphysical, spiritual, or celestial vehicle now in rapid evolution. *This is true alchemy.*

To grasp the concept of true ascension, we must realize the goal is not to escape this earthly domain but to ascend into higher consciousness and return with our higher levels of awareness intact. The concept of "ascending to go free," to escape, is a glamour — but behind each glamour is a seed of truth. An imitation is but a cheap copy of some treasure. So now we may have a distorted view of this precious attainment, seeking it like an easily acquired, cheap phenomenon.

The truth is, each of us is to create this light body — out of sight — so we can move into higher reality, gather what we can and, as our mental mechanism can register it, bring back what we have learned, to be integrated into physical life. We do not have to die to function in the new celestial body. Our goal is to make increasingly smoother shifts into higher consciousness, somewhat like we "shift" with our seed-thought work, returning with more clarity, new realizations, and useful insights for both ourselves and others.

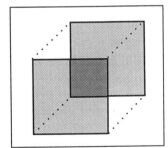

Fig. 51. Ascension — Two Realities. This diagram might clarify this analogy. Just as first one square seems more pronounced and then the other, so too does the physical plane, then the spiritual. Our disciplines and practices gradually form connecting lines between two realities (squares). As clear, smooth practices are integrated, we shift more easily from one square, or frame of reference, to the other. The clearer, more conceptual the mind, the better it will retain higher perceptions to be stepped down and conveyed to the world.

Teachers often receive new information or insights, even in the midst of sharing with others. Having built the necessary concepts within mind and having learned to move easily into altered states, they are able to make such shifts in the midst of inspired activities. This demonstrates two bodies functioning in harmony — one physical, one celestial — when they are relatively free of barriers at either level.

Free from restriction of the lower vehicles at least for a period of time, the lower "square" (as in fig. 51 on p. 194) aligns with the higher and continues to function. We realize liberation of spirit from the constraints of matter and encounter what appear to be phenomena to the world of matter, though natural to the other plane. Part of the purpose of this awakening to intuitive (soul) energies is to enable the passage of greater light into the greater group.

Individually and collectively, humanity struggles with light and dark. Since light and dark cannot occupy the same space, we clear away barriers in order to create more space within us to receive this light. These new energies intensify all that exists within consciousness, so we must be bold in confronting fears, ignorance, and unfinished business. But the same light provides awareness and resources to assist us in noting the work we need to do. We remember, "Every saint has a past, and every sinner has a future." Our task is to persist in doing the work.

Today, as we face traumas of the past — the human collective — from a more enlightened perspective, we seek to move toward a higher awareness most people barely perceive. We hasten to transmute destructive behaviors and habits. To become what it has glimpsed, humanity must move through a miserable time of confusion, unrest, and upheaval, breaking down old ways and creating new, always striving to sustain innovative concepts realized during this time of transition. This changing of the age, as it is known by many, is the end of the world *as it was*. It is the end of a world view, and those who can perceive and step down the vision of reconstruction are called to action.

> It was the best of times, it was the worst of times, it was the age of wisdom, it was the age of foolishness, it was the epoch of belief, it was the epoch of incredulity, it was the season of Light, it was the season of Darkness, it was the spring of hope, it was the winter of despair, we had everything before us, we had nothing before us, we were all going direct to Heaven, we were all going direct the other way.
> —Charles Dickens, *A Tale of Two Cities*

Creativity is necessary to guide us through this period — fresh ideas, innovative ways of doing things, and a new grasp of the power and potential of collective wisdom. To perceive our world and ourselves afresh frees the Self, the Christ-Within, to express its divine potential in new ways. *Greater things than these shall ye do* may yet come to pass. Are you not excited to be a part of a mission so vast?

> There is always a great need for political leaders, doctors, lawyers, and artists. But the greatest need is for higher psychics who are able scientifically to contact Higher Spheres of light and leadership and bring them to the world of [humanity] in the form of
> - new rules
>   - new laws
>   - new inspirations
>   - new directions
>   - new ideas
> to guide the steps of leaders in all fields.
> In the ancient world, every leader was guided by a true psychic, or he himself was a psychic.
> —Torkom Saraydarian, *Breakthrough to Higher Psychism*

Light workers improve themselves for the good of all. Dedicated to assist in purifying the collective karma of humanity, we dissolve personal barriers, we contact an abundance of energy with which to accomplish our next step. This surge of energy assists in building the light vehicle for the fourth dimensional light body, and the fifth dimensional vehicle, the light body for the collective, is wherein we know Oneness.

Remember, however, this is not a new concept; the mystical body is that entity in which we become one in group formation. Since ancient times, we have been told we are different parts of one body. (While we may call it the mystical body of Christ, it is known by other names. In Kabalah "Adam Kadmon" is the heavenly [hu]man.) The *kingdom of souls is to be the next kingdom to evolve on Earth, expected to manifest in the next cycle as an increasing number function as soul-infused beings. As humanity makes this important shift, the advanced draw others into alignment. Think of the hundredth-monkey concept, the critical mass needed for the leap forward in consciousness so often mentioned as humanity's future. The ability to sustain a higher vibration on each level attained is paramount to initiations which both humanity and the planet approach.

Awareness of the concept of planetary ascension is emerging.

> The Ascension is the evolutionary jump of the Planetary Consciousness (and its inhabitants) from one dimension to another. When planets Ascend, everyone and everything on the planet is affected, big time. Planetary Ascensions are so totally radical that as one approaches, beings that are identifying with the soon-to-be-outdated reality begin to feel very uneasy. "The End is near!" And, in a way, the end is near. The Old Way is passing. If, however, you're not attached to the old reality parameters, then the end is not the end, it's the Beginning. Ascensions happen all the time, all over the place. Now, Planet Earth seems scheduled to transform into "EarthStar", a fifth dimensional embodiment of the Christ Consciousness.[4]

Because it implies freedom from certain limitations, the concept of ascension provides exceptional hope. Being mindful of such a noble goal keeps us dedicated. Many are currently able to make such a shift (ascend), gain new awareness, and demonstrate a higher way through daily life. Yes, those who ascend the consciousness pyramid discover new perspectives at each new level; in fact, they come to know the route and resting places of their specific ways and means of traversing life.

As we honor the Self, we may be drawn easily into glorifying personality, with its ego, charms, talents, and competence. At the same time, the alternative seems to be to deny any selfhood to avoid egotism, resulting in a limiting rigidity. The solution of the paradox of self versus Self, however, is found in seeing these opposites as complementary rather than antagonistic. The Higher Third concept — an apex of a triangle with correlative opposites at the base (fig. 52) — is a valued tool for spiritual application. This apex is not a synthesis of the two, as many interpret Buddha's middle path to be. Each of the two establishes higher identification with the Source, the Absolute. As each moves closer to the Source, they find they also have moved closer to one another. The line of tension between the opposites is reduced.

> Behind every duality is a hidden Oneness, the Trinity.
> —Rudolf Steiner

The Higher Third concept is a method of reconciling opposites. Trying to solve the paradox of opposites at its own level does not work. Albert Einstein taught that no problem may be resolved at the level from which it originates. A compromise between two extremes of truth creates feelings of dissatisfaction. So we look for a higher understanding that includes the essence of each but allows each perspective to contribute from its proper place of decision-making. We may observe how both positions are correct in a particular context but not necessarily simultaneous. In contradictions related to meditation instructions, an attempt to see a higher perspective, as well as noting the relationship to levels of consciousness, often brings an intuitive answer which dissolves the conflict.

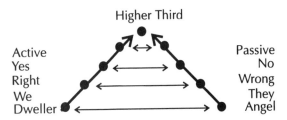

Higher Third

Active | Passive
Yes | No
Right | Wrong
We | They
Dweller | Angel

In order to settle . . . conflict, a new principle comes in, other and higher than the two conflicting instincts, and aiming both to override and to reconcile them. This third principle is the ethical ideal.
—Sri Aurobindo

Fig. 52. The Higher Third — the route of collision versus Higher Third reconciliation. This chart illustrates the opposites we encounter in life. When caught in any of them, we have difficulty making the best decision. If we can lift our consciousness to view the situation from a higher level, we often find a unique solution.

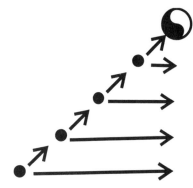

Fig. 53. Technique for Using Higher Third Principle.

The way to use this technique is to first see the maneuver.
Step 1. Opposite positions arise. Compromise may cause each to feel loss.

Step 2. Lift position to a higher level and nearer the treasured perspective. Both will feel progress is being made. Positions are closer, but without loss. Keep adding positive thought.

Step 3. Continue to focus upon unifying principles, and invoke more subtle perceptions.

Step 4. Each position moves to a more elevated perspective that allows for agreement. The new position gains much and suffers no loss. Creative thinking and respect for what each offers are the goals of this concept.

Higher consciousness would have us learn the art of negotiating, not compromise. Step by step, changes in thinking occur until the moment comes when ego resistance is no more. Those who shift now serve humanity, focusing on the Higher Plan. Ascension builds an appreciation of this dimension, its offerings, and its purpose. Remember the ascended one who said, "Lo, I am with you always." Since so many angelic beings, the Divine Mother, Masters, teachers, and saints are now appearing to humanity, we must be precious and worthy of their attention.

Now you have ascended the pyramid of techniques; hence, as a soul, your contributions are much needed. Such efforts lead to ascension and create the individual and collective rainbow bridge, an ongoing assignment. Rejoice that life has brought you this far. See with the eyes of your soul, and dare to continue. Remember, meditation is a lifetime commitment to your self and to your precious Self.

Master Djwhal Khul in *Discipleship in the New Age II* teaches, as do most traditions, that meditation gradually becomes a daily practice to continue for the rest of the student's life. However, a particular method may from time to time need to yield to more advanced techniques, seven of which are offered by The Tibetan to those who seek them.

The seven techniques Master Djwhal Khul offers presume considerable experience with seed-thought meditation and an awareness of soul alignment. Even so, the first three of these meditations enhance recapitulation and are of major importance in reestablishing the mental processes for invoking and evoking higher energy. The remaining four meditations[5] assist students to become sensitive to ashramic and triadic impressions. Students thereby qualify more rapidly for ashramic service and may become illuminated by the light of the spiritual triad — not simply by the soulstar.

The goal of the first three meditations is to bring about group unity rooted in love; this requires opening the heart center for greater potency. Since the heart center reacts only to "group impetus, group happiness or unhappiness, and other group relations,"[6] it is of ample significance in the Aquarian age.

Our meditation practice never ends for, as we become increasingly aware of inner life, we comprehend new reasons and new ways to serve. Indeed, service becomes our very reason for being.

> It is one of the most beautiful compensations of this life that no [one] can seriously help another without helping [one]self.
>
> —Ralph Waldo Emerson

Assignment

This advanced exercise for dissolving glamours and illusions as they are discovered is for mature students. Affirm your intent: *In the wisdom of soul and working as soul, it is my desire and will to eliminate from my inner and outer vehicles the obstacles, hindrances, and distractions to my true purpose.*

EXERCISE FOR DISPELLING INDIVIDUAL GLAMOURS

Disciples need to recognize recurring challenges in their lives. We decide what glamour is responsible and begin work to dispel the locked-in energy. The following technique uses soul and its energy to assist disciples in clearing personality.

TECHNIQUE OF LIGHT

As with all soul-infusion work, we begin by saying the long version of the I Am the Soul mantra:

I Am the Soul

I am the Soul,
and also love am I.
Above all else, I am
both will and fixed design.
My will is now to lift
the lower self into the Light Divine.
That Light am I.
Therefore, I must descend
to where that lower self awaits—
awaits my coming.
That which desires to lift
and that which cries for lifting
are now at one.
Such is my will.

In preparation for the clearing process:

Recognize the glamour to be worked with. Be willing to do what is needed to work in harmony with soul. Willingness must be actualized through the physical, astral, and mental levels. Deeply ponder the ways this glamour affects your personality and your relationships.

Then follow these steps:

In your mind, hold the soulstar over your head about ten inches. Focus its bright light on the mind. Then bring the light of matter (from solar plexus) up to blend with the mental light, merging the two into one.

Now focus the light of the soul with the two that have merged. We now have integrated three lights into one. Hold in meditative attention. Working as one purifying light, we have the light (intelligence) of body (solar plexus), mind (mental and soulstar), and soul as spirit.

In the first stage above, we blend soul and mind into one light, then personality, solar plexus, and mind into one light. Now we blend *all* into one light. The dedication of personality to soul (spirit direction) and the acceptance of personality by soul make this possible.

Now we pause:

We acknowledge the power of the one light of soul and prepare to turn this light upon the astral plane (not upon the body of the disciple but upon the astral plane about it where all glamours exist). The light of soul is used to burn away the connection between the seed in the disciple and the undesired attachment.

Proceed:

By creative imagination, the disciple seeks to hear the silent sound of soul sending forth its vibration — the *Om* — into the mind of the attentive personality. Personality receives and embraces the soul's outpouring and absorbs its liberating frequencies.

This vibration is embraced and generates an intense light, pictured as a searchlight of soul power to direct us. The light in the mind and the light of matter (solar plexus) are held in rapt attention.

The disciple invokes will and focus to send the energy of soul power as a light into and through the light of the mind. The mind is steadily held in the light as the glamour is recognized. Now meditate upon the reality of the glamour.

Next, the awareness that attachment restricts the life of the disciple is perceived — a most significant realization. A sincere desire to recognize it for what it is dawns upon the disciple. The realization that this attachment is no longer needed occurs. Choose liberation.

Now with keen concentration, the disciple, clear in consciousness, turns on the searchlight of soul and visualizes a broad beam of light streaming forth, piercing the glamour. The beam comes from soul to mind, and through mind to the glamour on the astral plane. Mind aligns to soul's purpose and sets itself free.

We Now Offer Two Techniques of Power

In the first, the disciple names the glamour and watches it dissipate. In the second, an important innovation results by identifying the desired quality and affirming it. Both methods are of value. Choose the appropriate one, according to the needs of a given situation.

The *first* is to dissipate glamour. Speak with will and focus:

The power of the light dissolves the congealed form of the glamour: _____ (name it: self-pity, fear, anger, manipulation).

The power of the light negates the quality of the glamour and sets me free.

The power of the light releases the life behind the glamour, dissolving the old form and freeing the energy, now to be used constructively.

In the *second,* the disciple recognizes the glamour and transforms it into a more desired quality, neutralizing the negative aspect. Speak with will and focus:

The power of the light affirms the appearance of the positive quality: _____ (name it: confidence, love, harmlessness, selflessness).

The power of the light affirms the positive quality of _____ and brings forth new awareness.

The power of the light affirms new life, new light, and new love within my being.

In this technique, soul and personality operate "as if" they are a working unit. Utilizing the power of soul to transform the nature of personality by bequeathing to it a quantity of its own energy, this infusion cancels negatives and emphasizes the spiritual facet to be developed.

The purpose of these powerful exercises is to use soul awareness by means of intuition, a faster process than natural evolution. We could say, conscious growth rather than unconscious.

Lightning Flashes:
Intuition and Illumination

As we wander, we change. The pilgrim who arrives
at the sacred place is not the same man who left home.
The seeker who returns to her family or tribe,
bringing gifts of power, healing, or vision,
is a transformed individual.
—Ralph Metzner, *Opening to Inner Light*

We turn in summary to one final seed thought, "illumination," and rejoice in its revelations. To conclude our journey, we must discuss intuition. Both words — intuition and illumination — encompass the essence of all our efforts. As we become better aligned to our soul, we draw closer to illumination; as we realize the ultimate nature of the themes and virtues we have penetrated; we grow increasingly sensitive to intuitive guidance — "straight knowledge," it is called. So it is fitting to conclude with these complementary topics.

What Is Intuition?

Each description of meditation attempts to fit this beyond-words experience into words. It is of course difficult to describe the indescribable. You probably agree, we must be intuitive to fathom what intuition is! It is so beyond intellect. Words contain meanings that stretch beyond their ordinary definition, so we use the language of symbolism and metaphor, a poetic approximation rather than literal definition.

It is valuable to identify what we mean when we try to use our intuition. Some teachers encourage developing (more correctly, opening to) intuition; some are satisfied with saying it is a vague way of knowing, affirming that some people seem to possess it more than others. One writer, Mouni Sadhu, bluntly states, we have it or we do not, that its presence is due to past incarnations, not anything in this life.[1]

If intuition really is the awareness of a higher, subtler level of self, or soul, then we all must have it. So, herein we orient our thinking. Knowing it is available to all, we acknowledge that people differ, primarily in the ability to recognize intuitive awareness. It is not a matter of having it or not, rather the degree of our experience with it and our ease of access to it.

We commonly recognize intuition as a hunch, an inspiration or flow of creativity, a sensing, basic instinct, gut reaction, flying by the seat of our pants, playing it by ear, an inner knowing without visible proof. While companies use computers and other data analysis procedures to reach objective decisions, executives study results and may proceed contrary to any objective decision — calling it "visceral override." Many of us act similarly when we know that we know but cannot say rationally how we arrived at this clear knowing.

Sadhu[2] calls intuition "cognition without thinking," or beyond the rational thinking process of mind. Assagioli[3] (a colleague of Jung and Freud in early psychoanalytic studies and a student of Agni Yoga) terms intuition a "sense organ for discovering analogies and promoting creativity." Humphreys[4] and Saraydarian[5] see intuition as representing the wisdom of our "Knower" on a higher plane, one of purer knowledge. This knower does not need mental processes to reach a conclusion or to provide information. As someone once said, "I know it with my Knower."

We can view the concept of straight knowing as a lightning flash, an illumination of cognitive mind by higher mind or by soul. If we consider the astral the feeling nature and each higher chakra more refined than the previous, we could say the highest level is where we *feel and know* with the essence of Self, a knowingness which feels exactly right: intuition — the faculty of spiritual knowledge reflected through higher feelings. Remember, behind emotion lives feeling, and behind intellect, knowing. Since intuition includes both, it resounds with uncommon clarity.

Our definitions of intuition, or straight-knowing, leave a lot unanswered. However, intuition is not a specific, isolated something within us. While it is related intimately to many aspects of our nature, clearly the closest relationship is to the feelings. We usually express intuitive insights as feelings — we feel and somehow know something to be so. This sensitivity seems connected with an increased openness to processing emotion, which in turn keeps us clearer and improves our ability to respond to our wiser level.

From levels of self and the interplay between them and maya, glamour, and illusions, let us construct a new image.

Current interest in right-brain functions has led to new ways of stimulating this awareness and processing. Creativity and the use of imagination are distinctly linked to this whole process of freeing us from limitations imposed by intellectual approaches and old programming. Those who seem to be clearer of restriction — societal, emotional, or mental — appear more intuitive and better able to connect unrelated pieces of data into a meaningful whole. Creative people tend to have a perceptual openness. Because

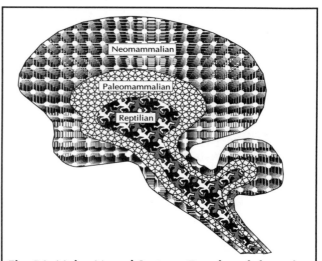

Fig. 54. Major Neural Systems Developed throughout Evolution. "Paul MacLean and his medical associates at the National Institute of Health's laboratory of brain evolution and behavior derived this description of neural systems through a synthesis of research from their own and other major centers, such as those headed by Karl Pribram and Wilder Penfield.* These three structures in our skulls represent the major neural systems developed throughout evolutionary history, through which we inherit all accomplishments that preceded and led to us, plus, may I add, a quantum-leap of additional potential we have not yet developed," Joseph Chilton Pearce has determined.

*Reprints of many of MacLean's works are available from the Laboratory of Brain Evolution and Behavior, National Institute of Health, Bethseda, MD 20014.[6]

of this, they are often more aware of various aspects of a situation, or intuitively attuned to wholeness.

Joseph Chilton Pearce has been most brilliant in his explanation of brain development and leads the field in explaining evolution's goal: divine beings. His book, *Evolution's End: Claiming the Potential of Our Intelligence,*[7] is highly recommended. A variation of his illustration regarding this helps us see stages of growth as reptilian, mammalian, neocortex, with evolution pressing us toward the development of prefrontal lobes.

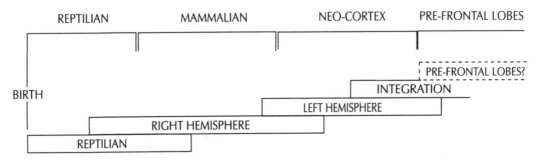

Fig. 55. The Brain in Evolution.

Intuition synthesizes, and a heart and mind united speak of a single-pointed reality. A powerful moment of truth dawns; it registers in consciousness, and we know. We say *we feel,* and at the same time *we know we know.* However, if we do not build the receiver set, transcendental knowing will never come. We remain locked into the ring-pass-not, the darkness of programming, old pain, or rational mind. This limitation seeks to make the material/physical the principal purpose of life. Because life will not be restricted in such a way, some turn in frustration against higher truth.

Openness with meditation begins the creation of a cup, or chalice, ready to catch droplets that precipitate into the receptive mind. When distortion is minimal, these droplets, or insights, register more clearly. People accustomed to gathering information in this way learn the sensation intuition imparts and generally accept such impressions more readily than others more rationally inclined.

While sensitivity to our feeling nature expedites the process, excessively powerful emotion may block the flow of intuitive ideas and inspirations. Intense emotionalism creates barriers to subtle feelings and dominates our attention, preventing the open perspective necessary for the intuitive process. Scars of past experiences block our perception. Thus, excess emotion and residue from past experiences must be cleansed and healed to support the synthesis needed for creative awareness to serve us.

Strongly held thoughtforms and emotionally charged memories, glamours, and illusions, as well as addictions, must be addressed before intuition flows easily. These barriers hold us captive until we respond with the purification work demanded by every path, though different in specifics. Lessons to be learned blend into the foundation of all spiritual disciplines.

Prior to the removal of barriers to awakening, the psychic level fluctuates between clarity and distortion, so it is often not to be trusted, except through careful discernment. Hard to fathom, this reflective, astral nature is quite a mystery, especially to the beginner. As careful training of psychic abilities, purification of our nature, and the development of discernment integrate, we acknowledge changes within and discover our spiritual senses speak much more clearly as a result of our efforts.

Let us recall: *psyche* means "of the soul," and indeed it is well accepted that personality can be assisted to reflect the light of higher consciousness more clearly. Flashes of straight knowing may be fairly clear in certain areas of our lives — usually where the fewest barriers or wounds persist. If, however, we have a great deal yet to learn in a given area, our unfinished business, we are apt to find our imagination creates havoc here. Scars of earlier experiences or old fears reflect in our feeling nature as readily as higher knowing, so it is wise not to trust all impressions. We readily remember when our impressions proved incorrect, and this makes us hesitate. At other times, we know our flashes are accurate, or soon discover so.

As we dissolve barriers, we increase the lucidity of our feeling nature, and much of the dichotomy is solved. Visualizations and other exercises strengthen cooperation between conscious mind and the knower as it attempts to guide us. We learn how to register

A Dream of Priceless Treasure

Martin Buber, the Jewish philosopher, enjoyed sharing a Hassidic parable that today's seekers would do well to heed. The story concerns a rabbi who lived in the ghetto of Cracow, the capital of Poland. He was very poor, his life was hard, but he was a faithful servant of the Lord his God.

One night the rabbi was told in a dream to travel to far-off Prague, the capital of Bohemia, where he was to dig for a buried treasure under a large bridge leading to the castle of the king. At first he ignored the dream, but after it recurred twice more, he gathered his courage and set off for Prague.

When the rabbi reached the bridge, he found it guarded day and night. He could only come daily, look over the bridge, watch the guards, and cautiously examine the soil. One day, the captain of the guards asked why he came every day. Being an honest man and quite naive, the rabbi told him of the dream. The guard broke into a great laugh, "You poor, ignorant man. No sane person would trust such a stupid dream! If I were so ridiculous as to follow my dreams, I would today be wandering futilely about Poland. I dreamed I was summoned to Cracow to dig for treasure behind the stove of a poor rabbi. Wouldn't that be the most useless thing to be doing in the whole world?"

Stunned by what he heard, the rabbi thanked the friendly captain and hurried home. As he dug in the neglected corner of his poor house, behind the stove he found the treasure that put an end to his misery.

This parable reminds us that the power of God and of Good is often nearby, but it seems a part of spiritual life to make a pilgrimage or journey to a distant place to discover valuable teachings of another culture or faith. To hate the journey or to ignore the inner voice may be the surest way to live in poverty, while precious treasure is close at hand. We may need the journey, a shift in consciousness, or a friendly guide to discover the riches that lay within.

Fig. 56. A Dream of Priceless Treasure.

impressions more readily and how to comprehend the signals and language of the inner self and the body. We learn to feel, see, or hear with the extended senses we cultivate consciously.

So we resolve to encourage our growth by doing two kinds of work. First, we consistently continue clearing, cleansing, and healing. We could call this diligently polishing the glass. We become conscientiously mindful of eliminating glamours and illusions as they emerge. Second, we learn how to use our extended or astral senses, just as we once learned how to use our physical senses. Our own nature contributes much to our subtler levels of development.

As we focus in new ways, much happens because we are all "naturally" psychic, although we have not been encouraged to believe so. As these levels bloom and flash their messages, we perceive and translate in accordance with our clarity and our efforts. If we are less naturally inclined, developmental practices help us clarify and more clearly comprehend what we sense. Dreams, metaphors, symbols, and the discovery of arche-types give meaning to subtler impressions. Our dreams become messages to be explored, impressions are contemplated, synchronicities examined, and life is viewed as a rich tapestry of many levels of consciousness interacting.

As we learn the language of symbolism, we learn to relate to our sensations, which in turn stimulates other sensing processes. Then tools such as astrology and numerology introduce us to concepts of detailed, subtle influences interacting. All of these connect in the psyche to expand our comprehension of the Great Life of which we are a part.

Imagination and intuition have similarities and differences. While imagination often designates the creation of alternative ways of dealing with situations or a flow of fantasies to satisfy desires, it may be directed toward specific goals as well. The term "image-making ability" suggests the real purpose of imagination and how it may be used. Our image-making ability is an expression of our divinity. *Made in the image and likeness of our Creator,* we too are invested with creative powers. We are entrusted with the ability to choose and shape life in wondrous ways. Imagination is a tool to cherish and to master.

Similarly, we all have had fearful moments when our imagi-nation preyed upon our fears, producing one dreaded drama after another. All the bad things that could possibly happen come to mind, flash after flash. But we do not have to allow this abuse. When these pictures start to roll like a reel of film, we must be wise enough to recognize our unexpressed fears are taking over and parading across our mindscreen. As we realize what is happening, we may refuse to accept this as intuition and openly acknowledge our fears. This provides a degree of relief and a renewed sense of the rational. In other words, we can face fears and invoke spirit help as we make the psychospiritual effort needed to free ourselves from the fears that arise. We need to do this for our psychological well-being, not just for more clarity in "sensing," although that is a wonderful result.

Intuition contains an element of *knowing* something to be, when compared to insights obtained during meditation or psychotherapy. While recounting past experiences and emotions, the client in therapy suddenly sees an important relationship, a meaning, or connection. When tears accompany this, we assume the negative emotional charge has been lessened or released. From this point on, such areas will be viewed from a new position. This flash of insight can be called *knowing with the Knower.*

Certain sensitive abilities — such as esp or the art of attuning to another individual (also called "reading") — appear to be related to intuition. The process for improving this sensitivity, as we will see in the *how-to* section of this lesson, has many similarities to the meditation process. In fact, meditation naturally encourages and prepares us to receive straight knowledge through intuition.

The use of *koans[8] (paradoxes) and meditation (such as the Higher Third technique[9]) requires reliance upon intuition — going beyond intellect and duality to "something more," "jumping into the abyss" to reach solutions. A classic koan is "What is the sound of one hand clapping?" The Higher Third method is a Buddhist concept whereby a duality is best seen as a *unity* from which two opposing factors spring (good/bad, cause/effect).

Intuition has been studied for many years by psychologists and other scientists. They call it "brain flash" when studying brain functions, or "inner visions," and "creativity" when they see it as the ability to know how to respond in complicated situations without being able to explain how. Scientists might use the word "inventiveness" comfortably enough.

> What has traditionally been labeled as extrasensory or as paranormal (intuition) is a universal human capacity which most people haven't chosen to exercise or develop.
>
> —Bill Kautz, *Portrait of a Prophet,* Omni

An outstanding prototype for studying intuition is found in the skill of Japanese chicken sexors.[10] Day-old male and female chicks ordinarily are not distinguishable, yet a sexor can accurately identify the sex of 1400 chicks an hour without looking at their sexual organs — with 98 to 99 percent accuracy. It is not known how they do it, but others have been able to learn this art by watching over the sexors' shoulders for a period of time — about three months.

Ancient mystery schools taught, as do the ashrams of the East, that the spiritual disciple is to be under a teacher's tutelage for an extended period of time. Such training consists of being together during meditation practices, even sitting together in absolute quiet, as well as to exchange information. The belief in energy transference and attunements occurring on subtler levels comprises an important part of the process. I would like to explain two valuable concepts with regard to creating just such an energy bubble to assist personal development.

The first relates to group meditation. When a group oversoul is being formed, if three participants have achieved an advanced level of initiation — open to soul/solar angel — they act as transformers and step down the energy to benefit the entire group. Members of such a group progress more readily in sensitivity practices than if meditating without proficient ones present.

> *We are all "naturally" psychic,*
> *although we have not been*
> *encouraged to believe so.*

The second is that when we place ourselves in a highly charged spiritual setting for three days and nights (sleeping in the energy bubble), significant opportunity for inner progress may occur. Leaders and teachers consciously create a unique environment for spiritual work by invoking spiritual forces and surrendering to holy and healing energies. In early ashrams, temples, and *abashkarels,* such techniques to assist a change of consciousness were sought deliberately. We are relearning the power of rituals and the skill of invoking energy consciously. Spiritual power becomes more real to us as our mind expands.

Thus, intuition appears to be a psychological — better said, a psychospiritual — function, a skill that may be learned. As we become more expert, we leave linear thinking behind and shift to viewing situations in their entirety. Psychologists agree with metaphysicians that conscious (intellectual) and unconscious (intuitive) activities complementing each other achieve the most effective functioning. Add regular spiritual practices to this, and we may glimpse some of the experiences of mystics who have provided guidance for humanity for centuries.

Today, many think humanity is rapidly advancing along a continuum from intellect to intuition as it learns coordinated right-left–brain interaction. In due time, we will develop the next brain, a new form now identified as the prefrontal lobe. Many believe this "new brain" — which will facilitate intuition and creativity in an advanced, new way of thinking — is to be realized by humanity.

Usually teachers suggest intuition works on two levels: day-to-day and spiritual. Intuition seems to pertain more clearly to areas of personal interest. We all have realizations or intuitive flashes that integrate pieces of information. We suddenly know just how a circumstance will turn out, or we realize a concept rings true at every level of our perception. Deep within our personality, we grasp a specific reality, and in a flash it integrates.

As these flashes occur, we begin to gain additional insight into life's grand truths. These flashes key us into impersonal soul patterns or realizations of truth relating to our greater life. Difficult to explain, these inner knowings are often insights to realities, principles, or even spiritual laws that elude easy integration. Due to its powerful legacy, we refer to a flash which brings such comprehension as "illumination." For a brief period the mind opens, the new reality registers, and an entire area of life is illumined.

The lesser level of psychism is confined largely to hunches and feelings — impressions pertaining to personality and its goals. Spiritual intuition reveals a broader cognizance of the true nature of reality and soul purpose. Assagioli believes we repress such functioning because it is not readily recognized or appreciated. Characteristics of an intuitive response distinguish it from linear thinking or feeling. It is immediate and direct, rather than deductive and progressive, as in reasoning. It is synthesized and holistic, not comprising parts we assemble later. It plainly presents itself and simply is straight knowing: "This is so."

Although many spiritual teachings postulate that moving from intellect to intuition is the goal of human consciousness, most agree we should not abandon intellect for intuition in all areas of life. The use of intuition has certain dangers and limitations, the most common being the difficulties encountered in distinguishing it from feelings and desires. Emotions are connected with instinct (conditioned responses) and intuition with clear knowing. The intensity of psychic knowing may be a product of fear, desire, unconscious drives, convictions, assumptions, or numerous ego needs, while, in fact, clear knowing does not depend upon such emotional reinforcement.

We reduce the danger of confusing emotions and intuition by seeking verification of our hunches and impressions through common sense — a combination of our feelings (pro and con), intellect, and experiences. We learn to avoid plunging ahead blindly to act on intuitive responses, assuming we are "more spiritual" or somehow "better" by doing so. We choose to evaluate the impression in an objective manner. Discrimination and discernment are also valuable tools of spirit provided to the receiver.

A wise teacher, Torkom Saraydarian, pointed out additional dangers. He believed blind stimulation of intuition may lead to development of ego rather than spirit. The nonself may profit by quick, direct insights, and personality may become resistant to doing the work required to dissolve its barriers. However, if used correctly, intuition provides a quick response to a real need in others and in ourselves without distortion by personality factors, because the intuitive level deals directly with the world of wisdom. Saraydarian also stressed the need for corroboration of decisions by consciousness and reason.

Having a trusted sounding board as we gain experience saves much misery. Mentors are useful in all fields of endeavor, and certainly the more uncharted the territory, the more beneficial they are. After gaining experience, we have less need of another's supervision. While it is certainly idealistic to believe we may become so in tune that we can intuit all the information we need for daily life, it is unrealistic. Let us always be wise enough to use trusted mentors, counselors, or therapists when needed.

The unique human nature is designed for multiple levels of life at once. The physical mechanism, with its responsibility for our autonomic processes and survival, belongs to the subconscious or basic nature, as do automatic emotional responses. Right and left hemispheres of the brain (the neocortex) balance mental capabilities with wholeness for the developing human personality. Certainly human life regulated by time and logic needs left-hemisphere skills; and we truly need the skills of *a relationship to the all* which the right hemisphere provides.

Development of increased creativity or a new mental mechanism, the prefrontal lobe, may be the instrument we are currently developing for an evolved, elevated expression of intuition. Many believe it is. Meditation and creative endeavors seem to augment the skill; intuition may be establishing a stronger base within our individual consciousness as we expand levels of awareness. All spiritual teachings suggest disciples are guided by "spirit"; we must ask how. The spirit within us seeks to refine our nature to fit more harmoniously with the great scheme of things. Our intuitive skills develop as the spirit part of our nature is accepted as real and meaningful. Now we can accept its guidance.

As we learn to receive our intuitive flashes and then take time to weigh our choices, we become more capable of responding appropriately. If we do not acknowledge and respond, we avoid accountability, perhaps claiming or blaming an outside force rather than aligning to a new level of self.

Use of intuition results in a release of energy which requires self-discipline. We all know quite creative people who dash in all directions at once and perpetually, or they plunge blindly into situations on the basis of a hunch. Intuition gives us a sense of direction; however, we also learn it is wise to wait for additional indications that the direction is accurate. This methodology allows us to integrate the gifts of both our rational and our sensing capabilities. In this way, we become truly whole, honoring our potential to be fully human and fully divine.

As we do our meditation practice, we regularly place our personality in the presence of the higher nature that is designed to provide additional energies on our behalf. Let us think of this as placing our maturing, in-process self in direct exposure to an energy beam. At a passive meditation level, this encourages receptivity between personality and High Self; at an active meditation level, we expose personality to the impact of solar angel. Once we have experienced the first initiation — birth of the Christ-Within — we labor to adapt personality to evolving this presence under the guidance of solar angel.

As we advance through our levels of growth, we also want to continue to be exposed to the love, light, and power of the Higher. As we subtly evolve, life's mysteries become clearer. We affirm, "I am the soul" (the human soul as the evolving Christ-Within), and we gladly stand in the presence of the solar angel, who knows the Plan and consistently vibrates (transmits) it to the edge of our developing mind. Regular exposure to such powerful influences acts upon the mindstuff, organizing our mental mechanism to perceive how to align with our purpose and the part of humanity's work in which we can participate.

If we would be world servers, we have three duties to perform:

- Cultivate intuition as the light of wisdom (knowing). In order to relate to higher will and purpose, all things must be seen in proportion: from the higher perspective, or God's Will.

- Similarly, we must unfold compassion (love-wisdom) to have the gnosis to link our aligned nature to the great heart. Only then may divine L-O-V-E link us individually (and collectively) to the larger universe.

- To achieve these goals we must each learn how to adapt and interface the lesser self — that part which evolves through interactions: physical, emotional, and mental — to the Mind of God.

So we see the advancing light as, first, information; second, knowledge; then third, wisdom to be used to realize our divine potential. As we add love, we become the one who can express love in its four manifestations: agape, humanitarian, philias, eros. Remembering, we acknowledge the power of choice: our will versus higher will, the option of good or not-so-good, only to evolve to choose between good and good and then to totally align our will to the Plan of the Creator. This entire process is to fulfill our goal — *intelligent love* — so we may advance on the path of conscious return.

How to Open to Intuition

When a man literally walks in the light of his soul and the clear light of the sun pours through him — revealing the path — it reveals at the same time the Plan. Simultaneously however he becomes aware of the fact that the Plan is very far as yet from consummation. The dark becomes more truly apparent; the chaos and misery and failure of world groups stand revealed; the filth and dust of the warring forces are noted, and the whole sorrow of the world bears down upon the astounded, yet illuminated aspirant. Can he stand this pressure? Can he become indeed acquainted with grief and yet rejoice forever in the divine consciousness? Has he the ability to face what the light reveals, and still go his way with serenity, sure of the ultimate triumph of good? Will he be overwhelmed by the surface evil and forget the heart of love which beats behind all outer seeming? This situation should ever be remembered by the disciple, or he will be shattered by what he has discovered.

—Alice A. Bailey

Meditation so stimulates our intuition, a thorough knowledge of it is certainly helpful. It is useful to improve our intuitive abilities for reasons we have mentioned. While each of us has these experiences sporadically and spontaneously, consciously cultivating the on-and-off experience may leave us feeling uncertain. With systematic attention to the process and its effects, we discover our senses do receive information on what works best for us. We must ascertain how our chosen methodology provides impressions.

Conscious participants upon the spiritual path aspire to make frequent and clearer contacts with the inner self. By accepting inner guidance and evaluating it, we become more sensitive to our deeper levels and how our inner communication functions.

We may receive a variety of data intuitively: information about ourselves, others, and situations; verification of knowledge received from an outside source; information regarding decisions; evaluations, such as acceptance or rejection, rightness or wrongness; a feeling for the direction of flow of events, thoughts, feelings; or alteration of feeling tone.

Our **rational mind** serves like a road map. We choose our destination, chart a course, mark our map, and travel forth. We can explain the route we take.

Intuition, however, is more like boarding an airplane. We take off, reach altitude, and soon land. We need not know the route, for we are in the hands of the pilot.

Neither method changes the destination. Both routes get us there, but our experience of the journeys differs greatly.

Fig. 57. Rational Mind and Intuition.

The effectiveness of any training that helps us become more intuitive depends largely upon our attitudes and expectations. Some teachers feel we have no control over intuition, but we can learn how to seek out and react to whatever comes. We can expand receptivity *and* the recognition of those flashes as they occur.

Years of teaching intuitive development classes have convinced me everyone has this innate ability, but we do not always recognize how it functions or when it communicates. Experimenting with various approaches with an experienced guide seems necessary in most cases (remember the chicken sexors). Master teachers sense some part of the Plan and work for and with their students until they sense it for themselves.

Ways of Thinking about Intuition

Whatever process we use to become more intuitive, our success is influenced strongly by our own attitudes and assumptions about this fledgling aspect of our nature. Here are keys to consider.

Be willing to accept guidance from within. To the degree we identify with body and ego, we tend to distrust anything inconsistent with ego's goals. It is human nature to limit possibilities to what we have already accepted as possible and in most cases already know. If we have low self-esteem, we may start with the assumption that we cannot do this, or that nothing worthy or reliable can emerge from us. So it may be necessary to clear some of the existing barriers in order to develop a positive attitude and the willingness to receive information not generated by ego or old programming.

Too often, people with low self-esteem tend to feel that any good which comes from within must belong to another intelligence (spirit guide, teacher, or spirit), but they claim any "error" as their own. We must be pleased to receive guidance and *allow the source to be our higher intelligence* or inner self until there is reason to believe otherwise.

Expect variability in your progress. Subtleties within the complexities of our nature may inhibit flow of communication at any given moment, so delicate sensitivity will fluctuate with time and circumstance. In other words, when we are settled and peaceful, we are more likely to receive valuable insights. When we are anxious or pressured, impressions may become quite distorted. The centering skills we have built help, but these need to be combined with healing areas of anxiety and dissolving barriers.

Expect confidence to build gradually, using whatever emerges from within. Counting your blessings helps, as does developing a deep sense of how loved you are by the universe. Know you are among the privileged to have earned the opportunity you find available. If the Lords of Karma love you so, welcome it. Rejoice!

Learn to recognize the quality of response as an indication of true intuition. The Source gives calm and impersonal but compassionate information and awareness. When this happens a few times, reliability to identify the subtle quality of messages from the Source can be developed. By journaling, we track our intuitive messages and feelings.

Realize that widely different states of feelings and attitudes affect intuitive responses. Tension and stress, even fear and desperation, may produce astonishing creativity, especially when our survival is involved. At other times, these same feelings may block the process. The peacefulness of meditation may generate a flow of inner communication. Flashes of intuition from stress tend to be spontaneous and intermittent, while responses from a calm mind regularly attuned are more consistent. This becomes increasingly apparent to the more experienced.

Just as necessity is the mother of invention, we find when we must know, it comes. This pressured awareness may result in wear and tear on the physical body, while more centered and regular meditation seems to foster physical well-being. Indeed, extreme sensitivity prevails when we are threatened, under stress, or highly anxious, as well as at the other extreme of deep peace. *It is preferable to explore this new skill while in a calm state,* even though a deadline or demanded response often provides enough tension to make impressions happen.

Be willing to accept whatever impressions come, while seeking to be open. Save judgment until later. As we embrace new creativity, we do not need a critic standing by. In fact, the more fun our experience is, with no sense of being judged, the more accurate we tend to be.

Practice without evaluating results at the same session. Practice will be fun when we maintain an attitude of lightheartedness conducive to results. Too much seriousness may spring from the effort to excel over others or to obtain skill for increased power — clearly ego domination.

Allow the revelation of the messages to evolve. Do not try too hard. Accept what you receive, and let it lie. Closely related to unconditional love, allowing is a significant part of the process. Allow thoughts, feelings, and knowing to just flow. Relax, receive, and savor impressions to recognize their gifts, not unlike symbology interpretation in dream study.

Consciously endeavor to *trust directions or answers given* to you. This does not mean to blindly accept or to avoid looking at them in the light of common sense. We are not punished for questions or for not following a hunch, so we are free to be open, to wait and see, as we build a confident attitude that we are receiving good responses, not discounting any answer.

After receiving an impression, *take time to see how it fits you:* Does it conform to your high principles? What will be the effects of following your intuition? How might that change your life? What are the various interpretations that can be weighed? How do you "feel" about the advice? How does it differ from solutions you have already considered? How can you verify its accuracy? Are there other steps which allow you to determine how the impressions relate to your usual way of thinking — feelings with which you are comfortable — and to your spiritual principles?

Be open and willing to look at your feelings and preconceptions about the situation you are exploring or the messages you receive. In this way we prevent discrediting our intuition through distorted feelings or preconceptions.

Remember, we can *return again to the inner source* with the same question. If we are given a different answer, this does not mean the first one was not right. It may have been all we could accept at that time, or it may mean the ego has had time to influence the response. It may indicate we need to explore further — or to just let it go for now.

Expect answers. A wavering attitude or serious doubt may make communication difficult. Remember, a part of us, as an extension of infinite creation, knows. Each piece of the hologram contains the entire hologram.

When you receive information quite different from what you expected, *look at your assumptions* about what "ought" to be. If we develop as broad a perspective as possible, we are more receptive to more areas of life, and our evaluations are more effective.

When you look for guidance from the intuitive level, hold in your mind that you *seek the best answers for all concerned.* This tends to weed out ego influences that distort.

Release preconceived notions about how an answer will come to you. Form varies considerably. It may be an inner voice; it may be visual images, dreams, or symbols, or comments made by another person or on a TV program. It is the response from within for which we wait, a sign we have come to identify through experience as our own way of receiving.

Remember, the final decision — the choice of what to do — is our own (if action is appropriate). In tune with our highest good, our intuitive level will never force us. High consciousness has complete respect for free will — ours and that of others.

Approaches to
Improve Openness to Intuition

Preparation for intuition is similar to creating a foundation for meditation. Some trained sensitives refer to this calming and centering time as meditation. Think of it as a time of releasing attention on other matters so a shift to a point of receptivity can occur. Physical relaxation and a quiet mind are basic requisites. You already have awareness techniques for doing this, so they will not be repeated here.

From here on, the process is similar to passive meditation, except the goal is becoming receptive to the voice of intuition, or whatever we might call our contact. It is not unlike tuning in to a particular radio station. Say what it is you seek, dialogue with your inner self, and ask to be given what you need or are open to at this time.

In other words, mentally or aloud, say something like, "I am now receptive to the inner part of me which knows. I am ready to accept guidance as needed for this time." Then quietly wait. Your insight may come immediately; other times it may be delayed or come slowly and piecemeal. Sometimes nothing comes, but having done this, you *will* receive the response later at an unexpected time and place. It will pop into your head as you walk down the street or take out the trash, or it may appear in a dream or in a book, and you recognize that word or message is in response to your request.

A similar approach is to attempt to just be or just blend with the Oneness, allowing the impression of response to form in its own way and time. You do not need to develop sending or asking skills. Just focus on building the receiver end of the communication process, then wait patiently.

"Building the cup" requires being receptive time and time again. Doing our part means taking the posture, becoming quiet, relaxing, and waiting, allowing the cup to form and the droplets to rain down. We do this each time we meditate, so we are participating in the ever-evolving process already.

To deal with a specific problem area, hold it gently in your mind, as if offering the total problem to a higher "someone." This is not "dumping" the issue but merely holding it, trusting that what is needed will come. We generally call this, "holding it in the light" or "in our consciousness." We hold the challenge lightly in mind, doing nothing "to it." As we image holding an object in our open palm, offering it up to solutions we do not have to form, we surrender it to a higher power.

As we stay open and nonjudgmental, our act becomes a prayer directed to our Inner Source. We need not ask for specific results, but by holding our request in consciousness, in time an answer begins to form. The key is in the gentle awareness of a love which allows all happenings and a complete knowing that insights emerge with right timing. Note the dichotomy of focus at one end of the spectrum and complete resting with it at the other.

Many intuitions are fleeting and easily forgotten. Even vivid impressions slip away, just as dreams may fade quickly upon waking. This is not surprising since we are usually in a slightly altered state of consciousness when impressions come. To assist in relating these to conscious mind, write down your impressions immediately. You already have experience in recording impressions from your seed-thought meditations. This aids in recall — short- and long-term — and provides a basis for evaluation, corroboration, and other interpretations which lend credence to what we receive over a period of time. If we do not record our guidance, we tend to recall only pieces and may lose significant information. Those valuable, often subtle feelings that accompany impressions are easily lost. Try to capture all these specifics in your notes.

Intuitive development classes stimulate creative communication; the best provide an environment for you to proceed with a spiritual ethic to guide your progress. Many spiritual teachers choose not to teach intuitive or psychic development without corresponding study in spirituality and/or the ethics of a chosen path.

As you work with these procedures, you will notice changes. In a short time, you will not need as much formal preparation in order to make contact. You can sit quietly and hold a mental conversation. Answers will pop into your head often before you have completed your question. Do not be shy about asking probing questions that expand your perception of what is being discussed. When you do not understand, explain what is puzzling you. Sometimes it helps to talk out loud to God as you take a walk — a kind of prayerful request or dialogue. You may find you receive an answer or new knowledge, but the signal to act has not yet come. Be willing to wait.

To confirm, evaluate, and interpret an insight, look at its aspects from intellectual, emotional, and practical points of view. Does it coincide with other things you have learned? Does it represent the highest ethical or spiritual principles? What is your emotional reaction to it? You may wish to check the insight with other familiar intuitive approaches — the pendulum, Shustah or tarot cards. You may want to return to a problem several times before taking action. You may use a seed-thought type of exploration of key words and themes in the impression. (Remember to create an impersonal seed thought.) A complex situation may take time to work out — perhaps in stages. Continue to monitor it, relative to impressions you had and continue to have. Seek the wisdom of a trusted advisor, but the responsibility for decision-making and responding is yours.

Do not be in a rush to identify the source of guidance and impressions with a particular entity. As we do these lessons, we are developing sensitivity to our own Knower. Alignment to soul is practiced regularly, hopefully daily, strengthening the bond between personality and soul. And, remember, intuition is not a substitute for thinking and common sense but a way of consciously deepening and broadening our responses to life.

We must keep our purpose in mind: to establish contact between the divine spark within our being and the Christ, teacher of angels and of humanity. We seek to strengthen our link to enable us to align our lives increasingly with the Lord Christ. We continue to work on areas that require healing (dissolving barriers). Thus personality transforms into an increasingly clearer vessel through which high consciousness expresses.

Dissolving barriers to light, love, and power, soul releases more energy as impediments are removed. Its subtle energy is called "joy." As we improve the inner connection, personality transforms; soul advances on the path of initiation. Illumined by higher awareness, personality aligns to a larger portion of the true self.

Most of us have been impressed, guided, or urged by a force that proved beneficial. In this personal and subtle way, we already know something about the power of spiritual reality.

Other types of encounters may occur. From time to time, some receive an impression of a spiritual name. Retain the name in writing; you may find it useful in aligning again to a particular spiritual level of self. Receiving a name does not necessarily mean you have a guide or teacher to contact; it may be a code or key for attuning to your own higher nature. Most do not realize this may be an introduction, let us call it, from our vibration at a spiritual level to our personality at the denser level. Before making assumptions, we need to spend time working with any name we receive to determine its purpose.

By developing our relationship to the Knower, we might say, we are realigning to the true self. Channeling the energy of another entity is quite different than becoming aligned to our soul and allowing what it knows to enter our consciousness. Spiritual initiation is a process of soul maturity—the goal of our humanness.

When we open to soul awareness and the energies of soul flow into personality, our own consciousness expands and emanates its wisdom. This is known as the teaching consciousness. It is easily entered by some, especially those who are seeking to realize their soul purpose. Often this experience occurs naturally in the midst of teaching and is evinced by "bringing through" previously unknown (to the conscious mind) information. When this happens, the "teacher" learns along with the listeners.

Such an occurrence depends upon a harmonization of the vibration of personality and soul and assists in building a closer rapport between the two. It feels similar to the attunement made in seed-thought work and, in fact, seed-thought work prepares us for easy access to our wiser level. This kind of shift can be controlled at will and may be beneficial to the host or others if ego identity is not a factor. An expression or style becomes recognizable.

Here, a name may be given for the altered point of consciousness to designate it as of a certain a vibration. Many call this a "soul name"; it is not meant to be taken as a new outer name, though at times such error is made. The heightened vibration of this name, when used at personality level or in everyday life, usually brings complications to the outer life; it is not considered part of a middle-road path but acts more to hasten the demise of personality. This is the reason new names are taken when one enters a convent, monastery, or ashram, where personality is denied in order to focus upon the spiritual self.

Concerns about channeling are many among spiritual teachers. Assorted phenomena occur under that term. Originally the word indicated that the consciousness of each plane could become a channel for a higher point of one's true nature. It was not thought of as serving another entity but to provide a channel for the grace of soul, among other attributes, to flow into human life.

Distinguishing Channeling from Seed-Thought Meditation

As we become more capable of extending our awareness into the vastness of the mental plane, we find we are also able to contact other intelligences, as well as the Cloud of Knowable Things. Part of the higher-wisdom training of the initiate includes learning to discriminate between channeling other intelligences and connecting with the higher mind of which every soul is a part.

At each level of our development, we experience the opportunity to associate with intelligences on our frequency. In our ascent to higher realities, we contact what is known as energies, entities, and influences. These definitions may help you distinguish the diffenences.

Energies are pools of emotion we contact; these may be good or not good.

Entities, usually distinct personalities, may be incarnate or discarnate, including intelligences such as devas or angelic or spacial beings.

An *influence* may be a thoughtform or even the will of another directed or built by manipulation, attraction, or karma. It may be a part of us — a memory or programming that has slipped below consciousness, or the suggestion of another (or often society) we may confuse as our own. In addition, there are demonic intelligences, but that is another issue and usually not what we encounter.

As we study, most of us experience some opportunity to contact at least one of these in our natural process of growth, especially if we are truly dedicated to our inner practice. The challenge is to be able to discriminate and to make intelligent choices as we respond.

When we connect with a truly rude or uncomfortable entity, we are quite clear that it is undesirable. If it is nice, we may have trouble determining that it is another intelligence; thus we offer these guidelines. Usually a loving entity is personal in nature. Supportive and encouraging, it often gives guidance or suggestions about our personality life. In this way we sometimes develop a "friend-in-spirit" relationship. In the Kabalistic tradition, these spirit teachers were called *Maggid;* many eminent Kabalists had such contacts. In the Greek tradition of Socrates, they were known as *Daimon,* as recorded by Plutarch. In the tradition of spiritualism, they are called spirit guides or teachers, or other names, according to roles they perform for the embodied one with whom they connect.

In recent years, popular usage of the word "channel" has been broadened to mean a channel for an entity other than the higher consciousness of the one who is the true builder of the channel, when we consciously or unconsciously allow another entity to enter the lower-vibrating levels of personality to deliver thoughts or discourses of its own. In such an instance the levels of personality are affected by the vibrations of the entity, and the psychic residue is considered a hindrance to soul who has to then do additional purification work in order to clear the foreign residue, as in all personality experiences.

Mediumship is withdrawing the larger share of one's own consciousness to allow another entity to enter the body and broadcast a message through the voice and structure. This might be, as in mediumship, but not necessarily. The less developed the invading consciousness, the more contaminated the unconscious becomes as it absorbs the foreign vibrations. Unconscious mediumship is considered an even less desirable experience because today humanity has a goal of expanded consciousness to correspond to its current advancing level of development.

Channeling, we see, may or may not be mediumship; it may be achieved by mental attunement to another entity or intelligence whereby the message is received telepathically. The receiver (channel) is conscious and passes the message through the mind mechanism built to receive soul's own messages. This mental psychism is considered the wiser and more modern way to work, with the least interference to soul development.

We must each take responsibility for the use of our own equipment and stop the broadcast should it become dogmatic or detrimental. This method is recommended for disciples who feel they desire to do this service. The opportunity comes to disciples; it is not forced upon them, but a choice is provided. When they consent, the method of working steadily develops with the free will of the disciple intact without manipulation, promise, or threat. As a service, the work does no damage to the disciple unless ego identity becomes exaggerated, which of course may easily occur.

Alice Bailey and Helena Roerich are examples of highly respected modern-day channels who are more correctly called the amanuenses of their respective Masters. Each of these special women is said to have taken dictation from a Master as a service to humanity, providing teachings for today's disciples.

While channeling and meditation lead to spiritual growth, the results are quite different. Seed-thought meditation, a process of a distinct kind of development, is not designed to contact outside intelligences but to focus our mental mechanism at increasingly higher levels, guiding us to attract a higher level of knowing from that vast reservoir, the Mind of God, as we build new god-like qualities into our nature. This intuitive awareness is the *gnosis*, the *sophia*, the gift of spirit in its ascending journey.

Torkom Saraydarian once proposed these questions: Do you choose to become enlightened, or do you want to be a telephone? Do you want to be a mouthpiece for another, or do you want to expand and grow as a part of higher mind, to be Christed? These wonderfully challenging questions illustrate *different works, different purposes.*

We must be able to recognize the difference. Let us use the concept of "personal" and "impersonal" to clarify. Personal guidance is encouraging and helpful. But if we are approaching the All-Knowing through the all-knowing part of ourselves, we are not vibrating at personality level; we are one with the Holy at the soul level. I-thou relationships do not exist there; one separate part does not guide another separate part. When that happens, we know our intelligence is integrating with the Great Intelligence. When we draw impersonal data to our focused and magnetized consciousness, we get *straight knowledge* vibrating to our seed thought or keynote. The thought we focus upon is the key that unlocks and attracts to us related data on its frequency.

In the process of building seed-thought skills, it is natural to touch into poetic rhythms or phrases of wonderful impact. Once the energy or information falls into a personal nature or recognition of the meditator, it is no longer as clear as originally precipitated from the Cloud; personality receives the teaching and that taints it. That is not bad — just limiting. A universal response, rather than a personal response, can be confused with channeling or personality guidance.

This is not to be critical of other "connections" but to distinguish the particular discipline and advantage of seed-thought work. As we work to build our individual and collective rainbow bridge from the minds of humanity to the mind of God, this is the tool we propose in these three volumes. Hopefully these thoughts clarify differences between channeling and piercing the veil.

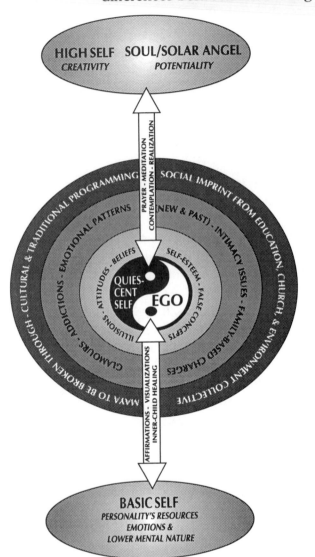

In the modern emergence of a middle-road path, personality and soul continue to interact; synthesis and advancement on the path of initiation are sought. The outer vehicles — body, emotions, and mind — are to conform to the work of soul, and regular alignment through meditation is most useful to create the interface.

People who feel they are mystics, heart-led by inclination, need to build the mind as discipline. People who consider themselves mentalists by inclination need mystical practices to bring gentleness and harmony. All mystics have learned some basic mind-expansion techniques to be able to open to their knowing, and all mentalists will someday join with compassion as true meditation is experienced. Two paths — merging and overlapping at times — lead to the one perfection.

The incoming energy of the current era pushes us to use wisely all the resources we can access. One of its promptings is to move us from intellect to intuition. The more we believe in the powers of mind and the more we experiment, we find — rather, rediscover — keys to our nonphysical aspects.

Fig. 58. Truth, Long Hidden, Is Revealed as all aspects are integrated. The work is to bring all parts of self into a point of rest where the quiescent self utilizes with clarity the opportunities of the life — achieved at last. Integration, after purification, registers intuition and illumination.

In these volumes, we have moved experientially from intellect, step by step, as we believed in it, to new realities we now intuit. We have harmonized our conscious mind and spiritual Self into a coworking relationship to lay a foundation for future discoveries.

If experience — naturally including intuitive flashes—is the mother of transcendence, who is the father? Consciousness.

Assignment

Seed Thought: ILLUMINATION

The seed thought for our closing lesson is *illumination.* Remember,

Let the mind be in you,
which was also in Christ Jesus.

Afterword
The Mysterious Call

For many are called, and few are chosen.

Matt. 22.14

L ord Christ, the teacher of angels and of humanity, calls all to high consciousness, but not all prepare themselves to be conscious participants in the great Plan. The effort we make is our response, and thus we prepare ourselves to be coworkers with the Divine.

Many of you have encountered new ideas in these three volumes, ideas and exercises which demand time and an open mind. Until we practice the exercises, we will never know whether or how they can facilitate self-realization, self-actualization, or any of those exalted goals so easily voiced but so elusive.

The proof of the pudding, they say, is in the eating. In this case I would add, in the experiencing. Even as I was writing these words, a wise woman called to discuss a breakthrough in her seed-thought work. She has been meditating in this style since 1981, and once more a shift has occurred to illuminate an entirely new understanding in her inner life.

While we are meant to shatter the glass ceilings built into our nature, intellect does not yield readily. With persistent inner work, devotion, service, and love, however, an alchemical process gently transforms our lives. The mind opens, and we *know.* Just as when we experience despair and all thoughts and words are inadequate to express our pain, this knowing has an elegance—not to be put into words, to be defined or interpreted by or for another—a life of its own perhaps, and too magnificent for this world.

Meditation is a process of building a relationship with God, a tool for creating intimacy with our Source. We enter into this tender pursuit as we would approach courtship. Both require love, time, attention, respect, and good communication. In return they deliver great moments, excitement, and expanded awareness. As we practice the meditation process, we advance in straight-knowing; we express Lots Of Vital Energy through sharing, experimenting, maturing. In the end, there is nothing of such value or with such substance as this romance of the soul. We cling to it faithfully, and it supports and protects us in the midst of the fire that transforms. No words can characterize the ultimate experience, but therein lies our adventure.

Esoteric teachings suggest we unfold nine consciousness petals as we come to full flowering: three love petals, three knowledge petals, three sacrificial petals. As they open, the three pearls of wisdom held within are revealed.

Since ancient times, the lotus has represented
the bud of high consciousness
waiting within each of us.
May the light of our awakened mind
and the fervor of our heart
bring forth its bloom.

Appendix

The Great Invocation

From the point of Light within the Mind of God
    Let light stream forth into the minds of men.
        Let Light descend on Earth.

From the point of Love within the Heart of God
    Let love stream forth into the hearts of men.
        May Christ return to Earth.

From the centre where the Will of God is known
    Let purpose guide the little wills of men—
        The purpose which the Masters know and serve.

From the centre which we call the race of men
    Let the Plan of Love and Light work out
        And may it seal the door where evil dwells.

Let Light and Love and Power restore the Plan on Earth.

Lead Us, O Lord

Lead us, O Lord,
        from darkness to light,
        from the unreal to the real,
        from death to immortality,
        from chaos to beauty. Amen.

I Am the Soul

I am the Soul,
and also love am I.
Above all else, I am
both will and fixed design.
My will is now to lift
the lower self into the Light Divine.
That Light am I.
Therefore, I must descend
To where that lower self awaits,
awaits my coming.
That which desires to lift
and that which cries for lifting
Are now at one.
Such is my will.

Healing Affirmation

Healing Affirmation for_____

In respect and appreciation for the innate healing intelligence, I make the following statements.

As this body invites healing help, it is open and receptive to the healing influence invoked. Only positive energy will be accepted, and the attention and care provided will create a positive healing experience. The body will mend easily and promptly. Each organ, cell, and tissue will accept the healing work, respond to it, and restore natural health.

_____ will be free from pain, experiencing only minor discomfort. Recuperation will proceed rapidly and without complications. _____ is open and receptive to the healing prayers and healing thoughts directed to her/him. Held in healing love, s/he responds to that love.

This blessed body, a temple of the Living God, is protected and assisted by the healing power of Christ (substitute: "of its Creator," if you so choose. Be aware of the belief system of the patient, and adjust appropriately.)

In our concern for others, we look for helpful tools. I created this affirmation years ago and use it regularly. It is designed to be read aloud by someone [surgeon, anesthesiologist, etc.] in the operating room prior to surgery. It has been well received by doctors when it is requested.

Robe of Light Prayer for Travel

I clothe myself in a robe of light
composed of love, light, and the power of God—
not only for my own protection as I travel
but so that all who see it or touch in to it
may be drawn to God and assisted.
Use me, Father-Mother God,
to the utmost capacity
for the coming of thy kingdom on Earth. Amen

Meditation is:

- An art, a science, a service. A shift and a touch to the divine.
- A method of getting in touch with God, the Divine Parent, and adjust our lives so we, like Jesus, can become a divine son or daughter.
- Useful in many areas of life: self-improvement, forgiveness, healing, centering, stress-reduction, just to name a few.
- Direct experiencing.
- A way to build a foundation for your own inner life and inner teacher to make itself known.
- A doorway to more clarity in understanding your purpose in life, your reason for incarnation.

Meditation is not:

- A cure-all or immediate enlightenment, but a recharge of higher energy.
- A way to escape responsibilities of life — to bliss out; a dedicated spiritual person is always responsible.
- The only solution to our problems, but it goes with our other steps toward improvement of our life that we become more of our potential.
- Not listening to someone else witness to their experiences.
- Not hypnotizing yourself but reviewing undesirable programs, glamours, and illusions, maintaining clarity and staying conscious.
- Not just relaxing — but that is a first step to going inward.

Procedure for Seed-Thought Meditation

1. Begin to relax with several natural breaths, singing softly or chanting.

2. Read a brief piece of devotional material.

3. Close your eyes, and turn your attention within. Use your opening gesture: select a bow, the sign of the cross, hands in prayer position (as you choose, but do adopt a gesture). Become still, and continue to relax.

4. Now visualize a point of clear, white light ten inches or so above your head—the soulstar, light of the soul. Focus upon this vibrating light, and cause it to expand its radiance, remaining clear and bright.

5. Draw the soulstar energy down to your heart. Magnify your feelings of love-caring. Allow love to flow. Feel it move through your emotional nature—clearing, cleansing, nurturing. Consciously bless the body. Feel love for it. This love and nurturing flows through the emotional nature and the body, healing past hurts, forgiving, and neutralizing all negativity. Fill yourself with the positive energy of the soulstar. Begin to radiate that love throughout your body; then emanate it into the space around you.

6. Now move your attention to the mind. Seek to lift your focus from personality mind to interact with Higher Mind. We guide this shift by taking a breath and thinking, "I would be lifted from limited mind to Divine Mind."

7. By focused intent and active will, we form a straight line of light to pierce the veil that separates the higher from the lower.

8. Lift your magnetized consciousness into the Cloud of Knowable Things.

9. Now imagine a line of light from the roof of the mouth upward and extending through and about ten inches beyond the forehead. If you feel with your finger just above the hairline, a tender place or slight indentation indicates a sensitive point. We draw this imaginary line of light from this point—arms extended in front, palms together, lift your arms to either side of your head at the temples, making the unicorn horn of ancient legend. (Normally you will not need to lift your hands and arms in such a way, but do it once to be aware of the WILL involved and the power needed to create this

focus.) With purity of mind, we form a magnetized consciousness by focusing on the seed thought, lifting, and magnetizing it by the power of the heart. When lifted into the Cloud of Knowable Things, this magnetized line of light precipitates droplets. Just as moisture collects and drops begin to fall when climatic conditions are just right, we are creating "precipitation."

10. Begin to draw to you that which you need. Ask to perceive, intuit, and know. Ask the great questions of the aspirant:

- How do I find my part in the mandala of human endeavors?

- How may I serve the higher cause?

- What is mine to do? What part of this is mine to do this day?

11. Using the technique of acting "as if," perceive yourself as a soul-infused personality, and focus upon your seed thought. _____ (Insert your thought here.)

12. Now bring the subtle impressions back to the conscious mind, for we would bring the passion of our heart and mind together within the chalice of our own being. To capture the thoughts you have contacted, jot down the phrases, ideas, concepts, or insights that come—also any symbols, designs, or forms that enter your mind. Mentally ask questions of these impressions, knowing responses will come.

13. Speaking as a soul-infused personality, say the Great Invocation (see appendix), both as a service and as a way of expressing thankfulness for all you have received.

14. Conclude this work by speaking the sacred tone, *Om,* aloud three times, and use your closing gesture.

(Refer to volume 2 appendix for a more detailed outline of a guided seed-thought meditation.)

Please copy this form, complete, and mail to the tutoring committee. This data is held in confidence. It is designed to help tutors serve you in your journey to high consciousness.

Meditation Correspondence Course Enrollment

Name (Please print)_____

Address_____

_____Phone (_____)_____

Date of Birth (month, day, year)_____

Gender_____Place of Birth_____

Occupation_____

Marital Status_____

1. Why do you want to take this course?_____

_____

2. What is your current understanding of meditation?_____

_____

3. Have you ever meditated?_____If so, with what group and in what way?_____

_____

4. When did you begin to meditate?_____

5. How long do you meditate?_____How often?_____

6. Do you try to maintain a pattern—same place, same time, same technique?_____

_____

7. How much time can you give this study?_____

8. Are you easily distracted by outer stimuli?_____

9. Do you tend to glance at the clock to see if the time is up?_____

10. Do you skip your meditation time on slim excuses?_____

11. Do you try to make up omitted meditations at a later time, or let them go?_____

_____

12. Is guided meditation (one led aloud by someone else) easier for you?_____

13. Do you discuss your techniques, experiences, findings, or reactions with others?

_____

14. When you hear of the experiences of others in meditation, do you feel you must be doing it wrong or that you aren't "as advanced" or "as spiritual"?_____

15. Are you ever discouraged and tempted to "forget the whole thing"?_____

16. Give a brief summary of the experiences and problems you have had with meditation. (Use additional paper if needed)_____

17. Have you ever practiced seed-thought meditation?_____

18. Have you used drugs: hallucinogens, alcohol, marijuana?_____

For how long?_____With what effects?_____

Do you now?_____To what degree?_____

19. Have you had psychic or ESP experiences?_____If yes, please describe.

_____

20. Are you familiar with Alice A. Bailey, H.P. Blavatsky, the Agni Yoga teachings? What level of exposure have you had?_____

21. Do you have significant racial, religious, or other prejudices of which we need to be aware?_____

22. What is your educational background?_____

23. Have you read the New Testament?_____the Old Testament?_____

24. Do you belong to a church or religious, metaphysical, occult, or meditation group?_____How long have you been affiliated?_____

25. Do you have a creative activity?_____What is it?_____

Note: Any other information you wish to share is welcome. You may use additional paper for your answers.

Date_____Signature of Applicant_____

Enjoy exchanges with a mentor who will provide personal attention and written responses to your meditation lessons. The enrollment fee is $5, and written assistance and guidance to deepen your spiritual life is $15 per submission. Please pay the $15 mentoring fee each time you submit correspondence. Mail to: Meditation Tutors, Sancta Sophia Seminary, Dept.M11, Sparrow Hawk Village, 11 Summit Ridge Drive, Tahlequah, OK 74464-9215.

Suggested additional reading for Volume 3

In addition to the Endnotes, some excellent books to enrich our spiritual sciences education and spiritual life are:

In *Three Remarkable Women* Harold Balyoz relates the amazing lives of Helena Roerich, Alice A. Bailey, and Helena P. Blavatsky, distinguished teachers heralding this era of light. Balyoz' *Signs of Christ* (for advanced students) is an anthology of many works by Roerich, Bailey, and Torkom Saraydarian. *Talks on Agni* is a collection of Saraydarian's lectures on Agni Yoga, teachings received by Helena Roerich from Master Morya, in addition to *Letters of Helena Roerich, Volumes I and II,* and the Agni Yoga Series. Specifically relevant to this meditation volume are Bailey's *From Intellect to Intuition;* Blavatsky's *Voice of the Silence;* and Saraydarian's *Breakthrough to Higher Psychism, The Science of Becoming Oneself, The Ageless Wisdom,* and *Christ, the Avatar of Sacrificial Love.*

More on Sophia

In Search of the Christ-Sophia—An Inclusive Christology for Liberating Christians, Jann
    Aldredge-Clanton
TheoSophia, Arthur Versluis
Sophia, the Wisdom of God—An Outline of Sophiology, Sergei Bulgakov

More on the shadow and on science and religion

The Gateway of Liberation, Mary Gray
Light on the Path, Mabel Collins
Make Friends with Your Shadow, William A. Miller
Beside Ourselves—Our Hidden Personality in Everyday Life—a psychological
    reflection on one's personality, by Naomi L. Quenk
The Adventure of Self-Discovery—Dimensions of Consciousness and New Per-
    spectives in Psychotherapy and Inner Exploration, Stanislav Grof
Ancient Wisdom and Modern Science, Stanislav Grof, editor
The Meeting of Science and Spirit, John White
Ray Methods of Healing, Zachary F. Lansdowne
Rays and Esoteric Psychology, Zachary F. Lansdowne

Dr. Leslie Weatherhead's *The Christian Agnostic* is one of the best bridge books from traditional to mystical Christianity, from exoteric to esoteric.

May learning and growth continue to excite you throughout your life. If you have questions or wish to share your experiences, write **Meditation Tutors, Sancta Sophia Seminary, Sparrow Hawk Village, 11 Summit Ridge Drive, Dept. M11, Tahlequah, OK 74464-9215**. We always are happy to grow in spirit with you.

Please see bibliography for publishing information.

Endnotes

Lesson 1

1. Excerpted from *Development of the Psychedelic Individual* by John Curtis Gowan (Brooktondale, NY: J. A. Gowan, 1974).

2. This subject is covered thoroughly in *The Book of Rituals—Personal and Planetary Transformation,* Carol E. Parrish-Harra (Santa Monica, CA: IBS Press, 1990); now owned by the author and distributed by Sparrow Hawk Press, Sparrow Hawk Village, 11 Summit Ridge Dr., Tahlequah, OK 74464.

Lesson 2

1. Manly P. Hall, *Self-Unfoldment by Disciplines of Realization* (Los Angeles: Philosophical Research Society, 1961).

2. Some of the ideas presented in this section are derived from volume 1 of *A Course in Miracles* (Tiburon, CA: Foundation for Inner Peace, 1975).

3. Sarah Leigh Brown, *Genesis: Journey into Light* (Tahlequah, OK: Sparrow Hawk Press, 1995).

4. One of the best bridge books from traditional religions to mystical is Dr. Leslie Weatherhead's *The Christian Agnostic* (Nashville, TN: Abingdon Press, 1965).

5. The Three Initiates, *The Kybalion, A Study of the Hermetic Philosophy of Ancient Egypt and Greece* (Chicago: The Yogi Publication Society, 1940).

6. Carol E. Parrish-Harra, *The Aquarian Rosary—Reviving the Art of Mantra Yoga* (Tahlequah, OK: Sparrow Hawk Press, 1988).

7. From *Science of Meditation,* a compilation in booklet form by Arcane School, New York, n.d.: "This is the living Christ, the teacher of angels and men, the eldest within that great family of brothers, humanity. The Christ, standing as the head of the spiritual Hierarchy, is the same great world Teacher who is known by many different names in the major world religions."

8. Ralph Metzner, *Opening to Inner Light* (Los Angeles: Jeremy P. Tarcher, Inc., 1986).

9. Richard M. Bucke, *Cosmic Consciousness* (New York: E.P. Dutton and Company, Inc., 1969).

Lesson 3

1. Vicki Underland-Rosow, *Shame: Spiritual Suicide* (Shorewood, MN: Waterford Publications, 1996).

2. Steve Wilstein, "Getting What It Takes to Win," *Hemispheres,* June 1994.

3. LGE Sport Science, 5700 Saddlebrook Way, Wesley Chapel, FL 33543-4499, 813-973-8022.

4. Mary Gray, *The Gateway of Liberation and Spiritual Laws: Rules of the Evolutionary Arc* (Tahlequah, OK: Sparrow Hawk Press, Expanded edition, 1992).

Lesson 4

1. Vera Stanley Alder, *The Initiation of the World* (London: Rider & Company Limited, 1939).

2. Alice A. Bailey, *Discipleship in the New Age, Volume II* (New York: Lucis Trust, 1955).

3. Torkom Saraydarian, *The Science of Becoming Oneself* (Sedona, AZ: Aquarian Educational Group, 1969).

4. Virginia Satir, *Conjoint Family Therapy* (Berkeley, CA: Celestial Arts, 1964).

5. Alice A. Bailey, *Discipleship in the New Age, Volume II* (New York: Lucis Trust, 1955).

Lesson 5

1. Perle Epstein, *Kabbalah The Way of the Jewish Mystic* (New York: Doubleday & Company, Inc., 1978).

2. Paul Carus, Ed., *The Gospel of Buddha* (Oxford, England: Oneworld Publishing Ltd., 1995).

3. Lawrence LeShan, *The Medium, the Mystic, and the Physicist* (New York: Ballantine Books, 1974).

4. The Halls may differ in name, but teachers present similar ideas. The names we are using are from Torkom Saraydarian's work; we particularly recommend *Christ, the Avatar of Sacrificial Love* (Sedona, AZ: Aquarian Education Group, 1974).

5. Triangles Bulletin 108, Lucis Trust, Inc., New York, June 1994.

6. An Alice Bailey transmission from teacher Djwhal Khul.

7. Emma Bragdon, *A Sourcebook for Helping People with Spiritual Problems* (Aptos, CA: Lightening Up Press, 1993).

8. Stanislav Grof, M.D., and Christina Grof, *Spiritual Emergency—When Personal Transformation Becomes a Crisis* (New York: G. P. Putnams Sons, 1989).

9. Christmas Humphreys, *Concentration and Meditation* (Baltimore, MD: Penguin Books, 1969).

10. William Gray (kabalist), *An Outlook on Our Inner Western Way* (New York: Samuel Weiser, Inc., 1980).

11. Carol E. Parrish-Harra, *The New Dictionary of Spiritual Thought* (Tahlequah, OK: Sparrow Hawk Press, 1994).

12. Haridas Chaudhuri, *Integral Yoga* (Wheaton, IL: Theosophical Publishing House, 1974).

13. Daniel Goleman, *Varieties of Meditation* (New York: Pocket Books, 1963).

14. Carol Parrish-Harra, *Messengers of Hope* (Black Mountain, NC: New Age Press, 1983, distributed by Sparrow Hawk Press, Tahlequah, OK).

15. Carol Parrish-Harra, *The New Age Handbook on Death and Dying* (Tahlequah, OK: Sparrow Hawk Press; 3rd printing 1993).

16. Richard M. Bucke, *Cosmic Consciousness* (New York: Citadel Press, 1970).

Lesson 6

1. Sri Aurobindo, *The Future Evolution of Man: The Divine Life Upon Earth* (Wheaton, IL: The Theosophical Publishing House, 1974; First Edition, 1963).

2. Helena P. Blavatsky, *The Theosophical Glossary* (London, The Theosophical Publishing Society, 1892).

3. This chart and paragraph of explanation are from *A Treatise on Cosmic Fire* by Alice A. Bailey (New York: Lucis Publishing Company, 13th printing, 1989).

4. Max Heindel, *The Rosicrucian Cosmo-Conception;* also quoted and paraphrased from *The Silver Cord and The Seed Atoms* compiled by a Rosicrucian student from Heindel's notes (Oceanside, CA: The Rosicrucian Fellowship, 1909 and 1968, respectively).

5. Alice A. Bailey, *Esoteric Healing* (New York: Lucis Publishing Co., 1986).

6. Two Disciples, *Rainbow Bridge II: Link with the Soul—Purification* (Danville, CA: Rainbow Bridge Productions, Third edition, 1988).

7. M.C. Nanjunda Rao, Cosmic Consciousness or Mukti, *Kundalini* (Vol. VI, No. 1, 1983).

8. Tricia Nickel, M.A., MFCC, "Wisdom Moons," *Welcome to Planet Earth,* Oct.-Nov. 1992, vol. 12, #s 5 & 6, p.43. Copyright 1992 by Tricia Nickel, permission to reprint. Tricia Nickel's private and group practice is in transpersonal psychology, hypnotherapy, and astrology. Writing and college teaching have heart and meaning for her. She has the Transformational Therapy Center, 3702 Mt. Diablo Blvd., Lafayette, CA 94549. Tel. 510 283 3940, e-mail 102362.642@compuserve.com.

9. Dane Rudhyar, *The Astrology of Personality* (Garden City, NY: Doubleday, 1970).

10. Alice A. Bailey, *Letters on Occult Meditation* (New York: Lucis Publishing Co., 1922).

11. Alice A. Bailey, *Education in the New Age* (New York: Lucis Publishing Co., 1954).

12. Readers may write to Sancta Sophia Seminary for the author's recommended seed thoughts for the current year. A fee of $3 for shipping and handling should accompany your request. If you would like a more complete understand-

ing of how we are attuned unconsciously to astrological and invisible energies, read *The Book of Rituals—Personal and Planetary Transformation.*

Lesson 7

1. *Multiple Reflections: Talks on the Yoga Vasishtha by Swami Venkatesananda,* compiled and edited by Swami Venkataramani (San Francisco: Chiltern Yoga Foundation, 1988).

2. Carl Jung, *Memories, Dreams, Reflections* (New York: Random House, Inc., 1965).

3. Alice A. Bailey, *Ponder on This* (New York: Lucis Publishing Company, 1971).

4. From *The New Dictionary of Spiritual Thought:* DUGPAS. Testing agents residing within the ego that resist light and seek to slow those on the path. The symbology of good and bad angels represents challenges presented by devas of light and dugpas—dark elementals of self-service that must become aligned to the soul purpose before advancement can occur. Dugpas are often called evil because they work on the path of involution, rather than evolution.

5. *Brotherhood, 1937* (New York: Agni Yoga Society, Inc., 2nd Printing 1982).

6. Rhonald R. Schlick, "The Rose and Cross—A Place for Unfolding," *The Rosicrucian Digest,* February 1986.

7. Matthew Fox, *The Coming of the Cosmic Christ* (San Francisco: Harper & Row, 1988).

8. E. A. Bennet, *What Jung Really Said* (New York: Schocken Books Inc., 1983).

9. Carol E. Parrish-Harra, *The New Dictionary of Spiritual Thought* (Tahlequah, OK: Sparrow Hawk Press, 1994).

10. Carol E. Parrish-Harra, *The Book of Rituals—Personal and Planetary Transformation* (Santa Monica, CA: IBS Press, Inc., 1990; now the property of Sparrow Hawk Press, Tahlequah, OK).

11. Ann Ree Colton, *Kundalini West* (Glendale, CA: Arc Publishing Company, 1982).

Lesson 8

1. William Irwin Thompson, thinker, historian, and prolific author who repeatedly exposes us to one central theme: Technology is making us one people of one planet whether we like it or not, and we are participating, shaping, and responding to nothing less than the transition from one civilization to another.

2. *The Quest,* Vol. 8, No. 2, summer 1995.

3. Larry Dossey, M.D., *Healing Words: The Power of Prayer and the Practice of Medicine* (Harper San Francisco, 1993).

4. from The Voice, a publication of Healthstar, Inc., located in Hooksett, NH.

5. Alice A. Bailey, *Discipleship in the New Age, Volume II* (New York: Lucis Trust, 1955).

6. Ibid.

Lesson 9

1. Mouni Sadhu, *Meditation* (North Hollywood, CA: Wilshire Book Co., 1972).

2. Ibid.

3. Roberto Assagioli, *Psychosynthesis* (New York: Viking Press, 1971).

4. Christmas Humphreys, *Concentration and Meditation* (Baltimore, MD: Penguin Books, 1969).

5. Torkom Saraydarian, *Breakthrough to Higher Psychism* (Cave Creek, AZ: T.S.G. Publishing Foundation, Inc., 1990) and *The Science of Meditation* (Sedona, AZ: Aquarian Educational Group, 1971).

6. Joseph Chilton Pearce, *Evolution's End: Claiming the Potential of Our Intelligence* (New York: HarperCollins Publishers, 1992).

7. Ibid.

8. Patricia Carrington, *Freedom in Meditation* (Garden City, NY: Anchor Press/ Doubleday, 1978).

9. Christmas Humphreys, *Concentration and Meditation* (Baltimore, MD: Penguin Books, 1969).

10. Jeff Meer, "Artificial Competence," *Psychology Today* (July 1986).

Bibliography

A Course in Miracles. Tiburon, CA: Foundation for Inner Peace, 1975.

Ainsworth, Stanley. *Positive Emotional Power*. Englewood Cliffs, NJ: Prentice-Hall, 1981.

Alder, Vera Stanley. *The Initiation of the World*. London: Rider & Company Limited, 1939.

———. *The Finding of the Third Eye*. York Beach, ME: Samuel Weiser, Inc., 1st American Edition, 1970. 16th Printing, 1984.

———. *Fifth Dimension*. York Beach, ME: Samuel Weiser, Inc., 1993.

Aldredge-Clanton, Jann. *In Search of the Christ-Sophia—An Inclusive Christology for Liberating Christians*. Mystic, CT: Twenty-Third Publications, 1995.

Amis, Robin. *A Different Christianity*. Albany, NY: State University of New York, 1995.

Arya, Pandit Usharbudh. *Superconscious Meditation*. Honesdale, PA: Himalayan International Institute, 1978.

Assagioli, Roberto. *Psychosynthesis*. New York: Viking Press, 1971.

———. *The Act of Will*. New York: Penguin Books, 1st Printing 1973, 4th Printing 1979.

Sri Aurobindo. *Future Evolution of Man: The Divine Life upon Earth*. Wheaton, IL: The Theosophical Publishing House, 1974.

Bailey, Alice A. *Initiation, Human and Solar*. New York: Lucis Publishing Co. 1st Printing, 1922. 16th Printing, 1992.

———. *Letters on Occult Meditation*. 1st Printing 1922, 15th Printing 1993.

———. *A Treatise on Cosmic Fire*. 1st Printing 1925, 14th Printing 1995.

———. *The Light of the Soul*. 1st Printing, 1927. 13th Printing, 1989.

———. *From Intellect to Intuition*. 1st Printing, 1932. 13th Printing, 1987.

———. *A Treatise on White Magic*. 1st Printing, 1934. 17th Printing, 1991.

———. *From Bethlehem to Calvary*. 1st Printing, 1937. 8th Printing, 1989.

———. *Glamour, A World Problem*. 1st Printing, 1950. 9th Printing, 1995.

———. *Esoteric Healing, Vol. IV, A Treatise on the Seven Rays*. 1st Printing 1953, 11th Printing 1984.

———. *Education in the New Age*. 1st Printing 1954, 10th Printing 1987.

———. *Discipleship in the New Age, Volume II*. 1st Printing, 1955. 8th Printing, 1994.

————. *The Externalization of the Hierarchy.* 1st Printing, 1957. 8th Printing, 1989.

————. *The Science of Meditation.* n.d.

————. *Ponder on This.* ("A Compilation by a Student Who Has Imposed His Own Punctuation on the Original Text.") 1st Printing 1971, 8th Printing 1991.

Balyoz, Harold. *Three Remarkable Women.* Flagstaff, AZ: Altai Publishers, 1986.

Bennet, E. A. *What Jung Really Said.* New York: Schocken Books, 1966.

Blavatsky, H. P. *The Theosophical Glossary.* Los Angeles: The Theosophy Company, 1892, reprinted 1973.

————. *The Voice of the Silence.* London: Theosophical Publishing Co., 1889.

Bloomfield, Harold H., M.D., et al. *Transcendental Meditation—Discovering Inner Energy and Overcoming Stress.* New York: Dell Publishing Co., Inc., 1975.

Bradley, Marion Zimmer. *The Mists of Avalon.* New York: Ballantine Books, 1982.

Bradshaw, John. *Healing the Shame That Binds You.* Deerfield Beach, FL: Health Communications, Inc., 1988.

Bragdon, Emma. *A Sourcebook for Helping People with Spiritual Problems.* Los Altos, CA: Lightening Up Press, 1993.

Brown, Sarah Leigh. *Genesis: Journey into Light.* Tahlequah, OK: Sparrow Hawk Press, 1995.

Bulgakov, Sergei. *Sophia, the Wisdom of God—An Outline of Sophiology.* Hudson, NY: Lindisfarne Press, 1993.

Brumgardt, Helen. *Contemplation.* Lakemont, GA: GSA Press, n.d.

Bucke, Richard Maurice. *Cosmic Consciousness.* New York: Citadel Press, 1970.

Burka, Jane B. and Lenora M. Yuen, *Procrastination: Why You Do It, What to Do About It.* Reading, MA: Addison-Wesley Publishing Company, 1983.

Campbell, Florence. *Your Days Are Numbered.* Marina del Ray, CA: DeVorss & Company, 1931.

Campbell, Joseph. *Hero with a Thousand Faces.* Princeton, NJ: Princeton University Press, 2nd edition, 1968.

————. *The Power of Myth.* New York: Doubleday, 1988.

Carrington, Patricia. *Freedom in Meditation.* Garden City, NY: Anchor Press/ Doubleday, 1978.

Carus, Paul, compiler. *The Gospel of Buddha.* Oxford, England, Oneworld Publishing, Ltd., 1995.

Cedercrans, Lucille. *The Nature of The Soul.* Whittier, CA: Wisdom Impressions, 1993.

Chaudhuri, Haridas. *Integral Yoga.* Wheaton, IL: Theosophical Publishing House, 1974.

Clarke, Jean Illsley. *Self-Esteem: A Family Affair.* New York: HarperCollins, 1978.

Collins, Mabel. *Light on the Path* (verbatim reprint of the 1888 edition) and *Through the Gates of Gold* (verbatim reprint of the 1887 edition) in one volume. Pasadena, CA: Theosophical University Press, 1976.

Colton, Ann Ree. *Kundalini West.* Glendale, CA: Arc Publishing Company, 1982.

Davis, Roy Eugene. *How You Can Use the Technique of Creative Imagination.* Lakemont, GA: CSA Press, 1974.

———. *Yoga Darsana: The Philosophy and Light of Yoga.* Lakemont, GA: GSA Press, 1976.

———. *An Easy Guide to Meditation.* 1978.

———. *The Teachings of the Masters of Perfection.* 1979.

———. *The Science of Kriya Yoga.* 1984.

de Purucker, Gottfried. *H. P. Blavatsky: The Mystery.* San Diego, CA: Point Loma Publications, Inc., 1974.

Dossey, Larry. *Healing Words: The Power of Prayer and the Practice of Medicine.* Harper San Francisco, 1993.

Eastcott, Michael J. *The Seven Rays of Energy.* Kent, England: Sundial House, 1980.

Edwards, Betty. *Drawing on the Right Side of the Brain.* Los Angeles: J. P. Tarcher, 1979.

Epstein, Perle. *Kabbalah The Way of the Jewish Mystic.* New York: Doubleday & Company, Inc., 1978.

Estés, Clarissa Pinkola. *Women Who Run With the Wolves.* New York: Ballantine Books, 1992.

Evans-Wentz, W.Y., ed. *Tibetan Yoga and Secret Doctrines.* New York: Oxford University Press, 1967.

Felser, Joseph M. "The New Religious Consciousness." *The Quest,* summer 1995, Vol. 8.

Fox, Matthew. *The Coming of the Cosmic Christ.* San Francisco: Harper & Row, 1988.

Frankl, Viktor E. *Man's Search for Meaning.* New York: E.P. Dutton, 1977.

Gibran, Kahlil. *The Prophet.* New York: Alfred A. Knopf, 103rd printing, 1979.

Goldsmith, Joel S. *The Art of Meditation.* New York: Harper and Row, 1956.

Goleman, Daniel. *The Varieties of Meditation.* New York: Pocket Books, 1963.

Govinda, Lama Anagarika. *The Significance of Meditation in Buddhism.* Wheaton, IL: Theosophical Publishing House, 1973.

Gowan, John Curtis. *Development of the Psychedelic Individual.* Brooktondale, NY: J. A. Gowan, 1974.

Gray, Mary. *The Gateway of Liberation and Spiritual Laws: Rules of the Evolutionary Arc.* Tahlequah, OK: Sparrow Hawk Press, 1992.

Gray, William. *An Outlook on Our Inner Western Way.* New York: Samuel Weiser, Inc., 1980.

Grof, Stanislav. *The Adventure of Self-Discovery—Dimensions of Consciousness and New Perspectives in Psychotherapy and Inner Exploration.* Albany, NY: State University of New York Press, 1988.

Grof, Stanislov, ed. *Ancient Wisdom and Modern Science.*

Grof, Stanislav and Christina Grof, eds. *Spiritual Emergency—When Personal Transformation Becomes a Crisis.* New York: G.P. Putnam's Sons, 1989.

Hall, Manly P. *Self-Unfoldment by Disciplines of Realization*. Los Angeles: Philosophical Research Society, 1961.

Heindel, Max. *The Rosicrucian Cosmo-Conception*. Oceanside, CA: The Rosicrucian Fellowship, 1909. 25th Printing, 1969.

Heline, Corrine. *Mystery of the Christos*. Santa Monica, CA: New Age Bible & Philosophy Center, 1961.

———. *Healing and Regeneration Through Color and Through Music*. Santa Monica, CA: New Age Bible & Philosophy Center, first combined edition 1883.

———. *Sacred Science of Numbers*. Marina del Ray, CA: DeVorss & Company, 1991.

Hittleman, Richard. *Guide to Yoga Meditation*. New York: Bantam Books, 1969.

Hodson, Geoffrey. *The Seven Human Temperaments*. Adyar, Madras, India: Theosophical Publishing House. 1st Printing, 1952. 7th Printing, 1981.

Houston, Jean. *The Possible Human*. Los Angeles: J. P. Tarcher, Inc., 1982.

Hubbard, Barbara Marx. *Birthing the Universal Human: A Guide for Evolutionary Circles*. San Rafael, CA: Foundation for Conscious Evolution, 1996.

———. *Evolutionary Journey: A Personal Guide to a Positive Future*. 1996.

———. *Happy Birthday Planet Earth: The Instant of Co-operation*. San Francisco: Evolutionary Press, 1982.

———. *Hunger of Eve: One Woman's Odyssey Toward the Future*. Eastsound, WA: Island Pacific NW, 1989.

———. *The Promise Will Be Kept: Gospels, Acts, and Epistles*. San Rafael, CA: Foundation for Conscious Evolution, 1996.

———. *The Revelation: A Message of Hope for the New Millennium*. Novato, CA: Nataraj Publishing, 1995.

———. *Teachings from the Inner Christ for Founders of a New Order of the Future*. San Rafael, CA: Foundation for Conscious Evolution, 1994.

Humphreys, Christmas. *Concentration and Meditation*. Baltimore, MD: Penguin Books, 1969.

Jampolsky, Gerald G. *Love Is Letting Go of Fear*. New York: Bantam Books, 1981.

Jeanne. *Numerology, Spiritual Light Vibrations*. Salem, OR: Your Center for Truth Press, 1987.

Judith, Anodea. *Wheels of Life—A User's Guide to the Chakra System*. St. Paul, MN: Llewellyn Publications, 1987.

Jung, Carl Gustav. *Modern Man in Search of a Soul*. New York: Harcourt, Brace & World, Inc., 1933.

———. *Man and His Symbols*. New York: Doubleday, 1964.

———. *Memories, Dreams, Reflections*. New York: Random House, Inc., 1965.

Keyes, Ken. *Handbook to a Higher Consciousness*. Berkeley, CA: Living Love Center, 1975.

Krishnamurti, Jiddu. *The World of Peace*. Meetings in Brockwood Park. England: Krishnamurti Foundation Limited, 1985.

Lamsa, George M., trans. *The Holy Bible from the Ancient Eastern Text, containing the Old and New Testaments, translated from the Aramaic of the Peshitta*. Philadelphia, PA: A. J. Holman, 1933.

Lansdowne, Zachary F. *Rays and Esoteric Psychology*. York Beach, ME: Samuel Weiser, Inc., 1989.

———. *Ray Methods of Healing*. York Beach, ME: Samuel Weiser, Inc., 1993.

Laubach, Frank. *Channels of Spiritual Power*. Westwood, NJ: Fleming H. Revel Co., 1954.

Leadbeater, C. W. *The Masters and the Path*. Adyar, Madras, India: Theosophical Publishing House. 1st Printing, 1925. 10th Reprint, 1973.

Lee, John. *Facing the Fire*. New York: Bantam Books, 1993.

Leichtman, Robert R. and Carl Japiske. *Active Meditation*. Columbus, OH: Ariel Press, 1982.

Lerner, Harriet G. *The Dance of Anger*. New York: Harper & Row, 1985.

LeShan, Lawrence. *How to Meditate*. New York: Bantam Books, 1974.

———. *The Medium, the Mystic, and the Physicist*. New York: Ballantine Books, 1974.

Levi. *The Aquarian Gospel of Jesus the Christ*. Marina del Ray, CA: DeVorss & Company, 12th printing, 1988.

Loehr, Franklin, et al. *Psychography: A Method of Self-Discovery*. Grand Island, FL: Religious Research Press, 1990.

Maltz, Maxwell. *Psycho-Cybernetics*. New York: Pocket Books, 1969.

Maslow, A. H. "A Theory of Human Motivation," *Psychological Review* 50, 1943.

Matthews, William. "Investment Advisory" Newsletter of *Sound Money Investor*, August 1989.

Meditation in Christianity, Volume I. Prospect Heights, IL: Himalayan Institute of Yoga Science and Philosophy, n.d.

Meer, Jeff. "Artificial Competence." *Psychology Today*, July 1986.

Metzner, Ralph. *Opening to Inner Light*. Los Angeles: Jeremy P. Tarcher, 1986.

Michael, Russ. *The Why and How of Meditation*. Washington, DC: Millennium Publishing House, 1975.

Miller, William A. *Make Friends with Your Shadow*. Minneapolis: Augsberg Publishing House, 1981).

Montgomery, Ruth. *Strangers Among Us*. New York: Random House, 1979.

———. *Threshold to Tomorrow*. 1982.

Moore, L. David. *A Personal Pathway to God—Our Song of Freedom*. Atlanta, GA: Pendulum Plus Press, 1995.

Muller, Wayne. *Legacy of the Heart*. New York: Simon & Schuster, 1992.

Naranjo, Claudio and Robert E. Ornstein. *On the Psychology of Meditation*. New York: Penguin Books, 1976.

Nickel, Tricia. "Wisdom Moons." *Welcome to Planet Earth*, Oct./Nov. 1992.

Ornstein, Robert E. *Psychology of Consciousness.* San Francisco: W. H. Freeman and Company, 1972.

Parker, William and Elaine St. John. *Prayer Can Change Your Life.* New York: Prentice Hall Press, 1957.

Pearce, Joseph Chilton. *Evolution's End: Claiming the Potential of Our Intelligence.* New York: Harper Collins, 1993.

————. *Magical Child.* New York: Bantam Books. 6th edition. 1986.

Peck, M. Scott. *The Road Less Traveled.* New York: Simon & Schuster, 1978.

————. *Further Along the Road Less Traveled.* New York: Touchstone, 1993.

Pelletier, Kenneth R. *Mind as Healer/Mind as Slayer.* New York: Dell Publishing Co., 1977.

Powell, James N. *The Tao of Symbols.* New York: William Morrow and Company, 1982.

Quenk, Naomi L. *Beside Ourselves—Our Hidden Personality in Everyday Life.* Palo Alto, CA: Consulting Psychologists Press, Inc., 1993.

Quest. The. Vol. 8, No. 2, summer 1995.

Ram Dass, Baba. *Journey of Awakening.* New York: Bantam Books, 1978.

Rao, Nanjunda, M.C. "Cosmic Consciousness or Mukti." *Kundalini,* vol. VI, No. 1, 1983.

Ravindra, Ravi. *The Yoga of the Christ.* Longmead, England: Element Books Limited, 1990.

Robbins, Michael D. *Tapestry of the Gods. The Seven Rays: An Esoteric Key to Understanding Human Nature.* Jersey City Heights, NJ: Seven Ray Institute, 1988.

Roerich, Helena. *Agni Yoga.** (*Part of the Agni Yoga Series) New York: Agni Yoga Society, Inc., 1954.

————. *Aum.** 1959.

————. *Brotherhood.** 1967.

————. *New Era Community.** 1926.

————. *Fiery World I.** 1969.

————. *Fiery World II.** 1946.

————. *Fiery World III.** 1948.

————. *Heart.** 1975.

————. *Hierarchy.** 1933.

————. *Infinity I.** 1956.

————. *Infinity II.** 1957.

————. *Leaves of Morya's Garden II (Illumination).** 1952.

————. *Leaves of Morya's Garden I (The Call).** 1953.

————. *Letters.* Volume I, 1954. Volume II, 1967.

————. *Supermundane I.** 1938.

————. *Supermundane II.** 1938.

Rossner, John. *In Search of the Primordial Tradition and the Cosmic Christ.* St. Paul, MN: Llewellyn Publications, 1989.

Rudhyar, Dane. *The Astrology of Personality.* Garden City, NY: Doubleday, 1970.

Sadhu, Mouni. *Meditation.* North Hollywood, CA: Wilshire Book Co., 1972.

Saraydarian, H. (Torkom). *The Science of Becoming Oneself.* Sedona, AZ: Aquarian Educational Group, 1969.

———. *The Science of Meditation.* Sedona, AZ: Aquarian Educational Group, 1971.

———. *Cosmos in Man.* Agoura, CA: Aquarian Educational Group, 1973.

———. *Christ, The Avatar of Sacrificial Love.* Sedona, AZ: Aquarian Education Group, 1974.

———. *Talks on Agni.* 1987.

———. *The Ageless Wisdom.* West Hills, CA: T.S.G. Publishing Foundation, Inc., 1990.

———. *Breakthrough to Higher Psychism.* Cave Creek, AZ: T.S.G. Foundation, Inc., 1990.

———. *Leadership, Volume I.* Cave Creek, AZ: T.S.G. Publishing Foundation, 1995.

Satir, Virginia. *Conjoint Family Therapy.* Berkeley, CA: Celestial Arts, 1964.

———. *Self-Esteem.* Berkeley, CA: Celestial Arts, 1975.Sc

Schlick, Rhonald R. "The Rose and Cross—A Place for Unfolding." *The Rosicrucian Digest,* February 1986.

"Service." *Triangles Bulletin* 108 (Alice Bailey teachings). New York: Lucis Trust, Inc., June 1994.

Signs of Christ. Collected by Harold Balyoz. Flagstaff, AZ: Altai Publishers, 1979.

Silva, Jose. *The Silva Mind Control Method.* New York: Simon and Schuster, 1977.

Smith, Bradford. *Meditation: The Inward Art.* Philadelphia, PA: Lippincott, 1963.

Smith, Geoffrey. "Meditation, the New Balm for Corporate Stress." *Business Week,* May 10, 1993.

Song of God, The Bhagavad Gita, commentary by Swami Venkatesananda. San Francisco: The Chiltern Yoga Trust, revised 1984.

The Three Initiates. *The Kybalion—A Study of the Hermetic Philosophy of Ancient Egypt and Greece.* Chicago: The Yogi Publication Society, 1940.

Tulku, Tarthang. *Time, Space, and Knowledge.* Berkeley, CA: Dharma Publishing, 1977.

Two Disciples. *The Rainbow Bridge.* Danville, CA: The Triune Foundation, Rainbow Bridge Productions, 3rd edition, 1988.

Underland-Rosow, Vicki. *Shame: Spiritual Suicide.* Shorewood, MN: Waterford Publications, 1996.

Venkataramani, Swami, ed. *Multiple Reflections: Talks on the Yoga Vashshtha by Swami Venkatesananda.* San Francisco: Chiltern Yoga Foundation, 1988.

Versluis, Arthur. *TheoSophia.* Hudson, NY: Lindisfarne Press, 1994.

Voice, The. n.a. Hooksett, NY: Healthstar, Inc., n.d.

Weatherhead, Leslie D. *The Christian Agnostic*. Nashville, TN: Abingdon Press, 1965.

White, John. *The Meeting of Science and Spirit*. New York: Paragon House, 1990.

Wilber, Ken. *Eye to Eye*. Garden City, NY: Anchor Books, 1983.

Wilstein, Steve. "Getting What It Takes to Win." *Hemispheres,* June 1994.

Wonder, Jacquelyn and Priscilla Donovan. *Whole Brain Thinking*. New York: Ballantine Books, 1984.

Wood, Ernest. *The Seven Rays*. Wheaton, IL: The Theosophical Publishing House, 1925.

———. *Yoga*. Baltimore, MD: Penguin Books, 1973.

Yogananda, Paramahansa. *Autobiography of a Yogi.* Los Angeles: Self-Realization Fellowship, 1946.

———. *Metaphysical Meditations*. 1982.

TAPES

Tapes designed as aids to the Meditation Course by Carol E. Parrish-Harra are available through the Village Bookstore, Sparrow Hawk Village, 22 Summit Ridge Drive, Tahlequah, OK 74464.

Guided meditations on tape: *Meditation Plus* (to be used first) and *Experience New Dimensions*.

Purification meditations on tape. Very powerful—follow directions carefully: *Coming to the Sunrise.*

LCCC Sings, a collection of chants used for meditation at Sparrow Hawk Village, performed by Light of Christ Community Church singers.

Sancta Sophia Seminary

A Contemporary Mystery School
How It Came to Be

I n 1982, Carol Parrish was revealed to the greater public by author Ruth Montgomery in the best-selling *Threshold to Tomorrow*. The book elaborated upon Carol's near-death experience, her remarkable psychic and spiritual abilities, and her current role as a messenger in the new era.

Just previously, Carol had received spiritual guidance to move the school she had established in 1978 from Florida to a remote location in the beautiful Ozark foothills of northeastern Oklahoma.

Today, in addition to her personal teaching of Sancta Sophia students, Carol is academic dean and oversees seminary classes, a post-graduate program, faculty, and advisors. She continues to minister at Light of Christ Community Church and has published widely acclaimed books and audiocassette programs. She is a highly sought international speaker and world traveler, leading many pilgrimages to sacred places.

Spiritually Charged Location

The magnificently wooded 400-acre mountain setting where Carol was inspired to build Sparrow Hawk Village is the home of Sancta Sophia Seminary. This spiritual community which provides a supportive environment for the practice of ethical living was founded by Reverend Parrish, her husband, Charles C. Harra, and her friend, Reverend Grace B. Bradley.

The church sanctuary is centered on a vortex of special energies created by a star-shaped convergence of Earth ley lines. This creates a unique enclosure of spiritual energies which enhance the synthesis of living, learning, and personal growth for faculty, students, and villagers. It is a sacred place which helps individuals heal and make their lives whole. Very importantly, the spiritual vortex provides an environment for the preparation and training of initiates for spiritual vocations.

The village is a harmonious environment of fifty privately owned homes, office buildings, church, and wellness center. It has wooded homesites, lovely gardens, and a sophisticated infrastructure. Villagers are independent, self-supporting people who live, learn, meditate, and worship together.

Personal Transformation

A combination of off-campus retreats, home-study, and residential programs forms the basis of participation in both graduate and undergraduate studies. The focal point of every student's program is a unique transformational process guided by master teacher Dean Parrish, together with skilled, dedicated faculty, advisors, tutors, counselors, and healers.

The integrative process begins with selected study and meditation techniques tailored to the disciple's personal goals. Month by month, an individually assigned advisor offers spiritual mentoring in telephone sessions, personal meetings, or by correspondence. The entire process is catalyzed during periodic class sessions when students visit to enjoy the eclectic and electric atmosphere of the campus and the village.

Five Levels of Certification Available

The distinctive process of home study, meditation, spiritual guidance, and periodic classes prepares students for planetary service on one of five paths. All programs are moderate in cost.

First, Practitioners earn certification as well-prepared lay ministers in counseling, spiritual healing, and teaching. Second, Teachers of Esoteric Philosophy become educators for the new paradigms of spirituality emerging around the planet. Third, ordination prepares ministers in Esoteric Christianity to bring the true Ageless Wisdom into both metaphysical and mainstream settings around the world. Light of Christ Community Church ordinations are endorsed by the International Council of Community Churches.

Additionally, the graduate school offers two levels of certification to a limited enrollment. For students with the requisite background, commitment, and high creativity, individually designed programs lead to one of several master's or doctoral degrees.

For More Information

Do you seek to serve as a healing practitioner, minister, counselor, or teacher? Would you like to earn an advanced degree? Sancta Sophia programs prepare you to contribute as an awakened leader in the era of enlightenment we are entering.

If you would like more information, you are invited to call the Registrar at 800 386-7161, or write to Sancta Sophia Seminary, 11 Summit Ridge Drive–Dept. 33, Tahlequah, OK 74464. If you wish, you may request the name of the affiliated center, church, or class nearest you. We would be happy to hear from you.

Adventure in Meditation–Spirituality for the 21st Century
Vols. 1 and 2
by Rev. Carol E. Parrish-Harra, Ph.D.
are recipients of the

1996 & 1997 Athena Award
"Book-as-a-mentor, Spirituality (over 200 pages)"

Rev. Carol E. Parrish-Harra, Ph.D.

Rev. Carol E. Parrish-Harra, Ph.D., author of *Adventure in Meditation, Spirituality for the 21st Century, Volumes I and II,* is recipient of the Athena Award for the second consecutive year—the 1997 Athena Award for Excellence in Mentoring competition, sponsored by *Mentor* newsletter.

Rev. Parrish-Harra, founder of Sancta Sophia Seminary and the spiritual community of Sparrow Hawk Village, draws to her like-minded seekers of higher consciousess and ethical living. Parrish-Harra is a leader in the World Network of Religious Futurists whose aim is to bring the ageless wisdom teachings to a greater, worldwide audience. *Call 800 386-7161 to order the books or for more information.*

Bestseller!

THE MYSTICAL MAGICAL MARVELOUS WORLD OF DREAMS

Wilda B. Tanner

Among the many books which offer insight into the meaning of dream symbols, I find Ms. Tanner's to be the most approachable and useful, especially for beginning and intermediate explorers on this path.

The Leading Edge Review

Written for the spiritual seeker from a philosophical perspective, this bestseller, now in its 11th printing, presents a proven method for using dreams to heal, solve problems, and attain guidance for health, wealth, happiness, and understanding.

In the first section of her mystical, magical, marvelous book, Wilda explains such phenomena as lucid dreaming, ESP or precognitive dreams, death-and-dying dreams, past-life dreams, and nightmares. She also offers valuable insights on how to recall, interpret, and work with dream symbols. The second section of this comprehensive book features a 260-page glossary of dream symbols and interpretations, plus an extensive cross-referenced index.

Wilda's joy and enthusiasm are contagious, and her teachings, while deeply meaningful, are couched in simple language suited to every age.

Wilda B. Tanner is an ordained minister, teacher, and philosopher. She has taught dream interpretation throughout the United States and Canada and has also been a frequent radio and T.V. guest.

380pp / tradepaper / ISBN 0-945027-02-8 / $14.95

THE NEW AGE HANDBOOK ON DEATH AND DYING

Rev. Carol E. Parrish-Harra

Rev. Carol E. Parrish-Harra has written beautifully a book that understands death and dying from the holistic perspective of the New Age. It deserves a wide audience; I highly recommend it.

> Dr. Kenneth Ring
> *Director, International Association for Near-Death Studies*

"Each death is a poignant love story. Each drama is unique and special, just as each birth. We dare not avoid these powerful experiences because DEATH IS LIFE TOO."

With these words the author begins this profound offering of insights from her ministries with terminally ill patients and their families, from her own near-death experience, and from her grief following the sudden loss of her daughter and granddaughter. Join with Reverend Parrish-Harra as she seeks to facilitate a better understanding of spiritual teachings and inspired writings concerned with death.

"Rev. Carol E. Parrish-Harra helps guide our hearts towards healing resolutions. Her writing shines a light on grief, convincing us we can face death, and learn and grow in the process."

> BettyClare Moffatt, author
> Cofounder, Mothers of AIDS Patients

196pp /tradepaper/ ISBN 0-945027-09-5 / $10.95

Books and Tapes for Spiritual Growth

Please send the following books:
Quantity

	Price each	Totals

_____ Adventure in Meditation—Spirituality for the 21st Century, Vol. I – *a meditation guide to achieve soul infusion, by Carol E. Parrish-Harra, Ph.D.* — **$17.95** — _____

_____ Adventure in Meditation—Spirituality for the 21st Century, Vol. 2 – *a meditation guide to achieve soul infusion, by Carol E. Parrish-Harra, Ph.D.* — **$17.95** — _____

_____ Adventure in Meditation—Spirituality for the 21st Century, Vol. 3– *a meditation guide to achieve soul infusion, by Carol E. Parrish-Harra, Ph.D.* — **$17.95** — _____

_____ Adventure in Meditation—Spirituality for the 21st Century, 3-vol. set *Complete set of volumes 1, 2, and 3, by Carol E. Parrish-Harra, Ph.D.* — **$49.95** — _____

_____ The New Dictionary of Spiritual Thought – *1,100 definitions of esoteric and spiritual concepts, by Rev. Carol E. Parrish-Harra, Ph.D.* — **$14.95** — _____

_____ The Mystical, Magical, Marvelous World of Dreams – *a concise guide to dream interpretation, by Wilda B. Tanner* — **$14.95** — _____

_____ Do You Speak Astrology? – *great for astrology beginners, by Doe Donovan* — **$12.95** — _____

_____ The Book of Rituals – *to create personal & planetary transformation, by Rev. Carol E. Parrish-Harra, Ph.D.* — **$14.95** — _____

_____ The New Age Handbook on Death and Dying – *excellent resource for comfort & guidance, by Rev. Carol E. Parrish-Harra, Ph.D.* — **$10.95** — _____

_____ The Gateway of Liberation – *classic writings on the Ageless Wisdom, by Mary Gray* — **$ 9.95** — _____

_____ Genesis: Journey into Light – *an esoteric interpretation, by Rev. Sarah Leigh Brown* — **$ 7.95** — _____

_____ Messengers of Hope – *a transformative journey after a near-death experience, by Rev. Carol E. Parrish-Harra (autobiography)* — **$ 7.95** — _____

Please send the following teaching tapes by Carol E. Parrish-Harra:

Adventure in Awareness – *Ageless Wisdom concepts & teachings:*

_____ I - Breadth of Esoteric Teachings (12 90-min. tapes) — **$60.00** — _____

_____ II - Awakening Our Inner Consciousness (12 90-min. tapes) — **$60.00** — _____

_____ III - Toward Deeper Self-Realization (12 90-min. tapes) — **$60.00** — _____

_____ Meditation Plus – *12 meditation techniques for spiritual growth (6 tapes)* — **$30.00** — _____

_____ Coming to the Sunrise – *advanced meditation for self-purification (4 tapes)* — **$25.00** — _____

_____ Energy Ecstasy (book used with "Sunrise" Tapes) — **$12.95** — _____

_____ Healing – *realize your own healing potential & how to use it (6 tapes)* — **$30.00** — _____

_____ New Age Christianity – *discover the Christ-Within (6 tapes)* — **$30.00** — _____

_____ Experience New Dimensions – *techniques for psychic development (6 tapes)* — **$35.00** — _____

_____ The Aquarian Rosary – *stimulate heart & mind to greater love (2 tapes)* — **$12.95** — _____

_____ The Aquarian Rosary (book) — **$ 9.95** — _____

_____ Meditation & Group Work for the 21st Century (2 tapes) — **$15.95** — _____

_____ Reincarnation & Karma (2 tapes) — **$15.95** — _____

Subtotal _____

Shipping and Handling ($2.75 first item, $1.00 each additional) _____

TOTAL ENCLOSED _____

Payment by: Check ❑ Visa ❑ MasterCharge ❑ Discover ❑

Name_____
(please print)

Address_____

_____Daytime Phone_____

Card #_____ Exp. Date_____

Signature_____

VILLAGE BOOKSTORE
22 Summit Ridge Drive • Tahlequah, OK 74464
For phone orders, call 800 386-7161
If ordering by phone with a credit card, please have your card ready